TRADE PROTECTION
IN THE
EUROPEAN COMMUNITY

TRADE PROTECTION IN THE EUROPEAN COMMUNITY

LUDGER SCHUKNECHT

hap harwood academic publishers
chur • reading • paris • philadelphia • tokyo • melbourne

Copyright © 1992 by Harwood Academic Publishers GmbH, Poststrasse 22, 7000 Chur, Switzerland. All rights reserved.

Harwood Academic Publishers

Post Office Box 90
Reading, Berkshire RG1 8JL
United Kingdom

58, rue Lhomond
75005 Paris
France

5301 Tacony Street, Drawer 330
Philadelphia, Pennsylvania 19137
United States of America

3-14-9, Okubo
Shinjuku-ku, Tokyo 169
Japan

Private Bag 8
Camberwell, Victoria 3124
Australia

Library of Congress Cataloging-in-Publication Data

Schuknecht, Ludger, 1962–
    Trade protection in the European Community. / Ludger Schuknecht.
        p.   cm.
    Includes bibliographical references and indexes.
    ISBN 3-7186-5287-0
    1. Protectionism--European Economic Community countries.
2. European Economic Community countries--Commercial policy.
3. Europe 1992.   I. Title.
HF2040.5.Z7S38   1992
382'.73'094--dc20   92-442
                                                           CIP

Printed in Great Britain by Antony Rowe Ltd

To my parents

Contents

List of Figures   ix
List of Tables   xi
Acknowledgements   xiii

1   Introduction   1
1.1 The EC Trade Policy Rhetoric   1
1.2 An Alternative View of EC Trade Policy Making   2

2   Protectionism—An Intra-National Prisoners' Dilemma   9
2.1 The Reasons for Free Trade and Protection   9
2.2 International Prisoners' Dilemma Explanations   14
2.3 Intra-National Prisoners' Dilemma Explanations   17
2.4 Constitutional Constraints on Trade Policy Making   26

3   European Community Policy Making   31
3.1 Introduction   31
3.2 Historical Aspects   32
3.3 Constraints on EC Trade Policy Making   35
3.4 The Policy-Making Agents   37

4   The Trade Policy Instruments   53
4.1 Introduction   53
4.2 GATT-Conform Measures   56
4.3 Grey Area Measures   62
4.4 Internal Protection   70

5   National Protection Based on Article 115, Treaty of Rome   73
5.1 Introduction   73
5.2 Who Applies and Who Are the Targets   75
5.3 The Article 115 Procedure   82
5.4 An Empirical Analysis of Article 115 Protection   87
5.5 Why Some Industries Prefer Article 115   95
5.6 Conclusion: Article 115 and "Fortress Europe"   96

6   Voluntary Export Restraints   **99**
6.1   Introduction   99
6.2   The Voluntary Export Restraint Procedures   101
6.3   The Political Economy of Voluntary Export Restraints   104
6.4   Empirical Evidence   108
6.5   Why Some Industries Prefer Voluntary Export Restraints   114
6.6   Conclusion: VERs, GATT and "Europe 1992"   115
      Appendix   116

7   Antidumping   **119**
7.1   Introduction   119
7.2   Who Are the Targets of EC Antidumping Measures?   121
7.3   Antidumping Procedures in the United States and the
      European Community   130
7.4   An Empirical Investigation of EC Antidumping   139
7.5   Why Some Industries Prefer Antidumping   145
7.6   Conclusion: The Future Role of Antidumping   146
      Data Appendix Table   148

8   Antidumping Against Central and Eastern Europe   **149**
8.1   Introduction   149
8.2   The Institutional Nature of EC Antidumping Procedures   151
8.3   CMEA Trading and Pricing Behaviour   153
8.4   The Role of Undertakings   156
8.5   Empirical Evidence   157
8.6   Conclusion: Implications for the Transition from Socialism   168

9   The Single European Market   **169**
9.1   Introduction   169
9.2   The History of Integration   171
9.3   Integration as Cartelization   174
9.4   Pressure Politics and the Single European Market   175
9.5   The Constitutional Economics of the Single Market   189
9.6   Conclusion: The Dynamics of Trade Integration   191

10   Conclusion   **193**
10.1 Summary of EC Trade Policy Making   194
10.2 Policy Implications   199

Bibliography   205
Author Index   223
Subject Index   225

List of Figures

2.1   The Welfare Effects of Protection   11
2.2   Rent Seeking and Trade Protection   18

3.1   Organization of the Commission   43
3.2   Decision Making in the Council and COREPER   46
3.3   Checks and Balances in the European Community   49

4.1   The Hierarchy of Preferential Treatment   69

5.1   The Article 115 Decision-Making Process   83

7.1   The US Antidumping Procedure   131
7.2   The EC Antidumping Procedure   135

8.1   Foreign Trade Practice in the Former Soviet Union   154

List of Tables

2.1 The International Trade Game for a Small Open Economy   12
2.2 Trade Protection as a Prisoners' Dilemma   13
2.3 The Intra-National Prisoners' Dilemma   25

3.1 The EC's Policy-Making Agents   39
3.2 Voting Power in the Council   47

4.1 The European Community Trade Policy Instruments   55

5.1 Article 115: Total Applications and Approvals, 1971–1988   76
5.2 Shares of Article 115 Applications and Import Shares
by EC Member Countries, 1980–1989   77
5.3 Shares of Article 115 Cases and EC Imports for Selected
Countries and Country Groups, 1988   79
5.4 Article 115 Cases per Target Country and Sector, 1988   80
5.5 Article 115 Applications per Product by EC Member
Countries and Target Countries in Selected Years   81
5.6 Specifications of the Trend and MFA Variables, 1971–1981   90
5.7 Regression Results for the Determination of Applications
from EC Member Countries for Article 115 Measures   92
5.8 Regression Results for the Determination of the Commission's
Approval Rate of Article 115 Measures   94

6.1 Voluntary Export Restraints by the EC and its
Member Countries   108
6.2 Voluntary Export Restraints per Sector and Country, 1990   109
6.3 Shares of VERs (1990) and EC Imports (1988) for Selected
Countries and Country Groups   110
Appendix: Voluntary Export Restraints and Similar Restraint
Arrangements in the EC, as of Mid-1990   116

7.1 Number of EC Antidumping Cases and their Outcome per
Country, 1980–1990   122
7.2 Shares of EC Antidumping Cases and their Outcomes per
Country Group, 1980–1990   125
7.3 Shares of EC Antidumping Cases and EC Imports for
Selected Countries and Country Groups, 1980–1990   126

7.4 Percentage of EC Antidumping Cases per Sector and Country Group, 1980–1990   127
7.5 The Incidence of Preliminary and Final Duties per Sector and Country in 1990   129
7.6 Discretionary Decision Making in the EC and US Antidumping Process   132
7.7 Acceptance versus Rejection in EC Antidumping Cases   144
Data Appendix Table: Independent Variables Considered for Inclusion in Estimations   148

8.1 The Incidence of Antidumping Claims per Country   157
8.2 Acceptance versus Rejection in Antidumping Cases against Former CMEA Members, 1980–1990   160
8.3 Dumping and Injury in CMEA Cases Compared to Other Cases   162
8.4 The Correlation between Dumping Margin and Injury in CMEA Cases   162
8.5 Average Industry Wages   163
8.6 The Incidence of CMEA Antidumping Cases per Sector   163
8.7 Determinants of CMEA "Dumping"—The Hard Currency Shortage Hypothesis   165
8.8 Share of Acceptances, Undertakings and Reduced Levels of Protection   166
8.9 The Correlation between Dumping Margin and Instrument in CMEA Cases   167

9.1 Winners and Losers from the Single European Market   176
9.2 GDP, Trade and Interdependence in the EC   181
9.3 Labour Costs in the Manufacturing Industry, 1957–1977   184
9.4 Labour Costs in the Processing Industry, Selected Years   185
9.5 Labour Costs in the EC in Purchasing Power Standards (Processing Industry), 1971–1986   186
9.6 Intra-Industry Trade between Selected EC Member Countries, 1958–1970   188
9.7 Intra-Industry Trade within the EC, 1964–1977   189

10.1 The Specialization of Industries in Trade Barriers   196
10.2 Substitution and Supplementation in EC Protection   197

Acknowledgements

This study is part of the Special Research Project 178 "Internationalization of the Economy" at the University of Konstanz, Germany. I am grateful to my advisor Heinrich Ursprung who suggested writing on this fascinating topic. His comments and suggestions, the contacts he helped to establish, and not forgetting the funding I received through this project were invaluable for the successful completion of this study. My second advisor Werner Ebke also deserves my gratitude. As a lawyer he helped me to overcome at least some of the legal shortcomings of this study.

I am also most grateful to Angelika Eymann, who worked with me on antidumping. I benefited immensely from the various visits by Arye Hillman to Konstanz and two counter-visits to Israel. Discussions and a workshop with Michael Finger at the World Bank were most stimulating, as was the time I spent at the Public Choice Center at George Mason University, USA, and the discussions with Viktor Vanberg. I am also most grateful to Peter Holmes, and three anonymous referees for their comments and suggestions. Several members of the EC Commission also deserve my gratitude, although they may disagree with some of my arguments. I would like to thank Peter Moser for many stimulating discussions at the Center and in St. Gallen. He helped me particularly when I could not see the wood for the trees.

The participants of the Forum of International Trade Policy and the Law and Economics Seminar at the University of Konstanz, and those of the Silvaplana Workshop on International Political Economy, deserve my gratitude. Hannelore Weck-Hannemann, Günther Schulze, and particularly my colleague Joerg Stephan were always open for stimulating discussions. Brigitte Bacher helped to overcome my artistic deficiencies by drawing most of the figures and tables. Claire Gordon and Edel O'Halloran kindly corrected my English without making me feel bad about it. Claire Gordon, Susanne Holder and Oliver Lorz were invaluable in preparing the manuscript.

I would also like to thank my family and my friends—their encouragement, fun and affection cannot be praised enough and provided the balance to my academic life.

Chapter 1

INTRODUCTION

Imaginary Petition of the Candle-Makers to the French Chamber of Deputies:

...We are suffering from the intolerable competition of a foreign rival, placed, it would seem, in a condition so far superior to ours for the production of light that he absolutely inundates our national market with a price fabulously reduced. The moment he shows himself our trade leaves us - all consumers apply to him; and a branch of native industry, having countless ramifications, is all at once rendered completely stagnant. This rival, who is no other than the sun, wages war to the knife against us...   Bastiat (1922)

1.1 The EC Trade Policy Rhetoric

Economists have traditionally argued that free trade maximizes a country's national income. The EC claims that its trading system is based on this principle. The few qualifications in the trade literature, however, serve the EC rhetoric to justify its external trade protection. The exporters, according to the EC rhetoric, use unfair trade practices to prevent the emergence of EC industries or to drive existing industries out of the market. A new "war of industries" is being fought, as the French Prime Minister Cresson suggests.

The EC's antidumping policies, for instance, are supposed to secure a "level playing field" as Commissioner de Clerq (1988) suggests "...the Community has a vital interest in maintaining a liberal system of international trade. But liberal trade is only possible, in practice, if industries can be sure that they are adequately safeguarded against unfair trade practises. This is why antidumping has become an important feature of the Community's trade policy ..."

Occasionally, the EC appeals to the social consciousness instead of referring to commercial fairness when justifying its trade

1

protection. Adjusting to world markets imposes intolerable social costs on society through the loss of employment and know-how or through dependence on foreign imports. According to the EC logic, protection is beneficial because it gives companies a breathing space in which to adjust - even if it is not altogether efficient.

The EC also promotes a certain image of trade protection and its characteristics. It claims that a sophisticated system of technical rules governs the application of trade policy instruments and secures the implementation of commercial and social fairness in a comparably liberal and transparent manner. Commenting again on antidumping, de Clerq argues that "...the Community's policy... is incontestably by far the most liberal... [and] among the most transparent."

Within the EC, on the other hand, the beneficial effects of free trade are heralded. Efficiency gains from liberalization will lead to economic growth, rising employment, and more personal economic freedom. The goal of a Single European Market enshrined in the EC's founding document, the Treaty of Rome, is within sight. A community-wide competition policy and the European Court of Justice ensure that this freedom is not abused and various funds facilitate the adjustment to the Single European Market. But the advantages of the Common Market for its members are generated internally and should mainly be felt by its founders. As the President of the EC Commission Jacques Delors points out in the introduction to the Cecchini-Report (1988), "...the goal is a unified and strong Europe."

To summarize, the EC rhetoric implies that internal free trade is beneficial. External competition, on the other hand, can be unfair and unsocial because there is no international law or agency to monitor it. The EC therefore has to deal with such practices itself. In doing so it claims to apply only fair standards in a more liberal and transparent manner than its major trading partners.

1.2 An Alternative View of EC Trade Policy Making

This study is in strong disaccord with the EC rhetoric: the concept of social or commercial fairness is meaningless for the evaluation of trade practices, because "...what constitutes unfair, 'unreasonable', unacceptable trade can be invented in unending improvisations..." (Bhagwati, 1991). Fair trade is a handy concept which allows intransparent and highly protectionist non-tariff barriers and which, at the same time, appeals to the public sense of what is 'right' and to what some economists claim are new justifications for protection (Bhagwati, 1991: 14). The EC's trade protection which is administered by the EC Commission is in fact highly *politicized*. The rhetoric of fair trade or socially-oriented trade policy is just an excuse or a marketing device for the Commission and the import competing branches. It covers up the fact that relief from import competition is granted especially to *well-organized and politically influential producers*, such as the textile, steel, vehicles, or consumer electronics industries amongst others.

The EC import volume in 1989 was over one trillion ECU or 1.2 trillion U.S. Dollars, 450 billion ECU of these from non-member countries. Non-tariff barriers are currently the most important and dynamic trade policy instruments: in 1983, over 20% of EC imports were covered by non-tariff barriers with an increasing tendency (Noguès, Olechowski and Winters, 1986). If this share had remained stable till 1989, which is a rather conservative estimate, this would have meant 100 billion Dollars worth of imports covered by non-tariff barriers. On the other hand, average tariffs have been reduced in various negotiation rounds under the General Agreement on Tariffs and Trade (GATT).

The welfare effects of protection are significant. The costs of the agreement with Japan for video cassette recorders, for instance, amounted to approximately 1/2 billion U.S. Dollars for the whole EC for the year 1983 (Kalantzopoulos, 1985). The voluntary export restraint on Japanese car imports cost British consumers alone approximately 250 million ECU in the same year, not to mention other member countries (Greenaway and Hindley, 1985). Heitger (1987) estimates that protectionism depresses the growth rate of the world economy by almost 2% each year.

Important non-tariff barriers are quantitative restrictions in textiles, footwear, iron and steel, automobiles etc. Most of these are *voluntary export restraints* and national measures enforced by *Article 115*, Treaty of Rome. The GATT (1991) registered 51 voluntary export restraints in 1990. The EC's Official Journal reports over 2200 Article 115 measures in the 1980 to 1990 period. In the eighties, *antidumping* has emerged as another potent trade policy instrument. 75% of the over 900 antidumping claims resulted in either voluntary price increases by the exporter or duties on their products.

The protectionist margins for producers are significant. Tariff equivalents for affirmative antidumping decisions amounted to 23% contrasting with a mere 5% average tariff on manufacturing products

(Messerlin, 1989). Estimated tariff equivalents for selected voluntary export restraints range between 3% and 50% (Kostecki, 1987).

All of these instruments are discriminatory in that they apply only to imports from selected countries. The decision-making process is not transparent; it is cumbersome or goes through unofficial channels, and the results are poorly published or not at all. The claim that the EC's trade policy is less protectionist and more transparent than that of other countries does not rectify this fact.

Paradoxically, proliferating external protection coincides with internal liberalization. Why should special interests refrain from seeking trade protection at the EC level when they have successfully prevented widespread external liberalization through the GATT? The key to explaining these conflicting phenomena lies in the different levels of trade policy making. Special interests obtain *external* trade protection because the *given institutional framework* accommodates such pressure. Internal trade liberalization, on the other hand, became feasible when the EC *changed the rules* for internal trade policy making.

In a nutshell, *the study intends to explain the emergence of both external protection and internal liberalization.* The bulk of this study deals with the first phenomenon - protection within accommodating institutions. A lesson, however, can be drawn from the EC's Common Market Project. Ultimately, the rules determine the nature of the trade game. The change in the legal/institutional framework of the EC lent credibility to the liberalization programme.

The study's approach is strictly economic. EC trade policy is not analyzed for its consistency with GATT or its own legal standards. Nor does the study follow the naive assumption that politicians only serve the people's well-being. Instead it applies a public choice approach to trade policy making. This theory asserts that individuals pursue their self-interest in politics as they do in the market place. The political actors, i.e. bureaucrats, politicians, interest groups, and voters, and their degree of organization and representation determine trade policy making within the EC's institutional constraints. A thorough analysis of the EC decision-making process and supportive empirical evidence is set against the EC's rhetoric. A considerable amount of historical and legal background information, data on trade, trade protection or welfare costs and further literature are also provided.

Protectionism as a Political Response to Pressure Groups
The first objective of the study is to show that special interests in the EC have better chances of protectionist decisions being made in their favour when they can claim injury by imports and when this claim is supported in the political sphere. This is due to the EC's institutional structure. Although EC protection is de jure administered protection, politicians have the final word in most decisions.

The EC Commission investigates the requests for protection and drafts the decisions. It also administers the implementation of trade policies. The proceedings, however, are not based on some rigorously applied standard of commercial or social fairness but the rules leave significant regulatory discretion. The Commission, however, has to gain approval for most decisions by the forum of the EC member governments, the Council of Ministers. This makes the administration accountable to the politicians and in turn facilitates politicized decisions. The politicians put pressure on the administration to satisfy their clientele, i.e. domestic producer groups. This bias is reenforced by the lack of transparency in the procedures and the underrepresentation of important interests such as consumers.

The study begins with a theoretical chapter. Economic theory teaches us that free trade maximizes world welfare and, as a rule, is also the best trade regime for single countries. Internally, however, special interests have an incentive to seek trade protection. This can result in a protectionist Prisoners' Dilemma rooted at the national level, where every interest group is protected from trade competition. This view is contrasted with the less relevant view of protection as an international Prisoners' Dilemma where countries pursue protection to secure the gains from economies of scale or international market power. The theoretical argument for the use of rules as a remedy, binding politicians at the national and/or international level is also presented in this chapter.

Chapters 3 and 4 describe the EC trade policy. First, the decision-making process, its main actors and its national and international constraints are discussed. This constitutes the system of checks and balances which underlies the trade policy choices analyzed in the following chapters. Subsequently, a summary of the EC trade policy instruments is provided. The array of instruments makes up a network of protection which can benefit the most varied interests.

Chapters 5 to 8 are the core chapters of this study. They analyze in detail those EC trade policy instruments which have been responsible for most protectionism during the 1980s. The application of national protection under Article 115 (Chapter 5), voluntary export restraints (Chapter 6), and antidumping (Chapters 7 and 8). The institutional framework for the application of these instruments differs significantly, affecting the scope and suitability for protectionist interests. Due to the vastness of the topic only these issues are discussed in detail.

Article 115 mainly enforces national protectionist barriers. Political scrutiny is exerted at the national level. In final decisions, however, it gives EC bureaucrats some discretion to pursue their own interests. This issue is particularly important when the question arises where national protectionist pressure will shift to when the Single European Market is realized.

Voluntary export restraints are the EC's most politicised instrument because their negotiation is usually not constrained by administrative rules. They are often negotiated under the supervision of top politicians and bureaucrats. Very little is published about them. They protect the most important industries such as cars, steel or textiles. The secretive character of the negotiation process dissipates resistance to voluntary export restraints because there is hardly any information available and no official forum to address.

Antidumping measures have significantly increased in importance over the past 15 years. They can be applied very flexibly because antidumping decisions can be easily tailored to the political winds. Claims against developing countries are motivated by shifting comparative advantage and claims against industrialized countries aim to reduce intra-industry competition. Cases against the former members of the Council of Mutual Economic Assistance in transition from socialism to capitalism deserve particular attention. Chapter 8 analyses in detail the export of "soft" goods to the EC and the implications for these economies' adjustment to Western markets.

Internal Liberalization through Institutional Changes
The study, however, does more than just explain EC protectionism during the eighties. Internally, the EC intends to liberalize trade completely before the end of 1992. This goal could not be achieved with the given trade policy rules. Liberalization only became feasible and credible when the EC changed its institutional framework. *Endogenizing the choice of institutions* adds an important dimension to the analysis of EC trade policy making.

Chapter 9 analyses how the Single European Market can be implemented despite protectionist special interests. The first part argues that the interests of all actors (special interests, bureaucrats and politicians) in internal protection have decreased over the past decades. Popularity among voters has also induced EC bureaucrats, the European Court of Justice, and politicians to tackle the problem of internal protection.

A remarkably skilful assembly and timing of the integration - a package consisting of rule changes, commitment, compensation and publicity - gave the project credibility. Compensation for the costs of internal liberalization takes the form of regional funds for the EC's less developed areas, well-paid positions in Brussels for national bureaucrats or EC wide trade barriers replacing the national ones. The changes in the institutional framework were most important. The mutual acceptance of norms established by the European Court of Justice in 1979 reduces the EC's harmonization needs. The Single European Act of 1987 provides a time-table for integration and facilitates free trade legislation by introducing a qualified majority rule for most issues related to "Europe 1992". This is the EC's most important liberalization programme.

Does the EC follow the principles of "good" policy making? Internally, it has taken a major step by changing the rules of the game. Externally, it seems that many improvements are necessary to move away from protectionist discretion and discriminatory and intransparent policy choices.

Analogous Studies
Several studies which provide a detailed institutional and empirical analysis of trade policy making in certain countries have been published during the past years. The classic studies are certainly by Baldwin (1985) and Destler (1986) on the U.S. import policy. While EC and U.S. protection are granted in representative democracies, Weck-Hannemann (1992) discusses the political economy of protectionism in the direct democracy of Switzerland and Amelung (1989) examines protectionism under the changing political regime of Turkey.

Chapter 9 of this study discusses the choice of institutions to promote trade liberalization. It relates to the book by Moser (1990) on the role of the GATT as an institution enhancing free trade. His conclusion is equally valid for the European Community: "Only by changing the rules of the political game, may a more free trade-oriented policy be achieved."

How to Proceed with this Study
This study is directed to all readers interested in a thorough analysis of an important contemporary policy issue as well as an academic audience. An intermediate microeconomics background should be

sufficient to follow through. Students and professionals in economics, international relations, and political science can use the study as a basis for European Community and trade policy courses, research, and for policy analysis.

All chapters can be read independently. To understand Chapters 5 to 9, however, the reader should be familiar with the basic theoretical arguments of Chapter 2. The reader who is uninformed about the structure of EC trade policy making and its trade policy instruments, will find it useful to read Chapters 3 and 4. Chapters 5 to 7 provide a detailed institutional analysis of the most important protectionist instruments. Chapter 8 on Eastern Europe is based on the results from Chapter 7 which are briefly reviewed. Chapter 9 on internal liberalization is also independent. Some knowledge of the EC institutions or reading Chapter 3, however, may prove helpful for a better understanding of these chapters.

Chapter 2

PROTECTIONISM - AN INTRA-NATIONAL PRISONERS' DILEMMA

This chapter surveys the most important trade policy concepts with particular emphasis on the new political economy or public choice view of protection. In the latter approach, protectionism is a distributional problem. Although free trade is, as a rule, the welfare-maximizing trade policy, it is often not implemented because the political process does not compensate the losers from a policy change. On the contrary, special interests can gain from seeking protection at the expense of the rest of the economy. This can result in a Prisoners' Dilemma (PD) rooted at the national level where no interest group has an incentive to abstain from lobbying. The country as well as the special interests would be worse off in such a PD. A constitutional economics approach to this problem with rules constraining the protectionist options of policy makers is suggested as a remedy.

On the other hand, protectionism can be viewed as an international Prisoners' Dilemma. This can result when countries restrict trade to profit from their international market power or to secure a natural monopoly in certain industries. This view, however, can not explain the prevalence of protection.

2.1 The Reasons for Free Trade and Protection

Standard trade theory suggests that free trade is the optimal trade policy because it maximizes a country's welfare.[1] Comparative advantage and economies of scale result in gains from trade. The concept of comparative advantage has already been developed by David Ricardo. In autarky, countries can only consume on their production possibility frontier. With trade, a country is better off because it can extend its consumption possibilities through specialization. While concentrating on the production of the goods

---

[1] Strictly speaking, this applies only to small countries without world market power, market distortions, or natural monopolies, etc. The relevance of these qualifications for policy making is discussed in detail later.

9

with the lowest opportunity costs, it imports those products whose production costs are higher than those abroad. The relative price for the imported goods compared to the exportables declines domestically. In equilibrium, the world is in a so-called Pareto-optimum. No country can be made better off by additional trade without injury to somebody else.

Comparative advantage explains inter-industry trade with cost differentials. Intra-industry trade, however, can best be explained with the existence of economies of scale. In his famous story about the pin-factory, Adam Smith pointed out the advantages of the division of labour in realizing gains from economies of scale. The constraining factor is the size of the market which is extended by international trade. Scale economies lead to intra-industry trade and product differentiation. In small autarkic markets, for instance, only one make of car might be produced; trade between countries can lead to the production of differentiated cars with intra-industry trade.

Standard economic theory, therefore, suggests free trade as a policy rule in competitive world markets. The size of welfare loss from protection can be easily shown graphically. In Figure 2.1, at world-market price P, local production is at Pd and consumption at Cd. A tariff of the size PT increases domestic production to PdT and decreases local consumption to CdT. Consumer surplus is reduced from DPF to DTE. Only part of the reduction is social waste. Consumer surplus TPAC is transferred to local producers whose producer surplus rises from SPA to STC. BCEG is the government tariff revenue. "Only" the shaded triangles ABC and EFG constitute welfare loss due to inefficient resource allocation and distorted consumption patterns.

The traditional theory also assumes that governments as a whole are the decision-making units in the arena of international trade. Devoid of self-interest, they act in their countries' best interest. They should therefore refrain from protection -- independent of what other countries do. Internally, a shift to free trade would be accompanied by a redistribution of part of the gains from free trade to losers (formerly protected industries) so that no individual is worse off.

Trade policy making can be illustrated in the form of a game. The countries are the players who can either implement free trade or protect their home markets. The previous discussion showed that countries are better off when they do not implement trade barriers. The solution to the international trade game should then be free

Figure 2.1 The Welfare Effects of Protection

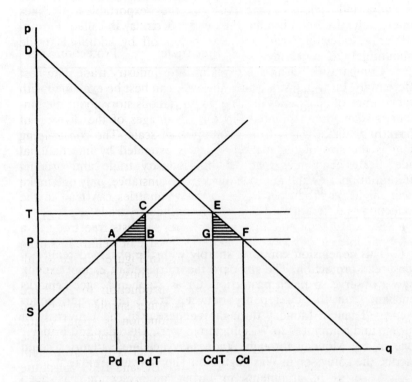

trade. When there are two small countries and two strategies, i.e. protection or free trade, the game can be illustrated by the 2x2 matrix in Table 2.1. The numbers in each cell represent positively valued payoffs to each of the countries.[2] The left-hand number indicates the payoff to country A, the right-hand number the payoff to B. When both countries protect, the payoff is lowest (for example (1) for both countries). Even if country A pursues protectionist policies, B is better off by allowing free trade. A profits from B's free trade policies and obtains the payoff of (2). But B profits more and receives (3) - even unilateral moves towards free trade increase national welfare. Since this result holds vice versa, neither country will restrict its foreign trade and thus obtain the highest payoffs of (4), (4).

---

[2] For simplicity, the ordinal payoffs for both countries are assumed to be symmetrical.

Table 2.1: The International Trade Game for a Small Open Economy

		Country B	
		Free trade	Protection
Country A	Free trade	(4),(4)	(3),(2)
	Pro-tection	(2),(3)	(1),(1)

This conclusion contrasts sharply with the observed reality of widespread protection. The standard theory therefore cannot explain why we observe so much protection. Or as Stephen Magee remarks trenchantly on the discrepancy between trade theory and policy practice: "I taught Monday through Wednesday at the University of Chicago and commuted to Washington to work Thursday and Friday... None of my Monday through Wednesday academic theories could describe the goings-on in Washington on Thursday and Friday."[3]

A series of arguments in favour of protection has been advanced. Trade barriers - for balance of payment, national security or prestige reasons, as retaliation deterring future protection, as a revenue source, or as a social policy instrument - are at the most second-best measures to achieve the intended objectives. Infant-industry protection to get domestic industries "off the ground" is also inappropriate to internalize "...the learning externalities associated with infant industries..." (Hillman, 1989). On national welfare grounds, only two arguments can be put forward to explain protection. These are discussed in some detail in the next section of this chapter. Optimum tariffs and strategic protection have been identified as wealth-enhancing protectionism in selected settings with imperfectly competitive international markets. The arguments are purely nationalistic, because world welfare decreases and conflicting national

---

[3] See the introduction of Magee, Brock and Young (1989).

trade interests may arise. More importantly the theoretical and empirical relevance is very limited.

During the eighties, the public choice view of protection gained increasing acceptance. *Trade policy making is about redistribution between winners and losers from protection who try to influence trade policy choices within the given institutional constraints.* Protection is seen to be mainly a consequence of rent seeking activities. It is the special interests within a country rather than the country's interest that give rise to the imposition of trade barriers.

The explanation of protection as a conflict between countries or special interests can be illustrated with the help of the classic Prisoners' Dilemma. Consider Table 2.2. If the game is only played once, player A, who chooses between rows, will select row 2. No matter what B does, he is better off with protection. He can get a payoff of (4) and (2) instead of (3) and (1) respectively. The same holds for B who chooses between columns: he also prefers protection. Although both would be better off with free trade as the payoff matrix indicates, the "uncooperative" protectionist scenario with the lower payoffs (2),(2) will prevail. If the players are two countries which both implement protection, the Prisoners' Dilemma is an international one. If the relevant players, however, are interest groups the Prisoners' Dilemma is rooted at the domestic level or in other words it is an *intranational* PD.

Table 2.2: Trade Protection as a Prisoners' Dilemma

| | | B | |
		Free trade	Protection
A	Free trade	(3),(3)	(1),(4)
	Pro-tection	(4),(1)	(2),(2)

While Sections 2.2 and 2.3 discuss these opposed concepts for explaining protection, Section 2.4 presents the constitutional economics approach to trade policy making.

2.2 International Prisoners' Dilemma Explanations

Optimum Tariffs and Strategic Protection

Optimum tariffs are the classical argument for protection. The essence of this argument involves the exploitation of monopolistic power by a large country at the expense of other countries. If a tariff is introduced in a country which is big enough to affect the world terms of trade, it will reduce demand in that country which in turn depresses the world price. If supply is inelastic, the benefits from lower world market prices can overcompensate the efficiency losses from protection and result in a welfare gain to the protecting country. A tariff is optimal when it is set at a level which maximizes the gains from protection.

The argument also applies to suppliers who can alter the terms of trade by taxing or withholding exports. The OPEC cartel, for instance, significantly raised export revenue by exploiting world market power. The OPEC policies, however, hint at an additional restriction of the optimum tariff argument. In the long run, alternative suppliers and alternative products enter the market and erode the protecting country's market power.

In recent years, the concept of strategic protection as a welfare-maximizing protectionist strategy has obtained significant attention. The basic notion is that economies of scale may result in a natural monopoly in certain markets. Governments can contribute to secure this natural monopoly for a domestic firm with the help of subsidies or trade barriers. Monopoly rents lead to net welfare gains for the protecting country because they overcompensate the losses from protectionist distortions.

The strategic component arises from the advantages of incumbents in markets. Market contestability is limited by economies of scale from minimum production capacities or research expenditures. In extreme cases only one producer can remain profitably in the market. Brander and Spencer (1983 and 1985) use the example of Airbus and Boeing (for the sake of the argument and not based on substantial evidence) as companies who export to a third country. Both incur losses initially and only one firm will survive. Why should the government not see that the lucky future monopolist is the domestic firm instead of the foreign one? To do this it would have to subsidise its domestic producer. World prices would then decrease because of increased production by the subsidised producer. Profits of the latter increase because of economies of scale. If the other country does not protect its industry, such a policy can lead to welfare gains for the protecting country.

The clue is that only one country can enhance its welfare at the expense of the rest of the world. However, more than one government can protect its industry and try to raise national welfare with the help of optimum tariffs or strategic protection. If the airplane market is really a natural monopoly, both governments of the producers of Airbus and Boeing have an incentive to subsidise. The most likely outcome is therefore that both governments subsidise and both countries are worse off.

Strategic trade policies or optimum tariffs then lead to a Prisoners' Dilemma as outlined in the previous section. Two countries may be better off by pursuing such policies unilaterally but they are jointly worse off if both pursue them. If A and B in Table 2.2 are countries, the payoffs imply that one country can increase its welfare at the expense of the other. The dominant strategy for both, however, is to protect its industry. They end up with a payoff of only (2),(2). The preferable option, however, is free trade paying (3),(3). The countries are caught in an international Prisoners' Dilemma.

In the relevant literature, Goldstein and Krassner (1984) and Stein (1982) support the international PD explanation of widespread protection: "All nations would be wealthier in a world that allows goods to move unfettered across national borders. Yet any single nation, or group of nations, could improve its position by cheating... and restricting imports" (Stein, 1982). While these economists and political scientists base their argument on optimum tariffs, Krugman (1987: 142) argues that strategic domestic protection may result in an international PD if several countries pursue such policies.

The Irrelevance of the International PD Explanation of Protection
International PDs based on optimum tariffs and strategic protection can neither explain the existence of widespread protection nor can they serve as a basis for trade policy making.[4] The reason why they are treated in such detail in this study is their extreme attractiveness among non-economists, who found that their protectionist views which

---

[4] For a more thorough discussion consult Krugman (1987), Baldwin (1988) and Siebert (1988).

were condemned by most economists, made sense after all. In analogy to Marx, free-traders provided the rope for their own hanging.

First, both optimum tariffs and strategic protection can only be applied in very restrictive settings. Only large countries facing inelastic world supply can implement optimum tariffs and usually only for a limited period of time. Strategic protection only works in natural monopolies. Market entry or product differentiation may dissipate monopolistic rents and gains from lower costs (Krugman, 1987). Furthermore, the threat of future retaliation by other countries significantly reduces the appeal of optimum tariffs or strategic protection ex ante. Repeated interaction in various markets deters from protection even more.

Informational problems limit the explanatory value of the international PD explanation. Implicit in studies using this approach is, for instance, a knowledge of foreign offer curves, the nature of the market structure, potential substitute products, to name only a few. "In reality, of course, even the best informed of governments will not know this much" (Krugman, 1987).

Thirdly, the notion underlying this approach of countries as unit actors maximizing their welfare is dubious. It would require politicians to be able to calculate the utility change of a country induced by a certain trade policy and then make their decision. Economists have tried to solve this problem by working with so-called social welfare functions knowing from very early on that utility can neither be compared nor added interpersonally and that no acceptable welfare function exists (Arrow, 1951). Even if a generally acceptable social welfare function existed, a welfare maximizing trade policy by goverments would not necessarily follow because protection redistributes income within society. We can only speak of Pareto-optimal changes in trade policy at the national level if the losers are compensated. Transaction costs for individuals to be informed and to participate in the process make compensation very unlikely.

On political economy grounds, Krugman (1987) argues that governments do not pursue strategic protection to further the country's overall welfare. He acknowledges the limited relevance of the international PD argument: "Nobody who has followed U.S. trade policy in sugar or lumber can be very sanguine about the ability of the government to be objective in applying a policy based on the Brander-Spencer (strategic protection) model" (p.142). Though theoretically a very appealing concept, Baldwin (1988: 229) points at the domestic roots of the protectionist problem while discrediting strategic protection: "The fact that optimal strategic trade policies may increase home welfare does not imply that the actual trade policies chosen are likely to improve welfare. On the contrary we might expect elected officials to systematically choose the wrong trade policies."

2.3 Intra-National Prisoners' Dilemma Explanations

Protection and Rent Seeking

Free trade is, as a rule, a country's wealth-maximizing policy. Why do countries then maintain trade barriers instead of introducing free trade and compensating the losers? Changing policies involves information, organization and decision-making costs. They lead to an unbalanced representation of interests (Hauser, 1986; Rowley and Tollison, 1986). Trade policies are then determined by the political influence of winners and losers from protection. In addition, the objectives of policy makers and the institutional setting constraining trade policy making influence the outcome.

One of the earliest books on the political economy of protection is by Frey (1984). Surveys of the relevant literature are provided by Ursprung (1987), Magee, Brock and Young (1989), and Hillman (1989). There is considerable empirical evidence in support of this approach to trade policy making as surveyed in Hillman (1989, Ch. 11).

The Motive: Rent Seeking

In a world of imperfect compensation, losers from free trade have an incentive to strive for protection in the political process of trade policy making. The motive, however, is not to maximize the country's welfare but to obtain a privilege. The motive is to *seek rents*, i.e. to seek receipt above opportunity costs for the factors employed in the protected industry (Krueger, 1974; Buchanan, 1980: 3). Markets are inherently rent seeking-oriented. New products and cost-saving inventions, specialized labour skills and locational advantages often yield rents. In a competitive setting these rents are transitory because of market entry. Such activities are utility maximizing and wealth-enhancing. Protectionist rents in contrast are gained in the political market. They usually take the form of government regulations which transfer income to special interests. In return for protectionist measures, special interests support protectionist policy makers. Redistribution, however, only comes at the cost of reduced overall welfare.

Figure 2.2 illustrates the distributive and welfare effects of rent seeking. The setting is even simpler than in Fig. 2.1 because supply is assumed to be perfectly elastic. A trade barrier causes the price to rise from E to A. Consumer surplus decreases by ABCE and producers gain ABDE.[5] The difference between the two is BDC, the so called Harberger triangle, which constitutes welfare loss due to inefficient resource allocation (Rowley and Tollison 1986).

Figure 2.2 Rent Seeking and Trade Protection

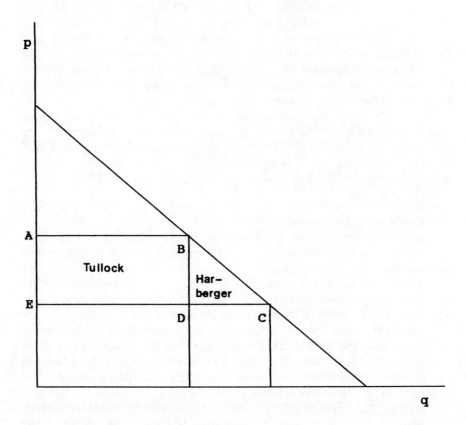

Social waste seems to be of little significance if BDC is the only loss and was estimated at only a minimal fraction of GDP (Harberger,

---

[5] We tacitly assume that the domestic price is not competed down to E.

1959). Tullock (1967) was the first to argue that this is only the case if rent seeking itself is a costless activity. Since producers invest scarce resources in the political process (lobbying, public relations, etc.) these resources are not available for productive employment elsewhere and constitute social costs as well.

In competitive political processes, rent seeking does not yield supernormal profits either. Rent seeking can amount the whole of rectangle ABDE in 2.2 or the total transfer. The Harberger triangle and the so called Tullock-rectangle together can reach significant proportions. There has been an extensive debate on how much of the transfer is dissipated by rent seeking. Tullock's observation that rent seeking is relatively low compared to what is redistributed in Western economies was the starting point of the debate. Hillman (1989) surveys some of the literature.[6] Although empirical studies have not resulted in satisfactory estimates of the extent of rent seeking activities, the relevance for explaining redistributive policies is widely acknowledged.

Winners and Losers from Protection
In order to explain the behaviour of certain interest groups in the political process and the trade policy patterns of a country, the winners and losers from protection have to be identified. This was first done with the help of the so-called Heckscher-Ohlin model. In this model, two countries are endowed with two mobile factors of production, i.e. labour and capital, and produce two goods. The country rich in captial specializes in the production of the capital-intensive good and imports the one that uses relatively more labour. Trade policy interests are identified by looking at the effect of free trade or protection on factor income. Labour's income increases when trade barriers obstruct the import and raise the price of the labour-intensive product (the famous Stolper-Samuelson theorem). The consequent relative fall in the price of the capital-intensive product depresses the income of the capitalists. Therefore, workers would favour protection and capitalists free trade in a country rich in capital. Empirically, however, we hardly ever observe that a dividing line between protectionist and free trade interests separates workers and capitalists. On the contrary, Magee (1980) found out that in the U.S.,

---

[6] Perfect competition in the political market should lead to complete rent dissipation. The underlying assumptions, however, are very restrictive. Risk averse agents, for instance, invest less than the expected value of the rents (Hillman and Katz, 1984). If the contested rent is a public good, free riding will also lead to underdissipation (see, for instance, Ursprung, 1990).

representatives of labour and capital from the same industry advocate the same trade policy.

The solution to this paradox lies in the fact that Heckscher-Ohlin models are only valid in the long term because factors of production are perfectly mobile only in the long term. Policy making, however, is oriented towards the short term for which some factors are industry specific and cannot move between various forms of production. This is taken into account in the Ricardo-Viner or specific-factor model. It again assumes two countries with two factors of production engaging in the production of two goods. The difference is that capital is specific to both industries while labour is mobile between the two. The mobile factor must get the competitive wage because otherwise it would switch to the other industry. The return to capital, however, depends on the price of the product because capitalists receive the residual after labour has been paid. The effect of certain trade policies on factor income again determines the trade policy interests. Raising the price of an imported product through protection is therefore in the interest of the specific factor while the owner of capital in the export sector is the main loser.

Consequently, specific factors in declining import competing industries in particular have an interest in market regulation. They can gain rents through domestic price increases induced by protection. The benefits are immediately visible to the protected industry and rent dissipation through entry into the market is not likely. If some of the protectionist surplus is transferred to labour within the firm, for instance via special union arrangements, capital and labour join together in favour of protection.

An import-competing industry has even more to gain from protection, when it is concentrated regionally (Cassing, McKeown and Ochs, 1987). If such an industry declines, location specific assets such as housing decrease in value because the supply of real estate from this industry and its workers make up a large share of the regional market. Workers not only incur the losses in real estate value but also face costly relocation. This raises their stake for seeking protection.

Export industries suffer from protection mainly through higher input prices and exchange rate adjustments. Large scale protection leads to a trade surplus and a currency appreciation, hitting exporters with lower revenues abroad. Exporters, threatened by retaliation, can lose indirectly from protection in the import competing sector. However, they get their own "protection" in the form of subsidies. Export subsidies, for instance, may be granted to dispel resistence to protection.

Producers of finished products oppose protection for intermediate or primary products because higher input prices decrease their competitiveness. They may be compensated with protection in their own product market. An example of this is the German "Kohlepfennig", a mark up on the price for electricity. This is a compensatory payment to the electricity producers granted for the high price of German coal which they are obliged to use.

Since domestic protection hurts the foreign exporting sector, foreign producers should resist the implementation of trade barriers. The choice of the protectionist instrument, however, can reverse the foreigners' trade policy interests. Carefully orchestrated "voluntary export restraints" can result in mutual gains for foreign and domestic producers because the foreigners get part of the protectionist rents (Feenstra, 1984; Harris, 1985; Hillman and Ursprung, 1988). Such arrangements can be observed frequently in the textile, footwear and automobile industries.

Ultimately, however, individuals in their role as consumers are the main losers from protectionism because they have to pay higher product prices. In addition, the benefits from free trade are generally not immediately visible. It is difficult for the consumer to differentiate between price increases due to inflation or external factors and those due to protection.

The Overrepresentation of Protectionist Interests
Trade policy is predominantly determined by interest groups and not by voters. It is only one of several issues in policy platforms for elections. In addition, voters remain poorly informed about trade policy issues because their votes have only a tiny influence on the outcome of an election. This can result in rational ignorance of voters about policy making which in turn facilitates the lobbying of policy makers by organized groups (Downs, 1957). Interest groups have an incentive to monitor and inform policy makers. "But that does not imply that voters do not count at all. Interest groups that can support politicians with *both* votes and resources have a comparative advantage over groups that can only provide the latter" (Moser, 1990).

The political process, however, is not only biased towards organized interests but also toward the protectionists ones among them. The visibility of benefits from protection as opposed to the hidden benefits from free trade to consumers has already been mentioned. More importantly, the main supporters of free trade - the consumers - are badly organized and rarely form lobbying interest groups due to free riding problems. As Olson (1965) points out, the formation of interest groups is biased toward small groups. Members of small coalitions will find it easier to provide collective action because the individual stakes are higher and monitoring costs against free riding are lower. Producers, for instance, are relatively easy to organize since they are well informed, often small in number and endowed with the necessary funds to finance their lobbying efforts. The free riding problem among diverse exporters to organize resistance against protection, however, is higher than for single industries striving for protection for a narrow range of products.

The special attraction of trade policy for redistributive purposes stems from the limited participation rights of foreign producers in the domestic political process. They are relatively well organized and can lobby in the same way as domestic producers. However, they do not have a right to vote. As a consequence, policy makers have an incentive to shift part of the costs of redistribution on to foreigners through trade barriers (Moser, 1990).

In summary, trade barriers against the imports of finished consumer goods are most strongly promoted in declining concentrated industries. Protection against raw materials and intermediate products is likely to face more resistance from free trade interests.

Objectives of Policy Makers
The Ricdardo-Viner model does not have a political sector nor does it consider consumer interests (which are assumed to determine voting behaviour). Political economicst have tried to overcome these shortcomings with several approaches. One group assumes that politicians are only intermediaries balancing political interests. The assumed objective of policy makers is to *maximize political support*. The basic model has been provided by Stigler (1971) and Peltzman (1976). The adaptation to an international trade setting is given by Hillman (1982). Politicians receive support from voters and interest groups. At the margin, they balance additional support from protected industries with losses from consumers/voters damaged by protection. Magee, Brock and Young (1989) call this the political equilibrium which is politically but not economically "efficient".

Declining industry support is particularly profitable because "...policy makers seeking political support from the declining industry confront a readily identifiable set of gainers from protection" (Hillman, 1989). The possibility of an industry suddenly collapsing can be introduced when industry decline and the erosion of political support mutually reinforce each other (Cassing and Hillman, 1986).

The Stigler-Peltzman model also suggests cyclical variations in the level of protection. During a recession, support of import-competing industries is relatively more profitable because industry problems are more severe. Voter interest in free trade is likely to lead to less protection at times of economic recovery.[7]

Since monitoring of politicians and bureaucrats by political interests is imperfect, there may be scope for the pursuit of personal interests. Bureaucrats interested in more power for their agency and higher budgetary appropriations will expand the application of administered protection (Niskanen, 1971). If bureaucrats balance the utility from higher budgets and less effort at the margin and if protectionism requires effort, bureaucrats will apply trade protection more restrictively (Breton and Wintrobe, 1975). Both politicians and bureaucrats may pursue ideological objectives or follow long term instead of short term policy interests.

Institutional Constraints
Institutions form the constraints within which policy makers accommodate trade policy interests. Protection in industrialized countries, for instance, is granted within the legal/institutional framework of representative democracy.[8] Two types of protection can be distinguished, depending on the agent who implements it. *Political protection* is granted in the legislative process as for example in the US by Congress. Trade regulation can also be undertaken by bureaus. It is then called *administered protection*. Policy makers have varying degrees of political control of bureaucrats. This blurs the distinction between the two types of protection. If there is much political scrutiny of the administrative process, administrative protection de jure becomes political de facto.

The legal/institutional framework also determines the set of trade policy instruments available to policy makers. The regulations governing their application determine their position on the scale between purely political and purely administered protection. This question will play an important role in the later analysis of the most important EC trade policy instruments.

Most existing studies deal with trade protection in the U.S. and assume that protection is granted by the legislature. Messerlin (1980)

---

[7] More recent approaches have modelled the interaction between policy makers, lobbyists and voters. The so-called rent seeking models are surveyed in Rowley, Tollison and Tullock (1988). Hillman and Ursprung (1988) introduce the interaction of voters and interest groups with policy makers in a candidate competition model.
[8] For the exception of Switzerland see Weck-Hannemann (1990).

and Finger, Hall and Nelson (1982) analyse bureaucratic or administered protection. There is a sporadic debate on the amount of protection that can be expected in the different regimes.[9] Institutional and empirical studies on administered protection and the amount of political control exercised over it are provided by Finger, Hall and Nelson (1982) and Moore (1990) for the U.S. and Schuknecht and Ursprung (1990) and Eymann and Schuknecht (1991) for the EC.

While legislative protection can be effectively constrained by the formal rules of law making and constitutional bounds guaranteeing freedom of exchange, bureaucracies may be restricted by strict technical rules in their conduct of trade policy making. The bias towards small well-organized interest groups can also be overcome institutionally. Institutions which facilitate large-scale negotiations at an encompassing level impede protection. "Large interest associations will tend to 'internalize' the indirect effect of their activities... and be more concerned about [society-wide] collective goods" (Lehmbruch, 1986; also see Olson, 1982). The power of institutions is never absolute as they can not guarantee free trade. Economically speaking, however, they determine the level of costs for redistribution. Institutions can be designed in such a way that they make protection more difficult.

The previous discussion tacitly assumed that institutions are static; however, they can be changed in the political process. They can be altered slowly through changes in the application of regulations, or policy makers can change them intentionally. This issue will receive more attention in Section 2.4.

Protectionism - an Intra-National Prisoners' Dilemma
If trade policy can be explained as a struggle between interest groups within nations, "...trade policy instruments are major means for interest groups to extract wealth-transfers from other domestic groups..." (Moser, 1990). Waste results from allocation inefficiencies. In addition, resources will be spent on attempting and resisting wealth transfers. Protection for one group may not reduce overall welfare significantly, but all interest groups have an incentive to lobby for transfers.[10] Foreign protectionist responses can worsen the situation further and provoke a trade war. As a consequence, everybody may be

---

[9] While Messerlin (1980) argues that bureaucratic regulation is more protectionist, Schuknecht and Ursprung (1990) claim the opposite. Nelson (1981) claims that administered protection is preferable to political protection because it is more stable.
[10] Repeated interaction in the political process provides an incentive for seeking a solution to this dilemma as discussed in Section 2.4.

worse off than they would be with free trade, even those who obtain protection. This is a PD setting but its origins are in the domestic rather than the international realm!

The 2x2 matrix in Table 2.3 illustrates the intra-national PD game. Industry A as shown in the table is assumed to be protection oriented. As in all PD games, the dominant strategy is to seek protection. No matter what the other players do, industry A is better off by striving for protection. However, all players favour a free trade/no-lobbying outcome to the protectionist outcome if everybody abstains from rent seeking activities. If everybody engages in free trade, payoffs to industry A rank second highest (3). This is even higher (4) if A gains protectionist rents while the others abstain from lobbying. If trade in general is much impeded and A does not seek transfers, A receives the lowest possible payoff (1). However, it can improve its position to (2) if it obtains protection. Even if the game starts with free trade, the incentive to seek rents will cause the free trade game to collapse.

Table 2.3: The Intra-National Prisoners' Dilemma

| | | Other domestic players | |
		Free trade	Protection
Industry A	Free trade	(3)	(1)
	Protection	(4)	(2)

Young and Magee (1983) develop a formal model of the intra-national PD with two goods, two parties and two lobbies. Both interest groups have an incentive to lobby although both would be better off by cooperating and refraining from lobbying. In a later paper, Young and Magee (1986) show that "...all groups can end up worse off when account is taken of the resources absorbed by the political activity bringing about the trade distortion ... when the opposing groups are evenly balanced in strength."

The PD relationship has not yet been tested empirically. Magee, Brock and Young (1989), however, find support for the PD relationship in simulated models with two factors lobbying in the political process. The particular setting and its parameter constellation result in a 5% and 7% wealth reduction for both factors. This does not discern prosperity from poverty. 5-7% national income at the aggregate level, however, is quite a lot of money.

Both points of view, that of an international or an intra-national Prisoners' Dilemma, can be relevant to explain protection, depending on the focus of analysis. The arguments, however, should be carefully applied so that no confusion arises.[11] Looking at domestic political processes as the main cause of trade barriers, Young and Magee (1983, 1986), Abbot (1985), Magee, Brock, and Young (1989), and Schuknecht (1990), to mention only a few, acknowledge the domestic PD character of protection.

2.4 Constitutional Constraints on Trade Policy Making

The Role of Rules in International Trade

If rent seeking by domestic special interests leads to protectionist trade policies and redistributive wealth destruction, what kind of constraints can prevent policy makers from giving in to protectionist pressure? How can we improve the international trade game? This is the normative question which political economists have to deal with.

In order to discuss remedies for the protectionist dilemma, a distinction between two levels of policy making has to be introduced. Trade policy making is governed by a certain institutional framework which is comparable to the rules of a game. Rules result in a pattern of predictable events and guarantee that interactions are conducted in an orderly fashion. Political rules govern exchanges within markets as well as the intervention by governments in individuals' choices. Different sets of rules lead to different patterns of exchange. The analysis of the *consequences* of certain rules as well as the *choice between alternative sets* of rules is therefore an important issue which is investigated by the constitutional economics literature (Buchanan, 1975 and 1986).

---

[11] There is some confusion in the literature with respect to separation between the two types of PD. See Schuknecht (1990) for a thorough discussion of this issue.

The rules of the trade policy game involve, for instance, the institutions discussed previously. What is important is that the network of institutions makes up the trade policy rules which determine single trade policy decisions. The delegation of trade policy making to the legislature or to the bureaucracy can make a big difference. Details can be very important. Administrative rules for trade protection can be liberal or favour protection, they can leave little or signifiant discretion to the administrators, politicians can have tight or little control over the bureaucracy. A recurrent theme of this study, i.e. Chapters 5 to 8, is the fact that every-day trade policy making (within the given institutions) in the EC is protectionist. It sometimes provokes threats to start a trade war which reflects the protectionist Prisoners' Dilemma outlined in this chapter.

Constitutional rules are the strongest institutional constraint on interest groups and policy makers. It is very expensive to change them. A relaxation of constitutional constraints in Western democracies is frequently lamented. It has facilitated the expansion of government redistribution, for instance through trade protection, during the past decades (Moser, 1990).

Trade policy analysts should recommend rules which favour free trade. Rules can contribute to solving the domestic protectionist PD if they raise the costs of implementing protectionist policies. Petersmann (1988), for instance, argues that the GATT rules commit governments to transparent, non-discriminatory and least distortive means of protection. Moser's studies on the role of the GATT (Moser, 1989, 1990) provide empirical evidence that this had a constraining effect on U.S. policy makers. The completion of the Single European Market is also based on this logic. Chapter 9 shows that the EC's most important changes towards internal free trade were changes in the trade policy rules.

An important obstacle to the credibility of *international* trade rules is their limited enforceability. International trade involves exchange partners in different jurisdictions. In the absence of a common enforcement agency, this may cause a problem. An international order safeguarding free trade and enforcing claims is a public good, calling for an international government, argues Kindleberger (1986). Considering the problem of controlling an international government, alternative means of maintaining the international trade order are preferable. International claims can be enforced spontaneously, for instance through international trade agencies. Joining such agencies builds up trust between trade partners (Moser, 1989). The "...coordination of private foreign trade activities in the shadow of the territoriality of law..." is also discussed by Schmidtchen and Schmidt-Trenz (1990). Alternatively, Tumlir (1983) suggests "vertical" enforcement, i.e. international commitments being enforceable in national courts. Free trade then becomes a private right. The recent US-Canadian free trade agreement and the developments in the EC apply this dual approach of international negotiation and national enforcement.[12]

At the national government level, free trade commitments are easy to enforce but difficult to negotiate because of diverse domestic interests. International commitments are easier to negotiate because countries can trade concessions. This adds to the weight of free trade interests in the political process (Moser, 1990, ch. 4). Internationally, politicians buy "...secure access to foreign markets" by offering commitments for.. [their] own trade policy..." and, thereby, gain political support from exporters (Hauser, 1988). Reciprocity is even more likely to further free trade when trade liberalization is negotiated for broad product categories instead of for single products (Moser, 1991). Reciprocal negotiations within the GATT framework, for instance, were very successful in promoting free trade (Finger, 1991a). In support of this approach, Bhagwati and Irwin (1987) argue that GATT negotiations should make the trade policy rules more liberal instead of aiming at some outcome, for instance, more balanced trade or fair market share. The latter approach would not be beneficial.

The constitutional economics approach is fruitful in analysing and comparing institutional settings in which trade policy making takes place. Constitutional solutions to the protectionist question are also suggested by Abbot (1985), Petersmann (1986), Roessler (1986), Krugman (1987), Hauser (1988), and Tumlier (1983) amongst others. Milton and Rose Friedman (1979) suggest a free trade constitutional amendment for the US.

Implementation Problems
It is also on the constitutional level that free trade has a better chance of being *implemented*. A necessary condition for the agreement on free trade rules is that the involved parties are informed about the effects of such changes. If consumers/voters know that prices decrease with trade liberalization and if producer groups know about the danger of a Prisoners' Dilemma and the opportunities of extended markets, this increases the prospects of liberalization. The EC, for

---

[12] See also Vanberg (1991) for a discussion on national versus international rules.

instance, invested heavily in informing the public about the benefits of the Single European Market to gain public support for "Europe 1992".

Wealth-enhancing free trade rules, however, can be prevented by distributional conflicts. When the rules are rewritten, the political economy constraints, i.e. the interests of pressure groups, have to be taken into account. The latter may have an incentive to embed rent-seeking opportunities in the constitution through protectionist escape clauses. On the other hand, agreement on freer trade is facilitated by the fact that international trade games are repeated games (Axelrod, 1984). Politicians and special interests may anticipate the protectionist PD which would prevent many beneficial future exchanges. They then realize that a free trade agreement can solve the intra-national PD problem. Since rules are usually valid for a long period of time, certain policy makers and special interests who would profit from trade barriers in the short term, may also be uncertain whether their long term interests still lie in protection. They may then rationally agree on free trade as the policy which maximizes the expected net payoff to society.

The voting rule on the constitutional level is crucial. Ideally, such choices should be based on unanimous consent because this would ensure that losers are compensated. Unanimity, however, raises the decision-making costs because too many interests may have to be compromised and single actors may exploit their veto power. A qualified majority rule can therefore be optimal (Buchanan and Tullock, 1962).

A rule with the stated purpose of free trade does not automatically lead to its implementation. It must be translated into numerous laws and regulations. Qualified majority rule was introduced in the EC for the many single decisions that are necessary to implement the Single European Market. Considering the numerous implementation problems that may arise, it is interesting to see in Chapter 9 how the EC has gone about solving them.

Chapter 3

EUROPEAN COMMUNITY POLICY MAKING

3.1 Introduction

A new level of international government such as the European Community is based on a distinct system of checks and balances between the agents involved in policy making. This in turn determines the potential for trade protection. This chapter presents the EC's system of checks and balances with its policy makers, their interdependence and their constraints with emphasis on the implications for trade policy making. It therefore provides a basis for understanding the detailed studies of EC trade policy making in the following chapters. There is bias in this system towards the interests of member governments. They have to approve almost all decisions which allows a strict control over the EC administration, the Commission, and its work. The dominance of national policy makers is a noteworthy feature of EC politics because it is the root of the EC's politicized protection.

Hine (1985) and Dudley (1989) provide excellent surveys of EC trade policy making as does Nugent (1989) of the EC policy institutions. A public choice analysis of international organizations and governments is provided by Vaubel and Willett (1991).

The EC and its authority over trade policy was not created overnight. It emerged over a 30 year period. A brief introduction to trade policy history is presented in Section 3.2. The EC does not operate in a political vacuum. Internationally, it is constrained by the General Agreement on Tariffs and Trade (GATT). Internally, residual domestic sovereignty over trade matters also puts restraints on the EC. These are discussed in Section 3.3. The EC's particular legal/institutional framework and the resulting interaction between policy making bodies and special interests is analysed in Section 3.4.

31

3.2 Historical Aspects

In 1958, the EC member countries signed the Treaty of Rome and decided to delegate trade policy making to the European Community.[1] In this treaty, the member countries commit themselves to implement a Common Commercial Policy (Article 113, Treaty of Rome). This includes a Customs Union and the free movement of goods, services, capital, and labour within the community. Since then, the scheduled completion of the Common Market has been postponed several times and is now envisaged for the end of 1992. In the meantime, the Common Commercial Policy has become the policy which has received the greatest deal of attention. It represents an important constraint on domestic policy makers.

EC trade policy developed in four stages.[2] During the transition period from 1958 to 1968, internal tariffs were dismantled and the Common Customs Tariff was implemented. National non-tariff barriers towards non-member countries, however, still prevailed. A common system of value-added tax replaced the previous inconsistent systems of indirect taxation. The levels of value-added tax still differ. This requires tax adjustments and border controls between member countries. During the transition period the U.S. initiated two GATT negotiation rounds because it feared that the formation of the EC would result in discriminatory trade policies and the formation of trading blocks (Hine, 1985; Moser, 1991). The GATT negotiations successfully reduced tariff barriers from an average of 12.5% in 1958 to 11.7% after the Dillon Round in 1963. A further reduction to 8.1% was negotiated in 1967 in the Kennedy Round.[3]

Member governments had delegated their international responsibilities concerning trade to the EC. The GATT negotiations were the first important forum where the EC gained experience and authority as a negotiating party on the international floor. The Commission also negotiated international agreements to succeed national commitments, for instance, to former colonies.

---

[1] The original member countries were Belgium, Luxembourg, the Netherlands, Italy, France, and Germany. Denmark, Ireland, and the United Kingdom entered the EC in 1973, Greece in 1980, and Spain and Portugal in 1986. Currently, Austria, Cyprus, Malta, Norway, Sweden and Turkey are applying for membership.

[2] For a description of the historic stages see Hine (1985). The publications of the European Research Associates (1981, 1982) and various issues of the Economist also provide valuable detailed information.

[3] For the impact of the Kennedy round on international trade and the U.S. see Marvel and Ray (1983) and Baldwin (1985).

The second phase from 1968-73 can be called the emergent phase. The Common Customs Tariff had been introduced and the EC had established itself on the international floor as the new address for trade negotiations. Especially after the Kennedy Round was over, the EC felt it could interpret its GATT obligations more loosely. GATT was circumvented with various preferential agreements. The EC exploited the provisions for preferential treatment in Customs Unions claiming that each of its agreements was the first step to such a union (Henig, 1971). This web of preferences threatened "the whole GATT edifice" (Hine, 1985).

The dominant issue during this phase, however, was the enlargement of the EC in 1973. The international and domestic interests of Great Britain, Ireland, and Denmark were taken into account. Britain's membership furthered the EC's outward orientation because of its global trade links. On the other hand, it resulted in increased protectionist pressure by declining industries. The United Kingdom had suffered from chronic low growth rates and balance of payment problems before. Competitiveness of the industry was eroded by one of the lowest growth rates of labour productivity and one of the hightest growth rates for labour costs.[4]

During this period, regional trade preferences, national protectionism, for instance by Italy towards Japan, and declining industry protection prevailed (Hine, 1985). On the other hand, overall tariff levels after the enlargement remained approximately constant. Free trade for industrial products was established with the remaining EFTA countries at the end of this period.[5]

The third phase 1974-85 (recession phase) witnessed the two oil crises with subsequent recessions and the emergence of Japan and the newly industrialized countries of East Asia (NICs) as fierceful competitors in world trade.[6] Increased import competition coincided with sluggish growth and increased unemployment. This reversed trade liberalization not only on the EC level (Hine, 1985). National protectionism proliferated. Trade barriers even affected other member countries when disguised as national regulations, safety measures etc. This demonstrated that the EC's authority over trade

---

[4] For figures for the 1970s see Commission (1982).

[5] After the EC accession of Portugal in 1986, the EFTA members are Switzerland, Sweden, Austria, Finland, Norway, Liechtenstein and Iceland.

[6] Although there had already been tensions with Japan in the late 1950s, the EC trade deficit with Japan only increased rapidly during the seventies and early eighties. While in 1970 it was close to one billion ECU or 40% of the imports from Japan this share rose to 65% in 1983 (EUROSTAT, 1984).

policy was still incomplete. GATT evasions in the form of non-tariff barriers and differential treatment of GATT members increased. Internal pressure for protection rose while outsiders criticized excessive EC trade barriers.

The foundations for the fourth phase after 1985, the integration phase, were already laid in 1979. The European Court of Justice then ruled in the famous Cassis de Dijon case that national norms must not be used to disguise trade restrictions. Up to then, Germany prevented the import of French black current liquor on health grounds. This ruling was upheld in comparable cases, for instance, for certain sausages and beer which violated German purity laws. The ruling has a strong deregulative effect. It shifts the burden to the imorting country to prove that the import is a health hazard or in other ways dangerous. Before, the exporting firm had to prove the opposite (Curzon-Price, 1991). Thereby, the principle of "mutual recognition" of norms between member countries was established. Goods could not be kept out of one member country if they had been admitted for consumption in any other one (Dudley, 1989). This put an end to a large share of disguised national protectionist regulation and reduced the necessary amount of harmonization for internal liberalization significantly.

The protectionist trend of the late seventies and early eighties was fully reversed in 1985 when the EC drafted the Single European Act. By 1987, all member countries had agreed to implement the Single European Market before the end of 1992 and to pass a total of 279 regulations for its completion. The project has been strongly publicised, it contains clearcut and feasible goals and its implementation has so far largely taken place as scheduled. The EC even wants to extend the Single European Market to the EFTA countries and thereby create the European Economic Space.

Two other important developments increased support for and credibility of the Common Market Project. The EC's competition law dissipates the fears that internal competition could promote monopolization.[7] During the eighties, the European Court of Justice significantly increased its judiciary authority. In various rulings, for instance the ones mentioned above, it established the reputation that it can and will enforce the liberalization programme.

The expected gains in wealth from "Europe 1992" are significant and are estimated to be at least 2.5% to 6.5% plus long term gains from increased industry dynamics (Cecchini, 1988). Most

---

[7] See Bael and Bellis (1987) for a detailed discussion of the EC's competition law.

firms have anticipated the completion of the Common Market in their corporate strategy (Jacquemin and Sapir, 1991). This suggests that the project "Europe 1992" is perceived as being credible.

While EC member countries are mostly enthusiastic about the Common Market, outsiders fear an increase in third-country protection under the catchword "Fortress Europe". Controversies over the EC's agricultural policy and industrial policy for cars and high-tech products have even threatened the successful completion of the GATT Uruguay Round. Free external trade, however, is crucial for foreign exporters and EC consumers alike. Jacquemin and Sapir (1990) provide empirical evidence that external openness is more important for maintaining competitive markets and prices within the EC than internal free trade.

3.3 Constraints on EC Trade Policy Making

The Alleged Primacy of the GATT

In principle, the European Community is bound by the General Agreement on Tariffs and Trade (GATT).[8] The supremacy of the GATT law, however, has neither been fully incorporated in the EC trade policy practice, nor has it been enforced in the European Court of Justice. However, GATT had and still has a strong influence on the evolution of EC trade policy. Article XXIV of the GATT treaty document allowed the formation of a European Customs Union. It permits preferential treatment for union members but requires non-discriminatory treatment of non-members. The formation of a Customs Union should not affect the average tariff level. As mentioned, the EC abided with this Article. In another attempt to comply with GATT rules, the EC had completed its implementation of the Common Customs Tariff by the year 1968. GATT contains a list of fixed national tariffs. In various negotiation rounds under GATT auspices, the EC has also agreed to significant reductions of these tariffs.

The EC's external trade barriers as stipulated by the Treaty of Rome are all in line with GATT rules. The GATT allows antidumping and counterveiling duties (Article VI), protection for

---

[8] On the GATT: "...the most extensive legal analysis... is still Jackson (1969), while his recent contribution (1989) is an updated and more policy-oriented version. The economic aspects of the GATT are discussed in Dam (1970) and Senti (1986). Roessler (1985) surveys precisely scope and limits of the GATT" (Moser, 1990).

agriculture and primary products (Article XI and XVI) and infant industry protection (Article XXVIIIC). It provides a waiver from GATT obligations under certain circumstances (Article XXV) and escape clauses for manufacturing protection (Article XIX and IV). However, it prohibits the imposition of quantitative restrictions (Article XI).

In many instances, the EC has disregarded the GATT's main principles, i.e. the principle of non-discrimination and the principle of most-favoured nation. Non-discrimination means that protection should not discriminate between trade partners. The most-favoured nation principle requires that concessions granted to one member country automatically apply to all other members.

Firstly, GATT law is interpreted in a manner that is conducive to the EC. Its vague language has to be translated into the language and law of national jurisdictions and this together with the many exceptions and safeguards provisions certainly facilitates abuse. Stegemann (1991) identifies a codification ratchet between protectionist countries. Referring to antidumping, he asserts that the contracting countries periodically accept new standards for applying GATT regulation thus leading to more "legal" protection.

Secondly, the EC imposes trade barriers in the so-called "grey area" of GATT. Many quantitative restrictions from pre-EC times have been "grandfathered" but additional ones have sprung up both on the EC level and on the national one. Voluntary export restraints, for example, boomed as a result of bilateral negotiations. These can be negotiated "legally" under GATT after a complaint has been filed and an investigation has been undertaken, but those of the EC are almost all negotiated outside the GATT legal umbrella. This points to a severe shortcoming of the GATT. Effective persecution of evasions and violations is impossible. Finally, preferential treatments were implemented with the pretext of future customs unions.

The reinterpretation and evasion of the GATT has resulted in a deterioration of its rules since the Kennedy Round (1964-67). As one of the most important contracting parties and rule makers, the EC has contributed to this development with the codification ratchet, grey area measures and preferential treatment. The Community also devalued the GATT's dispute settlement procedure by rejecting unfavourable findings. However, GATT still maintains considerable control over EC protectionism mainly through monitoring and international reciprocity.

Residual Domestic Sovereignty over Trade Policy

Domestic sovereignty of member countries constitutes the other important constraint on EC trade policy making. Although the Treaty of Rome documents the primacy of EC trade policy over domestic policy, member countries can request exemptions under its Articles 115 and 36. Article 115 permits deviations when community-wide measures are impracticable or "create difficulties". Article 36 permits domestic measures in case of "essential interest of a country". Article 115 in particular is still applied frequently. Other domestic policies which indirectly affect trade are tax policies, border controls, national norms and administrative barriers, public procurement, subsidies etc. (Hine, 1985: 66). However, national sovereignty in these issues has declined over the past 30 years and will largely disappear by the end of 1992.

The full implementation of the Common Commercial Policy was also prevented by the national representatives in the EC Council. In this chamber, national policy makers have a veto power for important decisions. Until 1987, this comprised all detailed regulations regarding trade. They used or threatened to use this power in cases where national and EC interests conflicted. Trade policies against important national interests are also difficult to pursue because of the threat of member countries to withdraw from the EC. As long as there are no legal provisions against "exit" or no army to enforce membership, countries have the option to withdraw if they (or their politicians) do not find the arrangements profitable any more. This option will de facto remain after 1992. Bernholz (1990) argues this the right to exit should not be abolished in a political union because it is a valuable means of protection for minorities in principle.[9]

3.4 The Policy - Making Agents

The supremacy of EC law over national law gives policy makers a strong legal position in implementing common policies. The principle of subsidiariness, however, limits the competence of policy makers to selected areas designated for EC policy making. One of these areas is trade policy.

The EC has various legal means for policy making at its disposal, such as regulation, directives, decisions and

---

[9] Greenland, for instance, a self ruled Danish territory, was the first and only one to do so in 1985, but not because of trade policy.

recommendations.[10] Regulation is the most powerful instrument for developing general and abstract rules. Trade policy is implemented through regulations and decisions.

Four bodies determine EC policies including trade: the European Parliament, the Commission, the Council of Ministers, and the European Court of Justice. The Commission, the EC's administering agency, and the Council, the forum of member governments are the main policy makers in the EC. The EC is lobbied by powerful interest groups, working through officially recognized associations and private lobbying firms. These four bodies and interest groups are discussed in turn. In particular, the responsibilities, the organization, the modes of decision making, the terms of appointment of members, and the interdependence with other agents are described. Table 3.1 provides a summary of the agents involved in trade policy making.

The European Parliament
Article 137 states that the European Parliament shall represent the people of the EC. The European Parliament's responsibility is, first, to *advise* the more important policy making institutions, the EC Commission and the Council. The European Parliament has a right to hearings in both institutions. The Council has to consult the European Parliament for instance on trade policy issues.

The European Parliament also decides on aid programs, association agreements and EC enlargements. It discusses the EC's annual report. It has some control over the Commission which it can dissolve with a two thirds majority. Its main power lies in the fiscal sphere since it approves the budget. In the future, however, the European Parliament may play a more important legislative role within the EC.

518 parliamentarians are elected directly for renewable four year terms. The Parliament decides with simple majority rule. It is assisted by committees, but as long as the legislative role of the Parliament is negligible they can only support its advisory duties. The larger countries France, England, Italy, and Germany have 81 votes each in Parliament. Spain is represented with 60 votes, the Netherlands with 25 and Belgium, Portugal, and Greece with 24. Denmark (16 votes), Ireland (15 votes), and Luxembourg (6 votes) have the smallest national shares in the European Parliament. While the United Kingdom has approximately 506,000 voters per European

---

[10] Nugent (1989: 144-149) for a detailed discussion.

Table 3.1 The EC's Policy Making Agents

	Responsibilities	Organization
European Parliament	Advises Council; approves budget, EC associations and enlargements can dissolve Commission	518 members (1991), each country has between 6 and 81 members; assistance from committees
Commission	Agenda setting power for Council; EC executive for competition and trade policy; supervises implementation of EC treaties	President heads 17 commissioners; large members send 2, others 1 Commissioner; 23 Directorates General with 14 000 employees
Council	EC legislature which coordinates interests of member countries; changes "constitution"; delegates policy implementation to Commission; decides most trade policies	Total of 76 votes with 2-10 per country; over 10 forums under heading Council for different issues; COREPER (administrative staff) for low-priority issues
Court of Justice	Applies, interprets and develops EC law;	2 chambers; 13 judges and 6 general advocates in main chamber
Interest groups	Inform and lobby Commission and Council	189 members in Economic and Social Commitee; numerous "private" lobbying organizations

Table 3.1 The EC's Policy Making Agents (continued)

	Terms of appointment	Voting rule	Influence on other agents
European Parliament	Direct election in member countries for renewable 4 year terms	Simple majority	Small
Commission	Commissioners nominated for renewable 4 year terms, President: 2 years; others are lifetime state employees	Simple majority or "written procedure" = adoption when nobody objects	Major influence; mainly at executive level; some influence on Council through agenda setting power
Council	Elected national executives constitute various Councils; terms correspond to terms of national governments	Unanimity; 54/76 majority for most "Europe 1992" issues	Strong influence on decisions and all agents
Court of Justice	Renewable 6 year terms; nominated by Council but independent	Simple majority	Rulings develop EC law; supervises Commission's and Council's decisions
Interest groups	Members of Economic and Social Committee appointed for 4 years by Council	--	--

Parliament member, Luxembourg is much better represented per capita. Each parliamentarian represents only 34,000 voters. The unbalanced representation is due to the interaction of large countries and small countries which do not want to be dominated by the large ones. This may play a more important role when the responsibilities of the Parliament are extended.

The Commission

The Commission's responsibility is to promote the interests of the European Community as stated in Article 10.2 of the Merger Treaty. De facto, however, the Commission has to balance national interests with EC interests. It must avoid antagonism with the member states because it cannot work without their cooperation.

The Commission has four major responsibilities in EC policy making (Article 155, Treaty of Rome). Firstly, it has the right to *initiate legislation* (agenda - setting power).[11] The Commission drafts the legislation and conducts the relevant investigations. With respect to trade policy, the Commission drafts, for instance, the antidumping regulation or international agreements.

The agenda setting power of the Commission, however, is constrained significantly and, so far, gives the Commission little scope to abuse it to the discomforting extent outlined in the agenda setting literature (Peirce, 1991).[12] The Council has the right to ask for proposals (Article 152) and it has to approve of proposals with unanimous consent. This induces the Commission to propose more or less what is conducive to the member countries' interests. Although the Commission drafts the budget proposal the budget has to be approved by the Parliament and the Council. The time-consuming legislative process and the status quo, which continues if no decision is reached, further reduce the de facto agenda setting power of the Commission.

While the legislative role of the Commission is very limited, it has control over the *executive* function. It administers, for instance, competition and trade policy and the EC budget including various funds (agriculture, social, regional). The Commission, however, depends heavily on national bureaucracies in the implementation of its responsibilities.

---

[11] In some instances of agricultural policy making it has even acted as de facto legislature on an interim basis when the Council could not keep up with decision-making (Peirce, 1991).

[12] See for instance Romer and Rosenthal (1979) or McKelvey (1976).

The Commission is also responsible for the *external representation* of the EC and the negotiation of international agreements and treaties. With respect to trade policy, the Community undertakes all international negotiations, for instance, on voluntary export restraints or in the context of GATT. Representation at private events is done with the help of delegations.

Finally, the Commission *supervises the implementation of the Treaty of Rome* (watchdog function). The most important instrument for disciplining member countries (and the Council) is to start an enforcement proceeding with the European Court of Justice under Article 169 ff. Before going to the Court, the Commission must first ask the country in question to carry out its obligations and then order it to observe European Community law. Enforcement proceedings have been applied increasingly over the past decades. While the 1960s only led to one judgement per year on average, there were 20 judgements in 1980 alone.[13]

The Commission is headed by 17 Commissioners. The larger countries provide two, the smaller countries one Commissioner. The latter are nominated for renewable four year terms. The Commission is headed by the President who holds a two year office which can also be renewed. Decisions in the Commission can be made by simple majority rule. Normally, however, the Commissioners agree unanimously or by the so-called written procedure, i.e. draft decisions are circulated and adopted if there are no objections. A large number of advisory committees assist the Commission.

The most important Commissioners are:
- the President, currently Jacques Delors from France,
- the Commissioner for trade policy and external relations, currently Frans Andriessen from the Netherlands,
- the Commissioner for the Common Market and industrial relations, currently Martin Bangemann from Germany,
- the Commissioner for competition policies, currently Sir Leon Brittan, from Great Britain.

The last three come from countries which are characterized as less interventionist and as having the strongest interests in preserving open internal and external markets. Bangemann's position is somewhat ambiguous because he has to reconcile interventionist industrial policies with the liberalization requirements of the Single European Market.

---

[13] This issue is discussed again in the Section on the Court of Justice.

The Commission employs approximately 14,000 people with proportional representation of the member countries. It is divided into 23 departments called Directorates General (DG). These are headed by the Director General and consist of several directorates which in turn head several divisions. Two DGs deal with EC trade. DG VIII works exclusively on development assistance. DG I deals with external trade relations. Within this DG, six directorates deal with country groups from North America to Oceania. Three directorates work on GATT and OECD relations, agricultural and industrial trade, and trade policy instruments such as export credits and antidumping. The hierarchy of the Commission is illustrated in Figure 3.1 using the example of DG I for external relations.

Figure 3.1   Organization of the Commission

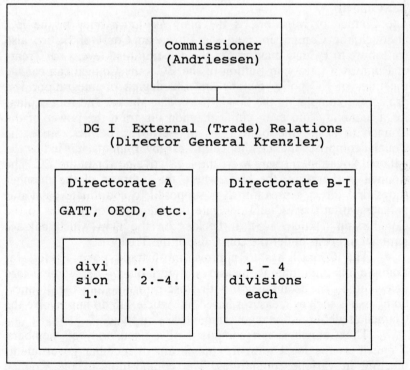

Compiled from Organigramme de la Commission des Communautées européennes, 1989

Although de jure independent, the Commissioners are national nominees who are fairly dependent on their national governments (Nugent, 1989). The Council nominates the Commissioners. Commissioners start out in national politics and often go back to a national political career. Reemployment by the member governments reinforces the dependence of Commissioners. The distribution of posts among member countries roughly reflects national policy preferences. Since the members' interests are quite diverse, the Commission has difficulties in developing a coherent policy. Holmes (1991a) describes, for instance, the conflict between the liberally minded Leon Brittan and his Directorate General (DG) IV (competition policy), the relatively protectionist DG I (trade) and the interventionist DG XIII (technology). The lack of a European-minded political base such as a strong European Parliament also forces the Commission to balance national interests. On the other hand, the Commission has to be impartial which is seen as a major advantage.

The Council
The Council of Ministers, is the main *legislative* body in the EC, although the Commission and the European Court of Justice also contribute to EC law making. On the constitutional level - the Treaty of Rome is a quasi-constitution of the EC - the Council can change the rules of EC policy making and the degree of integration. The project for completing the Single European Market and recent plans for a monetary and even political union illustrate the power of the Council to shape the basic rules of European politics. Since the Council comprises the member countries' governments, it is in fact the national governments who exert the legislative power in the EC. The Council is therefore, the body where the interests of the member states find direct expression. It is supposed to coordinate economic policies within the EC and delegate the execution of policies to the Commission (Article 145). It decides on the laws which balance national interests under the constraint of the Treaty.

The Council has to approve most trade policy issues, for example on antidumping measures. International negotiations are delegated to the Commission with close scrutiny from the Council. Some issues such as measures based on Article 115 do not involve the Council at all but national governments are involved.

The Council is not composed of a fixed body of members. "Council" is the legal term for the forum of member governments meeting in various committees. The composition of the Council therefore changes every time the various national governments are succeeded in their respective elections. The so-called democratic deficit of the Council stems from the fact that the member countries' executives constitute the EC legislature instead of a directly elected forum. Furthermore, the Council is physically remote from the people because it does not meet publicly.

There are over 10 different fora under the heading "Council". The issue to be decided determines the composition of the forum. The European Council consists of the leaders of all member governments and decides on more encompassing and general matters. Specific issues are decided by the respective ministers of the different countries. Ministers of agriculture, for instance, decide on agricultural issues. The Council of Foreign Ministers has an intermediate position and formally decides on most trade policy matters. The many fora further special interest legislation in the EC, particularly when the issues are very narrowly defined such as in agriculture. This bias is counter-balanced by the very diverse interests within the Community, for instance, between protectionist and liberal countries.

Hine (1985) mentions around 60 sessions of the Council per year for the early 1980s of which 15 were reserved for trade and 12 for agricultural matters. The European Council meets three times per year. Since then, the total number of sessions has increased significantly to around 80 per year (Nugent, 1989).

The Council has its own administrative staff, the Committee of Permanent Representatives (COREPER). The COREPER consists of country ambassadors (titulaires) and on a lower level, experts for each policy area. This triple level hierarchy of Council - Titulaire - expert is used to facilitate decision making in the Council. The COREPER has become a very powerful institution. The Ministers simply do not have the time to supervise the legislative process and therefore delegate it to the COREPER. In other words, the COREPER saves decision making costs and thereby allows the Council to concentrate on controversial and important issues. It is in close touch with the Commission. It arranges package deals together with the Commission to balance national interests.

Figure 3.2 illustrates the decision-making process in the Council.[14] Decisions prepared by the Commission are first debated by the experts of the COREPER. If they agree, the issue becomes an "A point" which is not further discussed by the Council. If the experts disagree, the Titulaires try to come to an agreement. If they agree, the issue is still an "A point" and is approved without further debate.

---

[14] The stages of law-making are described in detail in Nugent (1989).

Issues which have not been clarified by the COREPER become a "B point". They are the only ones which are passed on to the Council of Ministers and put to the vote there.

Majority voting, suggested in Article 148, was de facto abolished in 1966 in the Luxembourg Accord. The member countries agreed that all decisions of vital importance to a country (and all

Figure 3.2 Decision Making in the Council and COREPER

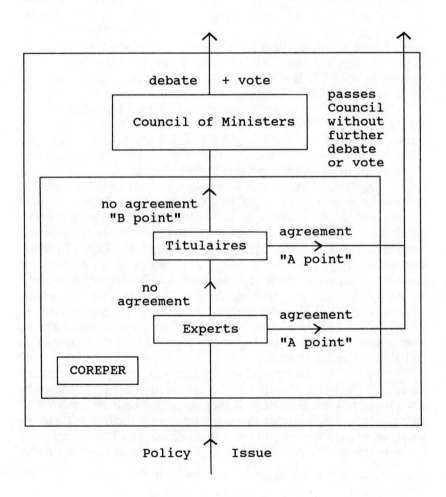

decisions are vital) should require unanimous consent. In 1987, the Single European Act did not reintroduce majority voting but explicitly excluded a selection of policy areas in the context of "Europe 1992" from the unanimity convention. Up to 1987, the decision-making process was so time-consuming and paralyzed by national vetos that the Council was close to being inoperable.

Most of the Council's (and COREPER's) decisions for the realization of the Common Market Project including trade require a qualified majority of 54 out of 76 votes. The number of votes depends on the size of the country's population with a bias in favour of the small member countries (Table 3.2). The four large countries each have 16-23% of the EC's total population but only 13% of the total votes in the Council. The smallest country, Luxembourg, has 3% of the votes but only 0.1% of the population. Interestingly, the voting power according to Shapley and Shubik (1954) is almost proportional to the share of the votes.

The majority requirement of 54 out of 76 votes allows two large and one small country to veto Council decisions. In trade issues, the combined votes of three liberal countries, for instance, Germany (10),

Table 3.2   Voting Power in the Council

Country	Votes	%votes	Voting power	Population millions	% of EC population
			(estimates for 1990)		
Italy	10	13%	13.4%	57.1	17.8%
Great Britain	10	13%	13.4%	56.6	17.6%
France	10	13%	13.4%	55.2	17.1%
Germany	10	13%	13.4%	61.0	18.9%
Spain	8	11%	11.1%	38.5	12.0%
Netherlands	5	7%	6.4%	14.5	4.5%
Portugal	5	7%	6.4%	10.2	3.2%
Belgium	5	7%	6.4%	9.9	3.1%
Greece	5	7%	6.4%	9.9	3.1%
Denmark	3	4%	4.3%	5.1	1.6%
Ireland	3	4%	4.3%	3.5	1.1%
Luxembourg	2	3%	1.2%	0.4	0.1%

Source of population data: UN Statistical Papers, July 1991.

Great Britain (10) and the Netherlands (5) or Denmark (3) would suffice to block protectionist decisions. Six of the small countries also have a blocking minority. Consensual decision making in fact remains the norm, even on issues related to "Europe 1992" (Nugent, 1989). The new voting rule is mainly a threat against countries who want to abuse their veto power.

The votes cast by member countries and dissenting views are not disclosed. It is therefore impossible to determine who has voted in favour or against a certain decision when it is rejected or accepted with less than unanimity. The official justification states that national politicians are protected from pressure by special interest groups when their vote is not known. It could also be argued that the lack of transparency serves to protect special interest policies from public scrutiny.

The member countries have significant control over the other EC decision-making bodies through the Council. The Council appoints the judges and general advocates in the European Court of Justice. It nominates the members of the interest group committees. Member governments also have tight control over the Commission. Figure 3.3 illustrates the "checks and balances" between the EC Council and the Commission. There are procedural and institutional checks between both. As mentioned, the Commission has mainly procedural means: it prepares and makes administrative decisions and prepares legislative initiatives. It has a right of speech in the Council. Enforcement proceedings through the Court are the most powerful device for furthering EC interests.

The Council's procedural rights are very powerful on the legislative level. It can request initiatives and decides on them either directly or through the COREPER. Institutionally, the COREPER is a powerful means of controlling the Commission. The politically nominated heads of the Commission, the Commissioners, also ensure that the Commission does not act against important national interests.

The Court of Justice
The EC judiciary is led by the European Court of Justice. The Court is the third important body in the EC's system of checks and balances. Being largely independent, it controls both the Commission and the Council through its rulings - although with limited means of enforcement. In recent years, the Court's authority has increased significantly. Authority increases the EC judges' utility because this results in more power, more prestige, more employees and more money.

Figure 3.3 Checks and Balances in the European Community

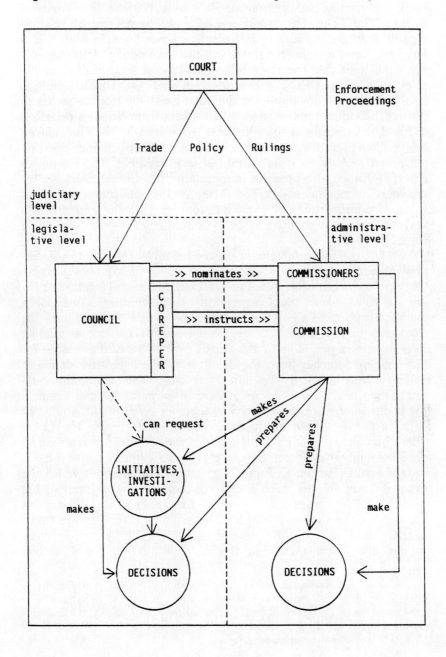

The duty of the European Court of Justice is to preserve EC law by *interpreting and applying the EC treaties* (Article 164, Treaty of Rome). The Court has to enforce EC law irrespective of political considerations, especially against member states (Article 169ff.). It is a referee between member states and the Community. Although it is not explicit in the Treaty of Rome, the Court has decided in the relevant cases that EC law overrides national law. This principle is hardly challenged any more. On the other hand, the Court also has to protect individual rights against infringement from Brussels (Hartley, 1980). The principle of subsidiariness has therefore been introduced by the Court recently. It requests that government activities must be performed on the most decentralized level possible. The European Court of Justice also provides interpretations of the relevant law for the courts in member states. This facilitates the application of EC law in national jurisdictions with very different legal systems and has been very influential in shaping European Community law (Barrington and Cooney, 1984).

The official enforcement procedure under Article 169 ff. has done more than enforce compliance with EC law. Ebke (1985) argues that the Court has contributed increasingly to the *development of EC law*. In cases where the Commission has taken the Council or a member country to Court for violation of Article 169 and 170, the Court has largely supported a supra-national perspective as distinct from a national one in its rulings (Ebke, 1985). One of the reasons for this development has been the deadlock in the legislative decision-making process since the late seventies. The unanimity rule established in the Luxembourg Accord often paralyzed the Council. Many decisions were vetoed because member governments could not approve due to resistance from national interest groups. The Court filled this vacuum with its rulings, helped the Council to overcome its deadlock and, at the same time, increased its authority substantially. In other words, in the EC, the Court makes the decisions which the Council is not able to make because of national special interests but which member governments would like to make.[15] From this perspective, the Council "delegates" trade liberalization to the Court because the Court is in the position to shape EC trade law. In three rulings, the Court prevented the disintegration of the Common

---

[15] This concept is analogous to Vaubel (1986) who claims that politicians try to delegate the "dirty work" to international organizations. It contrasts with the claim by Landes and Posner (1975) that in the U.S., the Supreme Court enforces the deals that Congress strikes. In the U.S., however, decision making in the legislature is not blocked by a unanimity requirement.

Commercial Policy and laid the foundations for the future Common Market Project: in the Kaufhof ruling (29/75), the Court enforced a narrow interpretation of quantitative restrictions against imports to single member countries. In the Donckerwolcke ruling (41/76), the Court prohibited tentative approval of national protectionist measures by the Commission with approval by the Council following later. The most important ruling was the Cassis de Dijon case, as mentioned in Section 3.2.

The Court has so far not investigated whether the stated purpose of a law is consistent with the results of its implementation. This inconsistency between the rhetoric of a law and its implementation is particularly prevalent in trade regulation as will be shown in more detail later. It reduces transparency and disguises the real intentions of a law.

The European Court of Justice consists of two chambers. The second chamber, the Court of First Instance has been recently installed. The main chamber consists of 13 judges and 6 general advocates. The Council can increase the number of judges by unanimous consent based on an initiative by the Court. The judges are drawn from the member countries and serve renewable six year terms. Judges are not allowed to hold political or administrative offices during their term as an EC judge. Every three years, half of the Court is replaced or reappointed. All governments have to agree to each appointment. This mutual veto power furthers the independent and impartial nature of appointments - and counterbalances the relatively short terms of office.

The Court decides by simple majority rule. The judges are protected further from political interference because their individual votes remain unknown. There is just one judgement. Concurring or dissenting opinions are not published. The means available to the Court are judgements, interim injunctions, testimonies and statements. Cases can involve individuals, firms and governments. Conflicts between member states, between the EC and member states, between EC institutions, between individuals/firms and the EC and cases from national courts can be decided by the European Court of Justice. It has not yet been fully determined which trade policy issues should go first to the Court of First Instance and which are simply judged by the main tribunal.

As mentioned, Community law is supposed to override national law but decisions against member countries cannot be enforced directly. The only incentive for member countries to follow the court rulings is the threat that other countries might also disobey, thus causing the Community to desintegrate. The lack of enforcement provisions prevents overly progressive rulings.

EC Interest Groups
The EC gives interest groups a strong position in policy making. Their official function is to inform the Council and the Commission about the opinion of national and EC wide interest groups. In fact, *lobbying* would be a less ornate term for what they are doing.

Interest groups are represented by many officially recognized EC wide associations as well as their national counterparts. They are supplemented by an array of industrial associations and lobbying organizations. Hundreds of private law firms, with many lawyers being former employees of the Commission, represent organized special interests. Some Eurolobbies are worthwhile mentioning: EUROFER for steel, COPA for farmers, CEFIC for chemicals, and CCMAC for cars. As the next chapters will show, some lobbies have even specialized in certain trade policy instruments: CEFIC in antidumping, the textile association in Article 115, to name only two.

EC groups have an organizational advantage over foreign producers because of the official organizational and legal support by the EC or by member countries. The official organization of special interest groups is the Economic and Social Committee which consists of 189 representatives: one third employer representatives, one third employee representatives, and one third for others (farmers, consumer, merchants). The large countries have 24 representatives, Luxembourg only six. The representatives are nominated by the Council for four years based on suggestions from interest groups and member governments. They have a right to be heard in legislative matters.

The Economic and Social Committee has much less influence than private lobbyists and industry associations. Well-organized and cohesive interest groups with significant political and economic weight are relatively overrepresented. The Commission facilitates lobbying by interest groups in order to gain information and support. This avoids conflicts and strengthens the Commission's position towards the Council (Nugent, 1989).

The previous discussion shows that the Council, the Commission and the Court - which are interdependent and lobbied by the organized special interests of the EC - determine EC policy making. The next chapter will look at the specific instruments available to the EC, their quantitative relevance, their legal basis, and their implementation.

Chapter 4

THE TRADE POLICY INSTRUMENTS

4.1 Introduction

The interest group that goes "policy shopping" finds a wide array of trade policy instruments in the EC. The size of the EC's political market allows a considerable product differentiation for redistributive trade barriers. The instruments are suitable for very diverse policy interests because of the institutional details regulating the application of each instrument. And as in many markets, specialized intermediaries (lawyers in lobby firms and associations) help the "shoppers" to find the right personal policy package. But can the EC afford to be protectionist?

In 1989, the volume of EC exports passed one trillion ECU. The EC is the world's largest trading unit with over one third of the world's merchandise trade (International Monetary Fund, 1988). Close to 60% of the trade is intra-EC trade. Over 50% of the external trade is conducted with the EFTA countries, the US and Japan. The developing countries including the newly industrialized countries and OPEC account for over 30% of EC trade. The EC typically has a trade surplus in manufactures and a deficit in primary products. Exports contribute 25% on average to the GDP with this share being much higher for the smaller countries. Since close to half of this share is external trade, the EC can hardly afford to become more isolationist. Nevertheless, external protection is significant.

Non-tariff barriers have replaced tariffs as the most important and most dynamic instruments over the past decades. Tariffs only constitute a major threat to foreign producers if applied under the antidumping regulation. Around 20% of the imports are covered by non-tariff barriers with the share having increased by 20% between 1981 and 1986 (UNCTAD, 1987). Imports from developing countries are hit twice as often as imports from industrialized countries.

The previous chapter outlined the central role of the Council and the Commission in European Community policy. While the

Commission exerts the executive functions and prepares legislative proposals, the Council has the final word in most trade policy choices. The Court preserves the supranational orientation of these policies.

This institutional framework suggests a politicized determination of the EC trade policy - despite the delegation of negotiations and investigations to the Commission. The following discussion will show that, in most cases, the Commission is bound by administrative rules which are vague enough to give it significant discretion. Political accountability of EC bureaucrats is high because the Council almost always has control over the final outcome. This makes administered protection in the EC much more political than in the US. On the other hand, protection is always influenced by the administration. Even voluntary export restraints, the most political instrument, are negotiated by the Commission and not determined exclusively by the Council.

The EC's trade policy instruments, their quantitative relevance, the dynamics, legal basis, and the institutions governing their implementation are surveyed in the following sections. Table 4.1 gives an overview of the current and probable future importance of these instruments. The survey is divided into GATT-conform measures (Section 4.2), external protection in the "grey area" or outside GATT (Section 4.3), and internal trade barriers (Section 4.4). Bael and Bellis (1990) provide an excellent legal survey of the EC trade policy instruments. Hine's survey (1985) of these instruments and the EC's international agreements from an economics perspective is also commendable. The GATT Trade Policy Review Mechanism (1991) provides valuable institutional and quantitative information on the EC. Schott (1990) includes a discussion of the instruments dealt with in the Uruguay Round including numerous policy recommendations.[1]

The direct instruments of trade protection are tariffs, quotas and voluntary price increases (so-called price undertakings). The EC also distorts world markets with internal measures such as subsidies, export credits or tax exemptions. It is, however, important to note that most of the measures discussed here are "indirect" measures in the sense that antidumping laws lead to tariffs or undertakings, Article 115 enforces national voluntary export restraints, and quotas and industrial policies result in subsidies etc. The categorization according to GATT conformity, however, is more relevant for trade policy making.

---

[1] These sources provide information on almost all the instruments discussed. They will, however, not be referred to in the discussion of each individual instrument.

Table 4.1 The European Community Trade Policy Instruments

Gatt-conform measures	Tariffs[1]	Anti-dumping*	Counter-vailing duties	Safe guards	New commercial policy instrument
Importance	+	+	0	0	0
Dynamics and future role	0	++	0	+?	0

Grey area measures	Quotas[2]	Voluntary export restraints*	Article 115*	Industrial policies[3]	International agreements	Internal barriers
Importance	++	++	++	++	0	+
Dynamics and future role	+	++?	0	++	0	0

0 = no/minor importance for protection, + = moderate importance, ++ = considerable importance

* Treated in detail in later chapters, VERs under safeguards and national protection grandfathered by GATT are GATT-conform.
[1] Only GATT-bound tariffs, not antidumping.
[2] Many under Article 115   [3] Leads mostly to antidumping, voluntary export restraints and Article 115 measures.

In the short term, the policy instruments are constant, but in the long term special interests can contribute to the development of suitable policy instruments. This process has been discussed theoretically under the keyword "erosion of constraints" in Chapter 2: The basic logic of this development is that special interests strive for easier access to trade protection. Cost saving inventions by the suppliers/policy makers in the form of new interpretations, new rules and new instruments then result in less external openness. Most of the time, however, changes in the rules lead to trade liberalization. The application of a trade policy instrument can then decline or even stop altogether, This happens, for instance, in preparation for "Europe 1992". The change in the application of policy instruments is presented in the following survey. The causes of such changes are not always referred to.

4.2 GATT-Conform Measures

The Common Customs Tariff
When the EC Customs Union was formed, the GATT required the simultaneous implementation of a Common Customs Tariff on an average level equal to or lower than the previous one. Customs authorities classify the import goods into one of 3000 tariff groups. The basis for the tariff is the transaction price. Tariff classification of imports is important when different rates apply to similar products. The rules of origin are important when, as practiced in the EC, international agreements give preferential treatment to some countries. To prevent the channelling of products through other countries with lower tariff rates, the products are classified as coming from the country where they have last been substantially transformed. This takes place when 1) the production process leads to a change in the tariff heading in the EC, 2) the tariff heading is changed and specific operations exercised, or 3) a certain percentage of value is added in the country.

The Common Customs Tariff is now of only moderate quantitative importance. The average tariff level for manufactured goods is currently approximately 5%. This compares to 4.5% for the US and 2.8% for Japan. The highest rates apply to footwear and certain motor vehicles, and amount to 20%. The effective rate of protection, however, can be more than double the tariff rate if the value added within the EC is low.[2] Several tariff reductions have been negotiated under the GATT auspices. The Kennedy and Tokyo Round reductions were most pronounced. Member countries have agreed in principle to cut tariff levels by another third in the Uruguay Round.

Tariffs are the second most important revenue source for the EC after its share from the member countries' value-added tax. In 1988, tariff revenues amounted to 8.6 billion ECU or 20% of the EC budget (Nugent, 1989). The planned tariff cuts in the Uruguay Round will reduce revenues by over 5%. The EC is likely to request compensation for this loss.

The legal basis for the Common Customs Tariff is Article 9 ff., Treaty of Rome. The Council can change the overall tariff level with the unanimous consent of the member states. This applies particularly to tariff reductions following agreements under GATT. The Commission leads the GATT negotiations under the scrutiny of the Council. Duties which are not tied to an international agreement can be suspended or reduced by the Council for the following reasons: in the context of preferential agreements (for instance Mediteranean countries, Lomé convention), in the case of supply shortages, and for reimporting outward-processed products. The Commission administers the tariffs especially when preferential rates apply to certain import quotas. The reduction in overall tariff levels has also reduced the relative importance of preferential treatment.

The EC can not easily raise tariffs unilaterally because most tariff rates are fixed in GATT negotiations and become part of the GATT treaty. Increasing them would be a breach of the treaty. Reducing remaining tariffs in the GATT, however, invokes resistance of special interests. With future levels being at only around three percent, the classic tariff will lose most of its political importance as a transfer device.

Antidumping

During the eighties, antidumping emerged as the EC's most potent trade policy instrument for certain manufactured products. It allows protection to be granted without retaliatory threats and at significant levels. The average antidumping measure is equivalent to a tariff of 23% (Messerlin, 1989). There were over 400 cases and over 900

---

[2] "The effective rate [of protection] expresses the nominal tariff on the final good minus the weighted average of the tariffs on its inputs as a proportion of value added per unit at free trade prices, where value added includes the non-trade content" (Corden, 1974).

decisions in the 1980-1990 period.[3] This figure compares to 389 cases initiated by the U.S. for 1980-87, one of the other major users of antidumping measures.

What makes antidumping so important is the rapid development of its application and the potential for extensive future protection. The first case was investigated in 1970 and only 26 cases followed in the next six years. Since 1976 the number of cases and also their importance has risen significantly. Most recently, single cases against dot-matrix printer or D-Ram imports from East Asia affected imports worth more than one billion ECU each.

GATT Article VI grants countries the right to implement an antidumping measure if the preconditions of the GATT antidumping codex are fulfilled. The last codex was signed in the Tokyo Round; another codex is in preparation in the Uruguay Round. The past antidumping codices were implemented in the EC with the help of regulations 459/68, 1681/79, and 2176/84 in 1968, 1979, and 1984 respectively. The results are published in the EC's Official Journal. The transparency provided, however, is limited by the scattered character of the published information which itself seems to be tailored to the political winds.

The EC distinguishes three kinds of dumping: product dumping, sub-assembly dumping and input dumping. Until 1987, only the dumping of finished products could be subject to an investigation. The evasion of antidumping measures in "screw-driver plants", in which only minor assembly operations of parts take place, resulted in regulation 1761/87 in 1987 against sub-assembly dumping. This is applicable if the assembly operations lead to less than 40% value added within the EC (local content rule).[4] Input dumping is not regulated (Bierwagen and Hailbronner, 1987). In 1986, the EC developed a rule to deal with unfair pricing practices in maritime transport, thereby applying the antidumping concept to services (regulation 4057/86).[5]

The investigation of an antidumping claim is conducted by the EC Commission. Only half of the claims, however, pass an initial

---

[3] A case is defined by country and product but decisions are made separately against each firm in a country. While cases against Eastern European countries only involve one firm, cases against Japan or the U.S. sometimes involve more than 10 producers.

[4] This regulation against circumvention has been ruled inconsistent with GATT (GATT, 1991a).

[5] See Bellis, Vermulst and Musquar (1988) for a discussion of the legal aspects of this case and Hoekman and Leidy (1991) for the problematic economic implications of extending this concept to services.

preselection. Several criteria must be fullfilled for a "successful" antidumping investigation. Most importantly, there must be dumping of foreign products causing material injury to domestic industries. Dumping occurs when exporters sell their products within the EC below their normal value, the normal value being defined as the price in the exporters home market, in a third country or the full production costs. None of these criteria is connected to one of the economic justifications of antidumping measures, i.e. predatory pricing (Viner, 1923) or sales below marginal costs (Ethier, 1982) which are the economic criteria defining unfair trade. This illustrates the arbitrariness of the EC's concept of fairness.

Injury can consist of decreases in profits, market shares etc. The investigation procedure leaves significant discretion to the EC's administering agency. It also guarantees some transparency for the involved parties in that the parties are heard in the course of the investigation and that the findings are published. The Council intervenes in the preselection and also has to approve of the Commission's findings.

Antidumping measures can consist of duties or voluntary price increases by the foreign producer, so-called undertakings. The Commission can negotiate undertakings with the involved parties, otherwise positive results of an investigation lead to a duty.

The significant discretion and political accountability of the EC Commission suggest a surprising hypothesis about the nature of the EC antidumping measures. The EC rhetoric and most of the literature claim that technical/administrative rules determine antidumping investigations. A thorough institutional analysis suggests that antidumping is largely politically determined. If this is true, antidumping is likely to attract significant attention from national governments and lobbying special interests. The large number of law firms specializing in antidumping cases and the attention in the media is casual evidence in favour of this hypothesis. Considering the importance of antidumping and the provocativeness of this hypothesis, antidumping is chosen for a more detailed institutional and empirical analysis in Chapters 7 and 8.

Countervailing Duties
Countervailing duties can be implemented against a foreign exporter when the exporter receives government subsidies. This is the twin instrument to antidumping with the same legal and procedural basis

and the same publication requirements.[6] A countervailing duty can be imposed if there is a subsidy on the export, the manufacturing or the transport of a good imported into the European Community. Secondly, the subsidized import must cause or threaten to cause material injury to domestic industries (Article VI, GATT). As with antidumping, the Commission investigates and prepares a proposal for the Council which the latter has to approve.

Countervailing duties are one of the least important trade barriers of the EC. Only twelve cases were recorded for the 1979-88 period, five of them against Brazil and three against Spain. In the U.S., countervailing duties are much more important. 389 proceedings were initiated in the 1980-87 period. This difference is due to the different government practices. While the U.S. subsidizes its domestic producers relatively little, the EC fears retaliation against its own highly subsidized industries if it applies coutervailing duties frequently. The EC therefore uses its political discretion to discourage applications for countervailing duties. Consequently, incurring lobbying costs for this trade barrier are not profitable for special interests.

Safeguards Measures
The quantitative importance of safeguard measures is similarly negligable to that of countervailing duties. There were only ten cases during the 1980-89 period. The only time they were important was in 1978 when they were provisionally applied against textile imports pending the formal conclusion of the second Multi Fiber Arrangement.

The EC can impose safeguards measures against imports based on GATT Article XIX which in turn is implemented in regulations 288/82, 1765/82, and 1766/82. The results of investigations under the safeguards clause are published in the Official Journal but the same holds as for antidumping regarding the quality of the publication.

Safeguards measures can, for instance, consist of surveillance of imports or quotas but there are no explicitly prescribed means at present (Bael and Bellis, 1990). The EC, however, is not allowed to discriminate between contracting parties. It has to prove serious injury (which is more than material injury under antidumping). The suspension of concessions - as the protection is called - must be limited to the duration and extent necessary to prevent or remedy the

---

[6] The economic literature for the EC case, however, is very scarce. An economic discussion and some figures are provided by Finger and Nogués (1987). Hufbauer (1990) discusses the relevant issues in the Uruguay Round.

injury. The EC must give written notice which is followed by consultations between the EC and the affected country. If the consultations do not lead to an agreement, the affected country can retaliate. To prevent this, the parties almost always negotiate a voluntary export restraint (VER). All these institutional barriers reduce the appeal for applying safeguard measures (Gard and Reidel, 1980; Jackson, 1989). The EC has therefore pressured hard for a relaxation of the GATT safeguard rules which is resisted by the East Asian countries (Hine, 1985).

The Uruguay Round plans important changes in the application of safeguards protection.[7] Most importantly, retaliation can be suspended for up to three years. This relaxation is counterbalanced by stricter standards for the investigation and the implementation of safeguards measures. A precondition for injury is an absolute increase in imports. The allotment of an import quota under safeguards must follow the pattern of previous market shares. The measure must not be valid for more than four years and must be degressive. Evidence of industry adjustment must be provided in a review after three years. Seeking VERs is outlawed unless other GATT provisions (e.g. antidumping) allow it. Although it is difficult to predict to what extent voluntary export restraints or antidumping will be replaced by safeguards protection, the prohibition of "official" VERs and the waiver for retaliation will make this alternative more attractive in the future.[8]

The New Commercial Policy Instrument
The new commercial policy instrument against "illicit commercial practices" was implemented in 1984 with regulation 2641/84. It does not specify the means of protection, but suggests recourse to the GATT dispute settlement procedure or safeguards measures under Article XIX GATT. In this sense it conforms to GATT although it is not explicitly part of the Treaty.

Initially, the new commercial policy instrument gave rise to significant fears of a "Fortress Europe". France requested a "...reinforcement of its trade defense mechanisms vis-à-vis non-member countries..." (Bael and Bellis, 1990) with the removal of internal barriers. The model was section 301 of the U.S. Trade Agreements Act of 1979. To put more pressure on the EC, France withheld its approval of the elimination of several technical barriers

---

[7] This assumes that the results are ratified in their current form.
[8] The reform of the safeguards regulation in the Uruguay Round and policy recommendations are discussed by Hamilton and Whalley (1991).

within the EC. Germany, Denmark, the Netherlands and Great Britain resisted and could have blocked the protectionist innovation. Log-rolling and the requirement of consensus resulted in France approving the technical liberalizations and in the introduction of a less strict version of the new commercial policy instrument.

The Commission investigates cases under the new commercial policy instrument and the Council decides within 30 days. The Commission, however, can terminate an investigation with an undertaking without further consent from the Council. The increased level of protection expected from this instrument has not yet materialized. The new commercial policy instrument has rarely been used. The other instruments suffised to cover all the important protectionist requests. However, the vague formulation and loose standards could lead to its application at the appropriate time.

4.3 Grey Area Measures

Quotas
8% of imports in industrialized countries are covered by quantitative restrictions (Finger, Olechowski, 1987). The EC applies over 500 quota restrictions against non-member countries, half of them in the context of the Multi Fiber Arrangement against clothing and textile imports from developing countries. Half of the quotas are national measures inherited from pre-EC times when countries could keep their national quotas for a transitional period in addition to EC wide protection (Hine, 1985: 87).[9]

There is no legal basis in the GATT or in the EC for the implementation of quantitative restrictions either; on the contrary, GATT Article XI explicitly prohibits quota restrictions.[10] Quotas are not discussed in detail here because they are implemented either under Article 115, Treaty of Rome, or under industrial policies such as the Multi Fiber Arrangement. In the future, quotas are likely to become less important because 1) national quotas must be abolished before 1993 and 2) the EC tends to negotiate VERs with foreign exporters instead of implementing retaliation-prone quotas unilaterally.

---

[9] A recent figure by the Commission (1990) states that there are still 2000 national quantitative restrictions.
[10] Although quotas under the Multi Fiber Agreemens in principle violate GATT rules, these agreements have been approved by the GATT.

Voluntary Export Restraints

Like antidumping, voluntary export restraints (VERs) have become a very important and dynamic protectionist instrument during the last decade. All kinds of trade restraint agreements fall under this heading. As a general feature of VERs, foreign exporters commit themselves to keeping their sales around a certain negotiated quantity. Often, they prevent the implementation of other measures such as antidumping.

Finger and Olechowski (1987) find that in 1984, 6% of the world import volume was covered by VERs. Kostecki (1987) estimates this figure to be 10% for 1986/87. The International Monetary Fund (1988) mentions 261 VERs in the world, 138 in the EC of which 51 are national VERs by individual member countries. Most VERs are negotiated in the textile and clothing, footwear, steel, vehicles and consumer electronics industries. Welfare costs are considerable. The VER on videorecorders to the EC, for instance, amounted to half a billion US$ (Kalantzopoulos, 1985). Winters (1991) surveys the results of other studies indicating considerable welfare costs of VERs for Great Britain.

The protectionist effect is significant as the example of the car industry shows. The market share of Japanese cars in the EC was 10% in 1986. In Germany, with a fairly lax VER, it was 14%. If the share of Japanese exports to the whole EC under free trade had been as high as in Germany, this would have meant another 400,000 imported cars, worth 3 billion ECU in 1986. This is a low estimate. The share of Japanese cars exceeded 20% in Sweden in 1986 and 30% in the U.S. in 1991. Smith (1989) estimates that the Japanese market share in the EC would at least double if the current national barriers were abolished.

VERs constitute an innovative means of evading international policy constraints under the GATT. The legal nature of most VERs is very dubious and some of them are called "memorandums of joint action" or "verbal notes". EC-wide VERs are often negotiated by the Commission in a "low key" way. There is no official procedure. Documentation is minimal and often limited to a couple of letters. Only VERs following safeguard proceedings include an investigation and a publication of the results and the details of the restraint agreement. Many VERs are negotiated on a national level. If they have a legal basis (regulation 288/82) they can be enforced through Article 115, Treaty of Rome. As mentioned, VERs are also popular as negotiated solutions to safeguards proceedings. Finally, VERs often result from trade agreements such as the Multi Fiber Arrangement in the context of industrial policies.

An institutional and empirical analysis, therefore, is much more difficult than for antidumping. The political nature of VERs can hardly be disguised. Nevertheless, the availability of various means of obtaining VERs and their current importance warrant a more detailed analysis. This is presented in Chapter 6.

National Barriers Based on Article 115, Treaty of Rome
Article 115 is the member countries' escape clause. It mainly enforces residual national trade barriers against non-member countries and thereby prevents arbitrage within the EC. The means applied are quotas and surveillance, although the underlying restrictions are often voluntary export restraints. Originally, Article 115 measures were used to enforce national protection which was grandfathered by GATT when the EC was founded. In the meantime, this original list of products has been extended significantly through the Multi Fiber Arrangement and a considerable number of barriers against other manufactured products. The categorization of Article 115 measures under "grey area measures" is not fully correct since it applies only to the latter barriers.

There were 2213 applications for the "non-application of Community treatment" in the 1980-89 period with an annual approval rate of between 62% and 86%. Over half of the cases involve textiles and clothing and thereby help to enforce the Multi Fiber Arrangement. Ireland is the main user of Article 115 for textiles but the measures are usually applied to imports of little value.

Article 115 also covers national quotas against industrial imports. Italy, Spain, and - most frequently - France have taken recourse to Article 115 against imports such as television sets, radios, cars, trucks and motorcycles. These examples show that Article 115 is another major conduit of the EC to curb imports. It is also a measure for national protectionist tendencies. The more liberal member states such as Germany, the BeNeLux countries, Denmark and, in the past few years, Great Britain hardly ever apply for Article 115 protection at all.

The implementation of Article 115 was regulated in more detail in 1979 and 1987 in decisions 80/47/EWG and 87/433/EWG by the Commission. The final decision is published in the EC's Official Journal. Transparency, however, is low since the few lines printed do not provide any clues about the criteria for approval or rejection of a measure.

Member countries can be exempted from community-wide treatment of imports with the help of Article 115 when community trade policy is "impractical" or creates "difficulties" for one or more member countries. The procedure does *not* follow the usual "Commission prepares - Council decides" format. The member governments must first approve of applications by their national industries which are then passed on to the Commission. The Commission has to give its final approval without further intervention by the Council. This suggests national scrutiny (as opposed to EC-wide control and log-rolling) and also leaves some room for bureaucratic self-interest.

Article 115 is both quantitatively important and procedurally interesting. Its prospects, however, are bleak. Although a complete abolition of Article 115 is not planned, national barriers should be abolished by the end of 1992. Making national protection unavailable releases significant national protectionist pressure which in turn requires compensation. A thorough understanding of the current determination of Article 115 is therefore crucial to understand how national protection is still possible despite a Common Commercial Policy and where this pressure will shift to after 1992. The most flexible instruments of compensation are antidumping and VERs - the recently negotiated EC-wide VER on Japanese cars is a forewarning of what can be expected in other sectors as well.

Industrial Policy and Managed Trade
The biggest threat to the international trade order and open markets arises from industrial policies which have become popular in the EC over the past two decades (Curzon-Price, 1991). The most renowned ones are policies affecting politically powerful declining industries, i.e. steel and textiles, agriculture and recently also growth industries such as consumer electronics. They have led to the regulation of large segments of world trade because trade protection prevents the undermining of these policies by foreign imports. This illustrates that domestic and international support of industries can often not be separated and one necessitates and supplements the other.[11]

In 1987, textiles and clothing comprised approximately 10% of world trade in manufactures; agriculture accounted for 13% of world merchandise trade. Import tariff equivalents for Hong Kong, for instance, averaged at 15% during the 1980s (Hamilton, 1991). These

---

[11] The emergence of industrial policies in the EC and its links with trade protection are discussed by Curzon-Price (1991).

figures show that the quantitative relevance of industrial policies for international trade is large.

The EC applies a broad array of measures to support and preserve their industries of the EC level. The most common support consists of subsidies or investment promotions (tax brackets etc.). Export credits play a major role in trade with developing countries (Pearce, 1983). State aid in the EC amounted to over 80 billion ECU for the 1986-89 period which is over 2% of the EC's gross domestic product (GATT, 1991). Industrial policy can result in cartelization (steel) or even nationalization of industries. If applied on the national level, they can also damage producers in other member countries. The coordination of industrial policy is one of the main issues debated in the context of the Common Market Project.

The legal basis for state aid is Article 92-94, Treaty of Rome. The aid must be approved by the Commission. Aid should only be used in the social sphere to solve adjustment problems. It must not lead to an increase in capacity. Repercussions on other member countries should be taken into account. Measures should result in the long term restauration of viability of the industry, they should be proportional to the problem, degressive and limited in time. In reality, industrial policies often lack coordination so that repercussions between member countries cause complaints and frustrations. German steel producers for instance complained about highly subsidized British and French firms which undercut less subsidized German firms. In many industries, subsidization has become quasi-permanent and has increased rather than decreased, as later examples will show.

Industrial policies lead to so-called managed trade which usually combines an array of protectionist instruments and products. The most renowned encompassing agreement is the Multi Fiber Arrangement for the textile and clothing industry which basically regulates trade for the whole industry. The alternative to an encompassing agreement is a bundle of measures against the importation of single products or product groups in the form of VERs, antidumping measures, etc. Such has been the practise of the steel industry.

The Council can request the negotiation of international agreements in the context of industrial policies. The negotiations are undertaken by the Commission and are under permanent scrutiny by the member countries through the Council which can involve highest level politicians. The Council finally has to approve of the negotiated agreements.

The Multi Fiber Arrangement has been negotiated between the 38 major developing country exporters of textiles and clothing and seven parties of industrialized countries (one of them being the EC) under GATT auspices. 66% of the textile and clothing imports from these countries are affected by bilaterally agreed quotas. Prices for clothing and textile products rose by 5% on average in the United Kingdom due to the Multi Fiber Arrangement. The costs for protecting one job amounted to three times the average annual earnings of a worker in this sector (National Consumer Council, 1990).

The industry is labour intensive and regionally concentrated and therefore particularly effective in lobbying (Verreydt and Waelbrock, 1982). When the recession after the first oil crises hit the industry, protection was quick to follow. The first agreement in 1974 limited the annual quantitative increase to 6%. The agreement proved to be too lenient to satisfy the special interests. France even introduced national quotas and others threatened to follow. The second agreement in 1978 allowed for "reasonable denegotiations partures" from the 6% rule. This resulted in many national quotas and VERs which had to be enforced with the help of Article 115. Attempts are being made to reintroduce GATT rules for trade in textiles and clothing.[12]

The sector that is supported most extensively is agriculture.[13] The official objective is to increase productivity, to raise farm incomes and to stabilize prices at a reasonable level (Article 38, Treaty of Rome). The means applied are manifold. Variable import levies and import taxes ensure a fixed threshold price for farmers. Surplus production is sold on the world market, stored, or destroyed. Mounting surpluses distort world prices. EUROSTAT (1988) reports 91 billion ECU value added in the agricultural sector. The economic costs are only marginally lower: in 1989, the consumers subsidized agriculture with 49 billion ECU and the tax payer paid another 40 billion ECU (GATT, 1991). 63% of the EC's 38 billion ECU budget in 1987 was spent on agriculture (Peirce, 1990; Hayes and Schmitz, 1988). This provoked both internal and external resistance against the Common Agricultural Policy. As a consequence, a quota system (dairy sector) and land closures were implemented.

---

[12] The history of the Multi Fiber Arrangements is briefly discussed in OECD (1983). For a discussion of the issues in textile and clothing trade in the Uruguay Round see Cline (1990).

[13] For a critical review of the Common Agricultural Policy see Hill (1984) and for the issues dealt with in the Uruguay Round see Hathaway (1990).

The first oil crisis also gave rise to protectionist demands from the steel industry when overcapacities and modernization requirements coincided with falling profits (Crandall, 1980). 40% of the antidumping cases in the 1978-80 period were launched by the iron/steel sector. Market cartellization was the result of the introduction of production quotas in 1980 and mandatory prices for 40% of the production in 1984. Overproduction by individual producers leads to hefty fines. Voluntary price increases, VERs, and duties for third-country imports enforce the cartel internationally. In the early eighties, state aid to the Irish and French steel industries exceeded the value added in this industry (GATT, 1991).

Recently, industrial policy has spread to high-tech and other fast growing industries. EC producers claim that subsidies, protection, government induced mergers and cartels give them a competitive edge or at least a chance to survive in high-tech markets. Their quest for counter-competitive state aid is mostly successful, their promise of improved competitiveness, however, is rarely kept. The future of industrial policies looks bright. Several countries have a ministry for such policies, the EC has a Commissioner for industrial affairs. The 1991 winner was the car industry with an encompassing policy support package against Japan.

Since industrial policies mostly lead to conventional trade protection (VERs, antidumping and Article 115 measures) the effect of such policies on trade is indirectly treated in more detail in later chapters.

The Hierarchy of International Preferential Treatment

The EC has signed various agreements with other country groups giving preferential treatment to their imports. The EC usually grants tariff concessions. The decreasing importance of tariffs, however, also reduces the importance of these agreements to such an extent that some are left with only a symbolic character.

Figure 4.1 illustrates the hierarchy of preferential treatment in the EC as presented in Hine (1985) and updated here. The most "privileged" countries are the EFTA members who enjoy a free trade area with the EC. The Single European Market will be extended to these countries in the EFTA's successor, the European Economic Space. The EC signed an association treaty with Hungary, Poland and Czechoslovakia which grants these countries access to the EC markets without tariffs or quantitative restrictions. The ACP countries which signed the Lomé convention still face some tariffs but these are the lowest in the EC. The Mediterranean countries profit from a mixture of tariff preferences which makes them more advantaged than the Asian and Latin American countries. The latter are only part of the United Nations' Generalized System of Preferences (GSP) which grants them tariff concessions mainly for manufactured products. The USA and Japan are subject to the GATT rules without preferential treatment. Trade with non-associated Eastern European countries is not yet covered by the GATT codex and is therefore not subject to liberalization under GATT.[14]

Figure 4.1 The Hierarchy of Preferential Treatment

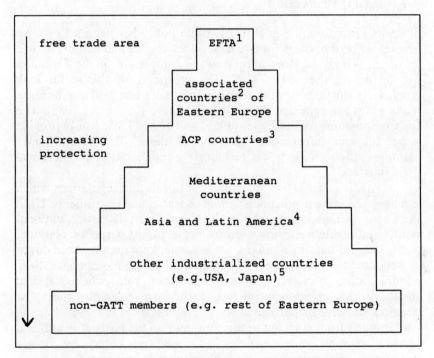

[1] future European Economic Space   [2] Poland, Czechoslovakia and Hungary
[3] African, Carribean and Pacific Countries which signed the Lomé Convention
[4] Countries with tariff concessions under the UN Generalized System of Preferences.
[5] Countries with regualar GATT treatment to which the most-favoured-nation principle applies.

---

[14] See Hine, Chapters 6.5, 6.6 and 8 to 14 for a thorough discussion of the EC's preferential agreements. Senti (1989) discusses the EFTA and its relation to the EC and the Single European Market in detail.

The legal basis for international agreements is Article 113, Treaty of Rome. Association agreements are based on Article 238. Preferential agreements are negotiated by the Commission. In its negotiations, the Commission is under close political scrutiny. The Council authorizes the opening of negotiations and establishes a framework for them. Ultimately, the Council has to sign the agreements. In the future, the importance of preferential treatment is likely to diminish further with decreasing overall tariff levels (possibly with the exception of Eastern Europe).

4.4 Internal Protection

Since its formation, the goal of EC trade policy has been a Common Market without barriers for goods, services, capital and labour. Article 8a of the Treaty of Rome requires the completion of the Common Market before the end of 1992. The prospects for this so far look good. It is worth reviewing existing internal trade barriers because major gains are expected from removing these (Cecchini , 1988). The EC Commission's White Paper (1985) and Hine (1985: 63-67) provide a helpful and informative overview of them. The White Paper identifies three major types: technical/ administrative, physical and fiscal barriers.

Administrative barriers consist of norms and regulations which can have the same protectionist effect as traditional instruments. Until the Cassis de Dijon ruling by the European Court of Justice, national norms and regulations were used for protectionist purposes. National purity laws for beer or sausages, for example, kept imports even out of self-claimed liberal Germany. Since then this abuse has declined. Still, administrative barriers play an important role when national standards lack clarity, change frequently, involve lengthy checks or penalize imports in particular ways. For instance, the 1990 ban on beef imports from England to the continent on the basis of health and security reasons under Article 36 caused an outcry by British producers and exporters against continental protectionism.

The costs involved in border crossings are the so-called physical barriers to free trade within the EC. Complex customs, tax and statistical formalities as well as the limited number of approved crossing points are examples of such internal barriers. Costs of border controls can be as high as 10% of the value of the traded products.

National standards, administrative practices and physical barriers sometimes result in strange conflicts with non-EC members.

The French once required Japanese VCRs to clear customs in just one customs office in Poitier where the few officials could not keep up with the work. The ban on hormone treated beef and pork from the U.S. officially served to protect the consumer while the U.S. denounced the EC's regulation as protectionist. These disputes usually raise significant public attention although they are quantitatively much less important than other types of protection.

Certificates of origin have become another subject of disputes. The percentage of value added that makes a product local is being discussed in the Uruguay Round. The future rule is very uncertain. The rule for cases of antidumping duty evasion within the EC is currently at 40%. France requests local content rules as high as 80% because Japanese cars produced in Britain would then not qualify as domestic any more.

Remaining fiscal barriers, for instance, consist of national export subsidies, tax brackets, preferential treatment in public procurement for national suppliers and different levels of value-added taxes. The EC now attempts to coordinate subsidization and to open up public procurement for competition within the whole EC. The GATT (1991) reports that national import penetration (imports as a percentage of national production plus imports) ranges between 19% (Italy) and 43% (Belgium). Import penetration in public sector purchases is much lower. It ranges between 1% for Italy and 21% for Belgium. Opening public procurement to EC-wide suppliers has so far only had very limited success. The large difference in value-added taxes between member countries initially constituted a major barrier to lifting border controls because countries feared the flow of demand (and tax revenue) from high-tax to low-tax countries. The EC has now agreed in principal on a minimum level for value-added tax of 15%. Governments can choose higher levels but excessive differences will result in international arbitrage.

The U.S. example, however, shows that large markets are hardly ever completely free of internal barriers. The EC population and producers are likely to experience some frustration when, for instance, health standards, professional qualifications etc. impede the free movement of goods, services, capital and labour even after 1992.

Chapter 5

NATIONAL PROTECTION BASED ON ARTICLE 115, TREATY OF ROME

In order to ensure that the execution of measures of commercial policy taken in accordance with this Treaty by any Member State is not obstructed by deflection of trade, or where differences between such measures lead to economic difficulties in one or more of the Member States, the Commission shall recommend the methods for the requisite cooperation between Member States. Failing this, the Commission shall authorise Member States to take the necessary protective measures, the conditions and details of which it shall determine. (...)

Article 115, Treaty of Rome

5.1 Introduction

Article 115 is the escape clause for member countries to circumvent the protectionist limits of the Common Commercial Policy. Although national quotas and the Multi Fiber Arrangement are the primary instruments of national protectionism towards non-member countries, many of these are enforced with the help of Article 115. It is, therefore, a barometer of national protectionist tendencies.

There have been 2213 applications for Article 115 measures by particular member countries during the 1980s. In the event of a positive decision, the EC can implement surveillance of imports or import blocks. The approval rate during the 1980s, for instance, was between 62% and 86%. This indicates a relatively good chance of success when seeking such protection. The most notable users have been the countries which also pressure for external protection and extensive industrial policies i.e. France, Ireland, Italy and, recently, Spain. Over half of the cases involve textile imports, but cars and

73

consumer electronics are also politically and economically important products which face national restrictions. The most important targets are the Newly Industrialized Countries of East Asia, China and Japan.

Article 115 is mainly applied to prevent the circumvention of national restrictions through trade deflection. Without Article 115, the Italian import quota for Japanese cars, for instance, could be evaded by importing more Japanese cars to Italy through France. In addition, this provision can serve to spread national barriers from one member country to another and thereby raise national protection. When barriers in one country (say against Japanese cars by Italy) lead to shifting exports (say from Italy to France), France can then request protection of its own market under Article 115. Finally, it can serve to distribute EC-wide quotas among member countries in a protectionist manner by forcing foreigners to allocate their quotas to their own disadvantage (for instance exporting winter coats only to Greece). Article 115 measures, therefore, are a good indicator of national protectionism towards non-member countries.[1]

Although Article 115 is one of the EC's instruments of administered protection, political scrutiny is important. However, the latter is usually exercised by the applicant's government which approves the protectionist claims before they are passed on to the Commission. This encourages national interest groups to seek relief from import competition through their respective governments. Political control on the EC level is only indirect. Since the final decision does not require approval by the Council, the Commission can use some of its extensive discretion in pursuing its own bureaucratic interests.

Article 115 reflects the failure of the EC to implement the Common Commercial Policy fully and to complete the Single European Market. Hine (1985) mentions 284 quantitative restrictions by member countries in 1982. The Commission (1990) even reports that over 2000 of them still exist. A significant number of barriers are in the grey area concerning GATT legality. They emerged after the EC was formed (and were therefore not grandfathered by GATT) and they were not negotiated under the Multi Fiber Arrangement (MFA) which regulates imports of textiles and clothing. Transparency and publicity have therefore been kept to a minimum. Publications are limited to a few lines in the EC's Official Journal.

---

[1] Other national non-tariff barriers such as administrative obstacles or discriminatory public procurement are briefly discussed in Chapter 4.4.

This chapter demonstrates the prominence of Article 115 in EC trade policy. Surprisingly, the economic literature has neglected this instrument.[2] The chapter investigates how Article 115 is applied by looking at the applicants and the targets (Section 5.2) and the institutional framework governing its application (Section 5.3). An empirical investigation into the determinants of decisions based on Article 115 follows (Section 5.4). Industries prefer this instrument to others because of its low lobbying costs and the little publicity it receives (Section 5.5).

In the light of the completion of the Common Market before the end of 1992, an abolition of national barriers is planned. Surveillance of imports to member countries has already declined from over 1200 measures per year in the early 1980s to less than 200 in 1991. This raises the delicate question of how industries are compensated when they lose their national protection. Understanding the current determinants of protection under Article 115 helps to predict what kind of protectionist pressure can be expected and whether this justifies the fears of a "Fortress Europe" (Section 5.6).

5.2 Who Applies and Who Are the Targets?

The number of Article 115 measures has risen from around 50 cases per year between 1971-1974 to over 300 cases for the 1978-1980 period (see Table 5.1). Recently, the number of applications has decreased to under 200. The sharp rise was mainly due to the negotiation of the second MFA for textile and clothing imports in 1978 which included many national quantitative restrictions. The MFAs were negotiated between developing and industrialized countries under strong pressure from the latter's producer lobby. The number rose from a mere 10 applications per year in the early 1970s to a peak of 273 in 1980 and declined again to a recent figure of around 100 applications per year. The use of Article 115 for manufacturing goods has also increased significantly. The pattern is similar to that for textiles and clothing but the fluctuations are not so extreme. From a low of 24 in 1974, the number of applications rose to 85 at the height of the economic crisis in 1982. In 1988, there were still 69 applications in the non-MFA sectors.

---

[2] Exceptions are Winters (1988), Hamilton (1991) and Schuknecht (1991). Winters (1990) investigates the effect of import surveillance on the behaviour of exporters.

Table 5.1 Article 115: Total Applications and Approvals, 1971-1988

Year	Number of applications				
	Total	Textiles/ clothing	Other	Approved total	%
1971	33	5	28	30	91
1972	63	11	52	59	94
1973	51	6	45	47	92
1974	36 MFA I	12	24	33	92
1975	78	40	38	64	81
1976	110	72	38	64	81
1977	121	75	46	79	65
1778	317 MFA II	258	59	197	62
1979	347	269	78	260	75
1980	356 Reform	273	83	222	62
1981	255	184	71	166	65
1982	241	156	85	174	72
1983	253 MFA III	176	77	188	74
1984	215	155	60	165	77
1985	211	143	68	176	83
1986	184	131	53	141	77
1987	182 Reform	122	60	157	86
1988	153	84	69	128	84

Source: EC Commission

In the early seventies, almost all applications gained approval from the EC. This rate declined to "only" 62% in 1978 and 1980 and has recently increased to almost the rate of the early seventies, i.e. 84% - 86%. The risk of a rejection therefore looks relatively small.[3] Table 5.1 also indicates two reforms in the regulations underlying the application of Article 115. They caused a dent in the number of applications, which will be discussed in more detail later.

The Incidence per Country and Country Group
Table 5.2 shows that 83% of the applications for the 1980-89 period come from France (40%), Ireland (26%) and Italy (17%). Recently,

---

[3] The rate of rejection in national bureaucracies which forward applications to the EC is not known. Some countries, however, have refused to forward any applications in recent years (Table 5.2).

Table 5.2 Shares of Article 115 Applications and Import Shares by EC Member Countries, 1980-1989

Country	Total number of cases	Share of total	Share thereof in		Share of Imports from non-members 1988
			textiles	other	
BeNeLux	121	5.5	78	22	15
Denmark	6	0.3	100	0	3
France	888	40.0	68	32	14
Germany	9	0.5	100	0	26
Great Britain	163	7.4	75	25	21
Greece	4	0.2	0	100	1
Ireland	575	25.9	97	3	1
Italy	367	16.6	33	67	13
Portugal	3	0.1	0	100	1
Spain	77	3.5	3	97	5
Total	2213	100	69	31	100

Spain has become a major applicant; 77 applications were filed in only three years. Great Britain and the BeNeLux countries on the other hand reduced the number of national measures significantly. After being major applicants in the early 1980s, they filed only one and three applications respectively in 1988. Germany, Denmark, Greece and Portugal hardly ever took recourse to national protectionism.

The share of French applications of 68% for textile and clothing protection and of 32% for other products is close to the EC average of 69% and 31% respectively. Other countries, however, show a distinct pattern of specialization. The Southern Europeans do not apply for protection in the textile and clothing sector; Italy and Spain, however, are the major applicants for other industry protection besides France. Ireland has almost exclusively "specialized" on using Article 115 for textiles and clothing. This pattern reflects the strong involvement of Southern European governments in running their industries and in industrial policies. Ireland, on the other hand, wants to protect its declining textile and clothing industries. This also holds for the other countries which occasionnally take recourse to Article 115.

Another way to assess the relative protectionist character of the member countries is to compare the share of a member country's applications with the share of its imports from outside the EC (Table 5.2). France, Ireland, Italy and Spain again appear to be the most protectionist countries in the EC. The French share of protectionist applications is 40% while her import share from non-member countries is only 15%. The share of applications for Article 115 protection by Ireland, Italy and recently Spain is also higher than their import share. The Irish ratio of 26% to 1% exaggerates its protectionism because restrictions against various textile products are relatively unimportant compared to for instance Italian restrictions against cars. Germany, Greece and Denmark and recently Great Britain and the BeNeLux countries are the member countries most oriented to free trade.

Table 5.3 presents the target countries of national protection for the year 1988. The pattern has been quite stable over the past 10 years. In 1988, 154 cases affected 18 countries. The main targets with 120 applications were developing countries. The sub-group of the Newly Industrialized Countries (NICs) was targeted 62 times. 15 claims were brought forward against Eastern European countries. The only developed country affected by national protectionism was Japan with 19 cases. Of the developing countries, Taiwan, China, Hong Kong, South Korea and India were the most important countries in descending order. They were targeted in 95 or 63% of the cases.

The relative impact of national protection on the affected countries can be assessed by comparing the share of cases against them and their share of merchandise imports in the EC. Table 5.3 shows that the developing countries are hit hardest. The three NICs account for 41% of the applications but for only 5.5% of the EC's imports. Thailand, China, and India are also affected relatively often with their combined share of imports being only 3% and their share of applications being close to one quarter of the total.

The Incidence per Sector
Some of the bias against developing countries stems from the fact that Article 115 enforces the Multi Fiber Arrangement. Table 5.4 shows that 54% of the applications in 1988 came from the textile and clothing industry with the NICs, China, and South Asia being the major targets. On the other hand, the table indicates that in 1988, 42 out of 71 cases against other manufacturing products, which amounts to 59% of all such cases, were also directed against developing countries. The most important sectors were consumer electronics and cars. Japan and the NICs were the only targets for electronics protection, Japan and Eastern Europe for cars. Protectionism against

Table 5.3 Shares of Article 115 Cases and EC Imports for Selected
Countries and Country Groups, 1988

Country	Total number of cases	Percentage of total cases	Share of EC merchandise imports 1988
Developed countries	19	12	62
Japan	19	12	11
Eastern Europe	15	10	8
Soviet Union	8	5	3.3
Romania	2	1	0.5
Developing Countries	120	78	30
(thereof NICs)	(62)	(41)	(5.5)
Hong Kong	21	14	1.6
South Korea	15	10	1.8
Taiwan	26	17	2.1
China	22	14	1.8
India	11	7	0.8
Thailand	4	3	0.5
Total	154	100	100

other miscellaneous imports was most frequently implemented against
China and Taiwan.

Table 5.5 illustrates the sector incidence of Article 115
protection for non-MFA products with their main user and target
countries over various sample years. The targeted products are shown
in the first column. The second and third columns indicate the
respective EC members applying for national protection in different
years. The last column shows the target countries by products. For
consumer electronics, France has been the main applicant (Italy does
not have an important national industry). In the vehicle sector, Italy
and recently Spain and Portugal have taken recourse to Article 115
(French and some other countries' imports are covered by VERs).

Trade Protection in the European Community

Table 5.4 Article 115 Cases per Target Country and Sector, 1988

Country group and country	Numbers of applications per sector				Total per Country
	Textile/ clothing	Vehicle	Elec- tronics	Miscell- aneous	
Developed countries (only Japan)	0	7	6	6	19
Eastern Europe	5	6	0	4	15
Czechoslovakia	2	0	0	1	3
Soviet Union	2	3	0	3	8
Romania	1	1	0	0	2
Poland	0	2	0	0	2
Developing countries (thereof NICs)	78 (37)	0 (0)	11 (11)	31 (14)	120 (62)
Hong Kong	20	0	0	1	21
Taiwan	12	0	4	10	26
Korea	5	0	7	3	15
Brazil	1	0	0	1	2
Caribean	0	0	0	7*	7
China	14	0	0	8	22
India	11	0	0	0	11
Macao	1	0	0	0	1
Pakistan	7	0	0	0	7
Philippines	1	0	0	0	1
Sri Lanka	1	0	0	0	1
Thailand	4	0	0	0	4
Yugoslavia	1	0	0	1	2
Total	83 (54%)	13 (8%)	17 (11%)	41 (27%)	154
		sub-total: 71 (46%)			

* Bananas

Table 5.5 Article 115 Applications per Product by EC Member
Countries and Target Countries in Selected Years

Sector/Product	1980	1981	1987	1988	Targets
	Applicants in the EC				
Electronics:					
Autoradios	F, I	I	-	F	Kor, J
Televisions	F, I	F	F, GB	F, E	J, Tw, Kor, C
Electronic instruments	F	F	-	-	J
Diodes, transistors	I	-	-	-	J
Videos*	-	-	E	-	Kor, J
Tuners	I	-	-	-	J
Radios	F, I	-	F	F	J, Tw, Kor, HK, Poland
Vehicles:					
Cars	I	I	I, E	I, E	J, EE
Cross country vehicles	I	I	I	-	J
Trucks	-	I	-	-	J
Busses	-	I	-	-	J
Motorcycles	-	I	I, Port	I, Port	J
Miscellaneous:					
Toys	F	F	E, F	F	Kor, J, C, HK, Tw, Singapore
Films	-	-	I	I	J
Sewing machines	I	I	I	I, E	J, Kor, Tw, Brazil, Yugos
Ball bearings	-	-	I	I	J, USSR
Microscopes	F	-	-	-	J

F=France, I=Italy, GB=Great Britain, E=Spain, Port=Portugal, Yugos=Yugoslavia, J=Japan, Kor=Korea, HK=Hong Kong, Tw=Taiwan, C=China, EE=USSR, CSFR, Poland and Romania
* There is also VER and Antidumping protection against VCR imports.

Other miscellaneous products have most often been the target of Italian protection. The table also shows that the range of products and the main applicants did not change much during the 1980s.

The sectoral pattern reflects the relative international trade performance of the target countries. The NICs and Japan have been very successful in penetrating the EC market for consumer electronics, textiles/clothing and cars - often at the expense of domestic industries. This indicates that the EC's member countries try to prevent loss of domestic production in some of their economically most important and politically most influential industries.

5.3 The Article 115 Procedure

The previous pattern of presentation of the incidence per sector and country suggests a politically motivated pattern of protection. Article 115 is captured mainly by the politically influential textile/clothing, vehicle and electronics industries. The following examination of the institutional framework within which Article 115 is applied reinforces this idea. In addition, the procedure reveals significant scope for the EC's administering agency to pursue its own objectives.

Article 115 protection involves a two level procedure which is presented graphically in Figure 5.1. The first level is the level of member countries. Member governments evaluate an application from a national industry or interest group for a restrictive measure against a non-member country, and decide whether or not to forward the application to the Commission. After this preselection on the national level, it is up to the EC Commission to accept or reject the application. The responsible Directorate General I for external relations investigates the request, and decides within five working days. The approved measure comes into effect, on average, three to six months after the decision. It usually applies for less than a year, which requires periodic reapplications. Approvals either result in surveillance of imports, import blocks or quantitative restrictions. Appeals are forwarded to the European Court of Justice.

The EC does not lay down any rules for the evaluation and forwarding of applications by national governments. Unless member states introduce their own rules, the decision is made politically. The final decision on an Article 115 measure is made by the Commission. From this perspective it can be defined as administered protection. However, if administered protection also requires the application of strict technical rules by the administering agency, the label does not fit. The Commission has significant discretion in the application of Article 115. Approvals require the existence or threat of economic difficulties. These need not be as severe for surveillance as for

Figure 5.1 The Article 115 Decision-Making Process

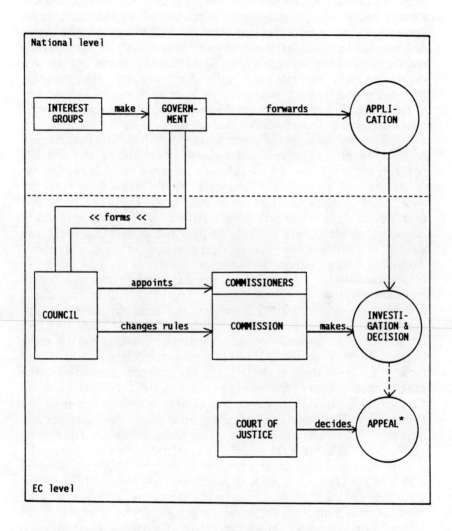

* Directly affected parties (e.g. national interest groups,
governments, foreign exporters) can appeal decision.

quantitative restrictions. Indicators of difficulties for measures of surveillance are: the importance of the good, the market share of domestic producers, producers of the affected third country, and the market share of all non-member countries. Additionally, price decreases or price increases prevented by imports, profits and losses and layoffs are used as indicators of "difficulties" for quantitative measures (decision on regulation, 80/47/EWG). These notions are vague enough to facilitate protection seeking (Hailbronner, Bierwagen, 1989) - each producer should be able to turn at least one of these criteria to his advantage. Protection seeking is also facilitated by the fact that industries' difficulties are not published.

The two main groups which can use the discretion in their own or their clienteles' interest are national governments and the EC bureaucrats (see Figure 5.1). Politicians influence the implementation of Article 115 through two channels. Firstly, they determine the *preselection* of applications on the *national* level. This alone suggests a fairly politicized application of Article 115 since politically unopportune claims are unlikely to pass this hurdle. Secondly, the Council of Ministers can exert indirect pressure on the Commission's decisions. It can request a *change in the regulation* governing the implementation of Article 115 at the EC level. It can also try to intervene through the Commissioners. The individual investigations, however, are not subject to direct political scrutiny. Since political accountability of EC bureaucrats is only *indirect* and *single decisions are made without further intervention by the Council*, they can use some of their discretion on the EC level in their own interest.

The application of Article 115 has changed significantly over the past twenty years because of intervention from the Court and the Council. Since 1968, national measures need authorization from the Commission. The practice of member countries to take measures and obtain subsequent approval by the Commission was ruled illegal by the Court in 1976.[4] In 1972, the Court held that Article 115 can not be applied against insignificant amounts of imports. This case involved 0.26% of the German imports of preserved mushrooms.[5] In 1975, the Court obliged the Commission to review the claims put forward by the member governments.[6] This ruling was one of the reasons for the Commission to introduce the requirement of economic difficulties and the rules for evaluating such difficulties in 1980 (decision

---

[4] Ruling 41/76 in Donckerwolcke versus Procureur de la République.
[5] Ruling 897 at 916/72 in Bock versus EC Commission.
[6] Ruling 29/75 in Kaufhof versus EC Commission.

80/47/EWG). The vague formulation of this decision was a major shortcoming. A narrower interpretation and a stricter application of the rules is required since 1987 (decision 87/433/EWG). Measures can now only be granted for a limited period of time and in "particularly serious" situations.

An institutional analysis has more weight when it is applied in a theoretical framework and yields testable hypotheses. This examination yields such hypotheses in a public choice framework. Politicians are assumed to be interested in political support maximization. The classical model to this approach by Stigler (1971) and Peltzman (1976) suggests that regulation favours producer interests in times of recessions when protection is more pressing. Consumers' free trade interests therefore find more support in booms. The effect of respective cyclical factors in U.S. regulatory activity is tested by Takacs (1981) and Shughart and Tollison (1985). In the EC, applications as forwarded by national governments to the Commission, may best reflect these short term political influences. An application is only forwarded to the national policy makers when the quota granted to the target country is or will be used up and when the protected industry cares to enforce the quota. This is more likely to happen during recessions.

Changes in the regulation of Article 115 requested by the Council reflect the strategic long-term policy goals of member governments. The reason is that member governments only meet a few times per year, which limits the frequency with which the rules can be changed. The threat to change the rules may already exert an ongoing controlling influence on the Commission's decisions. Finger, Hall and Nelson (1982) tested the influence of such institutional changes on the U.S. antidumping decisions.

The changes in the application of Article 115 in 1980 and 1987 are re-regulations of this kind. The change in 1980 occurred after the number of applications for national protection exploded in 1978/1979 threatening to lead to the collapse of the Common Commercial Policy (see Table 5.1). The 1987 reform was originally intended to facilitate the completion of the Common Market which requires the abolition of all national barriers before the end of 1992.[7] These reforms should have an adverse effect on the amount of national protectionism. They reduce the approval rate which in turn reduces the number of

---

[7] In the relevant literature, justified doubts exist whether all border controls will be abolished (Hailbronner and Bierwagen 1989). Various scenarios are briefly discussed by Neme (1988).

applications as applicants adjust their expectations about the availability of protection.

Bureaucratic self-interest is expected to affect the Commission's decisions because technical/economic rules are vague and direct political intervention is impossible. The main variable determined by bureaucrats is the approval rate. Since bureaucrats want to expand their budgetary appropriations (Niskanen, 1971), their interests lie in the expansion of the underlying output, i.e. the use of Article 115. If there was no political control, discretion would allow them to approve of (almost) all applications. As mentioned, political control can be exercised through the Commissioners and re-regulation. These constraints on the expansionary interests of bureaucrats suggest that the latter will try to prevent intervention by expanding the use of Article 115 only incrementally.[8]

The political determination of Article 115 is most obvious when looking at the capture of this instrument by the textile/clothing industry. The negotiation of protection in the context of the Multi Fiber Arrangements under severe pressure from EC producers significantly increased recourse to Article 115 because the latter became the means of enforcing the Multi Fiber Arrangements. This protection came as a demand shock for the Commission which in turn has an incentive to buffer such shocks by curbing the approval rate to divert attention from the political sector.

The administrative framework of Article 115 thus suggests that its objective is protection. The means to protection is administrative and political discretion rather than the application of strict technical/administrative rules. The main argument of this chapter is that the institutional structure leads to the accommodation of national protectionist interests - the most blatant political intervention being the incorporation of MFA protection under Article 115 - and the pursuit of bureaucratic self-interest. The following section presents the results of an empirical investigation of the determinants of Article 115 decisions.

---

[8] The role of political control for bureaucratic behaviour is discussed by Breton and Wintrobe (1975). The hypothesis about incremental expansion was first advanced by Wildavsky (1964) for budgetary appropriations and seems most appropriate in this institutional contest for predicting the bureaucrats' behaviour.

5.4 An Empirical Analysis of Article 115 Protection

The absence of clearly specified rules on the national level suggests that political factors, almost by definition, determine which applications are passed on to the Commission. On the EC level, the vague nature of the rules also allows the Commission to follow unstated objectives and unstated criteria. A thorough investigation into the determinants of each decision on the national and on the EC level with micro data is, however, impeded by a lack of published information. The Commission keeps transparency at a minimum by publishing only the results of each case. Nevertheless, an informative test can be conducted using macro data.

The following hypotheses on the determinants of Article 115 decisions have been put forward in the previous section for empirical testing:

1) Short-term political-economic influence is exercised on the national level. Cyclical factors influence the number of applications forwarded to the Commission by member governments.

2) Institutional changes in the implementation of Article 115 on the EC level reflect political long-term interests. They affect the approval rate of the Commission which then feeds back into the number of applications.

3) Bureaucrats try to expand incrementally the use of Article 115 by increasing the approval rate.

4) The ratification of the MFAs increases recourse to Article 115 significantly. However, the Commission prevents extreme rises in the number of Article 115 measures by adjusting the approval rate.

The message that emerges from the results is that special interests receive relief from import competitition with the help of Article 115. The underlying motive is the self-interest of the involved industries, politicians and bureaucrats. The results thereby demonstrate that an altruistic motivation of policy makers promoting for instance social welfare, social insurance or fairness is not needed to explain this sort of trade protection.[9]

Econometric Modelling

The level of protectionism emanating from the decision-making process is not directly quantifiable. National and EC decision makers,

---

[9] It has been argued that fluctuations during the business cycle can also support the social insurance explanation of protection. Hillman (1989) argues that this argument is both theoretically and empirically unconvincing. Strategic considerations were dismissed as a major explanatory factor for the EC's protection in Chapter 2.

however, determine the number of applications and the approval rate respectively. These figures therefore serve as a proxy for Article 115 protection. The data is presented in Table 5.1.

The sum of applications per year forwarded by national governments is used as a dependent variable in a reduced form equation to test for short and long-term political economic influences. The approval rate serves as a dependent variable in an estimation of bureaucratic and long-term political interests on the EC level.[10] The technique applied is Ordinary Least Squares (OLS). The results, unfortunately, have to be treated with caution because the time series contains only 18 observations with approximately 14 degrees of freedom.

The explanatory variables were selected to test for the impact of cyclical, long-term political, bureaucratic and MFA-related factors on the dependent variables. The sign of the coefficient indicates the direction of this impact on the number of applications and the approval rate. A positive sign indicates that a positive change in the explanatory variable also has a positive impact on the dependent variable.

Two-tailed t-tests were used to check whether the null hypothesis - that impact is in the opposite direction or that there is no impact at all - can be rejected. The significance level for each variable is indicated by one asterisk (10%) and two asterisks (5%) respectively. Additionally, the F-test and the goodness of fit-index R^2 adjusted reflect the relevance and the explanatory quality of the estimated model specification. The Durbin Watson statistics finally indicate the presence (or absence) of autocorrelation.

Description of Explanatory Variables
Four cyclical variables are used alternatively to capture changes in *short-term special-interest pressure* for protection changing over the business cycle.[11] Changes in the EC unemployment rate should be positively related to Article 115 applications and approvals. An increase in the unemployment rate puts increasing pressure on politicians to protect domestic industries and jobs. In the sample

---

[10] The dependent variable is the "logit" of the approval rate - "logits" being defined as $\ln(p/1-p)$ where p denotes the approval rate.

[11] The results for the studies by Shughart and Tollison (1985) and Takacs (1981) for the U.S. indicate a significant influence of cyclical variables although Feigenbaum et al. (1985) argue that the effect has been overstated by Takacs.

Cyclical data stems from the OECD indicators of industrial activity. Only one cyclical variable is used per estimation to avoid multicollinearity.

period, it can be observed that the unemployment rate of the EC tends to increase with a ratchet effect rather than being cyclical. To solve this problem, the relative change in the unemployment rate is used as an independent variable.

The Gross Domestic Product (GDP) growth rate of the EC is expected to be inversely related to the number of applications. If GDP growth is above average, it is less profitable to invest in redistribution. On the other hand, low growth will make protectionist rent seeking more profitable compared to productive investments. Alternatively, the production index for "total industry" and for "manufacturing" is used for the same purpose. The coefficient is expected to be negative because interest in protection will decrease with an improving industry performance.

The rate of response of the level of protection to changes in GDP growth, unemployment and the production indices may differ. While firms may already request protection when orders and/or production go down, reduced GDP growth is not observed until some time later. The GDP variable may therefore affect applications with a time lag. The same holds for unemployment because it takes time to feed back into the political process.

Looking at the *long-term political influence* on the use of Article 115, two changes in the regulations governing the implementation of Article 115 were identified in Section 3. They are expected to affect both the number of applications and the approval rate. Since 1980, more emphasis has been put on economic difficulties as a precondition for approval, and indicators have been introduced for this. It is expected that this reform would curb Article 115 measures significantly. In October 1987, the procedure was supposedly further tightened.

Two dummies reflect the reforms in 1980 and 1987. The first one takes the value of one from 1980 onwards and the other from 1987 onwards. The coefficients of both are expected to have negative signs.

Both variables are lagged by one period to test for their influence on applications. First, there is an information problem with respect to the new procedure. Many applicants may not know about it. Secondly, many applicants will test whether the Commission is really committed to toughening the procedure. The impact on the approval rate should be immediate because the Commission has to adjust its behaviour immediately. The respective dummy variables are used without a lag in the relevant equations.

The impact of *bureaucratic interests* is tested using a linear trend variable. This variable is supposed to capture the hypothesized tendency of the EC bureaucracy to expand incrementally. The expected sign of the variable is positive. Moreover, it is tested whether the variable for the 1980 reform can be incorporated into the trend variable. Table 5.6 shows the specifications of the trend variables. This new variable takes the value of one in 1971 which increases to eight in 1979. Several reductions for the 1980 value of the variable are introduced. These reflect the reduced availability of measures after 1980. After 1980, the trend picks up again.

If governments influence the ongoing decision-making process on the EC level, the approval rate is expected to vary over the business cycle. Since it was argued that governments can not exert direct pressure on the Commission, the coefficients for cyclical variables are expected to be insignificant for determining the approval rate.

The *most important external factor* which influences recourse to Article 115 is the series of *Multi Fiber Arrangements*. MFA I put a general ceiling on import increases. MFA II facilitated national agreements significantly. MFA III and IV do not differ much from MFA II. Table 5.6 also surveys the specifications of the MFA

Table 5.6 Specifications of the Trend and MFA Variables, 1971-1981

Variables	71	72	73	74	75	76	77	78	79	80	81
Trend	1	2	3	...							
Trend, includes 1980 reform	1	2	3	...			...	8	9	3	4
MFA I	0	0	0	1	1	1	1	0	0	...	
MFA I phased in 1974-1977	0	0	0	0.25	0.5	0.75	1	0	0	...	
MFA 75	0	0	0	0	1	1	1	0	0	...	
MFA 76	0	0	0	0	0	1	1	0	0	...	
MFA II-IV	0	0	0	0	0	0	0	1	1	1	1

variables. The effect of the MFAs is tested with the help of two dummy variables, one for MFA I (1974-1977) and one for MFA II-IV (1978-1990). They take the value of one for the time in which they are in force, and zero for the other years. A positive sign of the respective coefficients is anticipated. The history of the MFAs indicates that the EC member governments negotiated an increasing number of national measures over the 1974-1977 period. To reflect this, an alternative variable for the first MFA variable is phased in linearly over the four year period 1974-1977, taking the value of .25 in 1974 rising to one in 1977.[12]

As argued in Section 2, the expected response by bureaucrats to demand shocks such as the MFAs is a reduced approval rate. The dummy for the impact of MFA II-IV in 1978 is expected to have a negative influence on the approval rate, analogous to the 1980 reform dummy. Since applications increased gradually over the 1974-1977 period, due to MFA I, the variable which is phased in over this period is also used to test for changes in the approval rate.

Results

The results of the estimations support the above hypotheses. National preselection of Article 115 applications is determined largely politically. Short-term policy considerations help protectionist special interests to obtain more protection during recessions. Long-term policy considerations curb the number of applications through institutional reforms on the EC level.

On the EC level, short-term politics are not important, but policy makers exert influence through changing the rules. Bureaucratic interest in incremental expansion also finds empirical support. The MFAs - being themselves the result of lobbying by special interests - have a significant impact on both levels of decision making. The clear message of this is that the self-interest of interest groups, bureaucrats and policy makers explains EC trade policies based on Article 115.

---

[12] Additional negotiations after MFA II, on the other hand, took place immediately after ratification (OECD, 1983). The respective variable should therefore not be phased in.

Table 5.7 Regression Results for the Determination of Applications from EC Members for Article 115 Measures

Modelling technique: Ordinary Least Squares
Dependent variable is the NUMBER OF APPLICATIONS
Sample range: 1971-1988

Variables	Estimated coefficients (t-statistics)			
	(1)	(2)	(3)	(4)
Constant	81.6 (3.46)	393 (3.53)	420 (3.86)	39.2 (3.19)
Institutional changes:				
1980 reform 1 period lag	-129.5 (-6.66)**	-122 (-6.96)**	-116 (-7.76)**	134 (-8.42)**
1987 reform 1 period lag	-58.2 (-1.98)*			
Political protection (Multi Fiber Arrangement):				
MFA I	23.9 (1.09)			
MFA I, phased in 1974-1977		107 (4.33)**	107 (4.57)**	42 (1.57)
MFA II-IV	280 (12.3)**	352 (14.3)**	350 (15.5)**	294 (16.1)**
Cyclical Factors:				
GDP growth 1 period lag	-7.46 (-1.85)*			
Production total industries		-4.12 (-3.17)**		
Production manufaturing			-4.35 (-3.49)**	
Unemployment				1.53 (2.92)**
Observations	18	18	18	18
Durbin Watson	1.87	1.76	1.72	1.63
R² adjusted	0.93	0.95	0.96	0.95
F test	48.6	88.4	77.9	82.5

*(**) Rejection of the null hypothesis on the 90% (95%) level

In Table 5.7, the estimation results for *applications* as a dependent variable are given in estimations (1) to (4). The values for the F-tests and the goodness-of-fit indexes, R^2 adjusted, show the high overall relevance of the empirical investigation. The coefficients of the cyclical variables are in line with the hypothesis about short-term political influence on applications. The coefficients of the lagged "unemployment" and GDP growth variables and the production indices for "total industry" and "manufacturing" were all significant on the 5% level except for GDP growth (10%).

The estimation results also suggest that the coefficient of the 1980 reform variable has a significant effect on the number of applications for Article 115 measures. From these results it is not yet clear whether the 1987 reform variable also curbs the application of Article 115.

The coefficient of the variable for MFA II-IV indicates that these have a strong impact on applications. As expected, the effect of the first MFA is not immediate. Only the MFA I variable which increases linearly between 1974 and 1977 yields a significant coefficient in (2) and (3). The coefficient of this MFA I variable is not significant when estimated together with the unemployment variable in (4). 1974-1977 was also the period in which unemployment rose rapidly so that the variables may well be collinear.

When undertaking these estimations for the most important applicants France, Italy and Ireland separately, the results from the total sample are largely confirmed. The number of applications from Ireland is influenced by all the relevant variables including the second reform in late 1987. French applications are affected by the relevant reforms and MFAs but not by cyclical factors. Italian applications were not affected by the first reform in 1980 but the coefficients of all the other variables showed the expected sign at least on the 10% level of significance.

The estimation results for the logit of the *approval rate* are shown in Table 5.8. Again, the F-tests and the R^2 adjusted illustrate the high overall relevance of our hypothesis.[13] The most important result of equations (5)-(6) is the significance of the coefficient of the trend variable in both specifications. It supports the incremental expansion hypothesis for bureaucrats.

---

[13] The Durbin-Watson statistics in (5) indicate the presence of autocorrelation. In (6), the Cochrane-Orcutt technique is applied to correct this, yielding much improved results.

Table 5.8 Regression Results for the Determination of the
Commission's Approval Rate of Article 115 Measures

Modelling technique: Ordinary Least Squares Dependent variable is PERCENTAGE OF APPROVALS (logit)		
Sample range: 1971-1988 Variables Estimated coefficients (t-statistics)		
	(5)	(6)
Constant	2.36 (19.1)	2.48 (10.5)
Bureaucratic interest: Trend, linear	0.155 $(5.42)^{**}$	
Trend, including 1980 Reform		-0.47 $(-1.98)^{**}$
Multi Fiber Arrangement:		
MFA I phased in (1974-1977)	-2.85 $(10.5)^{**}$	
MFA 75 (1975-1977 = 1)		-1.02 $(-3.14)^{**}$
MFA 76 (1976-1977 = 1)		-1.02 $(-3.14)^{**}$
MFA II-IV	-2.74 $(10.1)^{**}$	-2.32 $(-8.18)^{**}$
Cyclical factors:		
GDP growth, 1 period lag		-0.05 (-1.11)
Number of observations	18	18
Durbin Watson	3.31	2.14
R^2 adjusted	0.90	0.87
F-test	38.9	23.6

*(**) Rejection of the null hypothesis on the 90% (95%) level

Political long-term influence represented by the 1980 reform variable has the expected negative effect on the approval rate, although only on a 10% level of significance. Estimation (6) incorporates the 1980 reform variable into the trend variable. Table 5.6 indicates a shift from 9 to 3. The pattern of the results, however, does not change compared to the previous estimations. In (6), the GDP growth variable illustrates that cyclical factors do not affect the approval rate.

Ratification of MFA I and MFA II-IV resulted in the expected lower approval rate. The two years 1975 and 1976 should have resulted in most of the negative impact of MFA I on the approval rate because the number of applications rose most rapidly during those two years. In estimation (6), two separate dummies (MFA 75 and MFA 76), therefore, take the value of one starting in each of the years 1975 and 1976 (see Table 5.6) to test for the impact of MFA I for these two years. The coefficients of the variables are significant and indicate that the bureaucrats prevented a rapid expansion of Article 115 measures by downward-adjusting the approval rate mainly in 1975 and 1976.

5.5 Why Some Industries Prefer Article 115

The prominence of Article 115 as compared to other trade policy instruments lies 1) in its relatively low lobbying costs and 2) in the little publicity it receives. Industries can lobby their own national governments. This facilitates protection seeking by small industries limited to national markets who would have difficulties in forming EC-wide organizations. This argument is supported by the numerous applications for narrowly specified products with a low turnover such as espadrilles or umbrellas.

Secondly, Article 115 protection can be obtained "low key" because the procedure is intransparent and not subject to GATT or other international scrutiny. This is abused by industries and policy makers who fear the publicity of antidumping and the popular mistrust towards EC-wide voluntary export restraints. As a consequence, some politically influential interests such as the car industry obtain protection under Article 115. A bundle of quantitative restrictions against Japanese cars enforced by Article 115, for instance, can have the same protectionist effect as an antidumping duty. But international and consumer/voter resistance is likely to be much weaker than against an antidumping measure.

The little publicity Article 115 receives is helpful when the special interests of different member countries can not agree. Article 115 allows for market segmentation and keeps internal conflicts and their exposure - for which the EC has been notorious - at a minimum. Lack of cohesion of interests would also increase the costs of EC-wide protection significantly. While the French and the Italian governments are under strong pressure for protection from FIAT, Renault and Peugeot, the Dutch and the Belgians without a national car industry want cheap Japanese imports without restrictions. With the help of Article 115, the Commission can keep all its customers satisfied.[14]

5.6 Conclusion: Article 115 and "Fortress Europe"

Article 115 measures capture most national protectionism against non-EC countries. It is the self-interest of pressure groups, politicians and bureaucrats and not political altruism which determines decisions under Article 115 by means of political and bureaucratic discretion.

The previous findings have two important implications. The first one refers to the fact that the rule change in 1980 significantly curbed the application of Article 115 while ongoing decision-making rather led to its expansion. This finding corresponds to the public choice argumentation of Chapter 1. The rules determine the nature of the trade game which is permanently under protectionist pressure from special interests. Countries have a stronger incentive to liberalize on the constitutional level of decision making than on the level of every-day policy making. The same pattern - increasing protection in the ongoing political process, liberalization through rule changes - is found again in Chapter 7, where the antidumping regulation is discussed.

Article 115 is one of the escape clauses included in the EC's founding document. As Baldwin (1988) argues in the context of GATT, such deviations from the Common Commercial Policy were necessary to accommodate particularly strong interest groups in the early days of the EC. Otherwise, the member governments would have vetoed the EC's commercial integration. Unlike in GATT, however, protectionism based on escape clauses has not led to a general crisis within the EC. On the contrary, the EC plans to abolish all national trade barriers before the end of 1992. A more thorough analysis of the underlying institutional changes is provided in Chapter 9 which is

---

[14] See also Simon and Garfunkel "Keep your customers satisfied".

exclusively dedicated to the description and explanation of the emergence of the EC's internal liberalization program.

The second important implication concerns post-1992 EC trade policy. If trade within the EC is to be free, Article 115 measures must be abolished. Although the "free" U.S. internal market shows that internal protection can prevail, for instance through health standards or subsidies, trade is likely to become more liberal within the EC after 1992. National producers who are currently protected on the national level will request compensation through EC-wide measures.

This tendency will be reinforced by the fact that Article 115 protection only allows national price discrimination in combination with internal barriers. Otherwise competition from substitutes produced within the EC would dissipate the protectionist rent. If, for example, French shirt producers are protected against Far Eastern exports they are only able to fully benefit from protection when Irish or Portugese competition also faces barriers to Ireland. If internal protection is abolished, national external measures under Article 115 will lose most of their protective impact, hence requiring an EC-wide measure instead (Hamilton, 1986 and 1991).

The fact that national policy makers accommodate protectionist presssure with the help of Article 115 on the national level suggests that this pressure will also be accommodated on the EC level. The next chapters demonstrate that the EC has the appropriate means. Only those producers who need protection for very specific products for which the other procedures are too costly, or those operating in national markets where the interests within the EC industry are not cohesive will have problems finding a substitute on the EC level. This, however, does not affect the bulk of products covered by Article 115. The French are even attempting to replace a national restriction on espadrilles (Basque summer shoes) by an antidumping measure. The voluntary export restraint negotiated between Europe and the Japanese car industry is a forewarning of what is likely to come. A "Fortress Europe" for vehicles, consumer electronics and textiles/clothing imports will take the place of "Fortress Italy" or "Fortress France". The fears of increased average levels of protection, however, have receded.

Chapter 6

VOLUNTARY EXPORT RESTRAINTS

6.1 Introduction

Voluntary export restraints (VERs) and similar arrangements are the EC's most important "grey area" measures. This label refers to the fact that they are not explicitly covered by GATT law. At the most, they are negotiated solutions to trade disputes with the backing of GATT in the context of safeguards and the Multi Fiber Arrangement (MFA).[1] The notion of fairness is rarely evoked, but it is claimed that VERs serve a social purpose in that they are supposed to reduce adjustment costs for the industry injured by import competititon and to save jobs in this industry.

This chapter deals in more detail with the prominence of VERs as protectionist devices in EC trade policy making. Most known VERs are negotiated by the Commission and, therefore, theoretically count as administered protection. De facto, however, they are the most politicized trade policy instrument used by the EC. It is argued that VERs are in most cases a shortcut to protection avoiding official legislative or administrative procedures. They are often the result of collusion between domestic producers and policy makers and established foreign producers.[2]

The latest mid-1990 count by the GATT reports over 50 restraint arrangements of this kind (GATT, 1991). An earlier count by Kostecki (1987) comes up with 68 VERs by the EC towards non-member countries. The coverage ranges from agriculture to textiles, steel products, consumer electronics, machinery, footwear and vehicles. Kostecki finds that 10% of the EC imports in the mid-eighties were effected by VERs, the corresponding figure by Finger and Olechowski (1987) for 1984 is 6%. A list of all VERs to the EC

---

[1] Voluntary price increases, also called price undertakings, are dealt with in the antidumping chapters.

[2] Hillman and Ursprung (1988); a VER, however, is not necessarily profitable for the exporter; it could just be his loss-minimizing protectionist alternative.

known to the GATT in 1991, is provided in the appendix of this chapter. The numerous VERs negotiated under the Multi Fiber Arrangement, however, are not included.

Tariff equivalents are between 3% and 50% with a trade weighted average of 15% which is significantly above the average EC-tariff of 5%.[3] Kostecki (1987) finds that VERs transferred 27 billion U.S. $ of quota rents into the pockets of foreign producers.[4] The only estimate for the EC is by Hamilton (1988) who found that Hong Kong's, Taiwan's and Korea's clothing exporters gained 200 million U.S.$ from their VERs on clothing exports.

The welfare costs of VERs are significant. They are estimated to be around 1 billion U.S. $ for the VER on clothing in 1980 (Kalantzopoulus, 1985). The costs of the agreement with Japan on video cassette recorders amounted to 80 million pounds sterling (approximately 120 million ECU) for British consumers (Greenaway and Hindley, 1985) and 1/2 billion U.S. $ for the whole EC in 1983 (Kalantzopoulos, 1985). The costs of the Japanese VER on car exports were 270 million ECU for British consumers in the same year (Greenaway and Hindley, 1985) and 50 to 100 million ECU for their French counterparts in 1984 (de Melo and Messerlin, 1988). The social costs of the British footwear agreement with several countries amounted to approximately 80 million ECU in 1979 (Takacs and Winters, 1990). These figures do not account for the additional lobbying ("Tullock") costs.

Whether the stated purpose of saving jobs has been successful is very dubious. In Britain, the footwear agreements saved 1000 jobs (Takacs and Winters, 1990). At most 1100 jobs were secured in the video cassette recorder industry. A layoff of beteen none and 13000 workers was prevented in the car industry through VERs with Japan (Greenaway and Hindley, 1985). The French quota on Japanese car imports only saved between 300 and 600 jobs. In Britain, the costs per saved job lay between 10.000 and over 100.000 ECU per year (Greenaway and Hindley, 1985). These figures are much higher than unemployment benefits or retraining expenses.

The discussion includes various restraint agreements under the heading of voluntary export restraints, i.e. the typical voluntary export restraint agreement, orderly marketing arrangements, voluntary

---

[3] Clothing imports from Hong Kong, for instance, faced an average tariff equivalent of close to 15 % during the eighties. This figure decreased from a high of over 20% in 1986 to little over 10% in 1989 (Hamilton, 1989).

[4] The way the quota rights are allocated determines who gets the rent. For a discussion of this issue see Hindley (1980).

restraint arrangements, export forecasts or industry-to-industry arrangements etc. Formally, VERs are quotas imposed by the exporting country unilaterally. The legal nicety, however, often covers up the fact that they are the response to political pressure from the importing country and its import-competing industry. The alternative to such a VER is not free trade but some other kind of trade restriction. For example Turkey refused to agree to a VER on shirt imports to France in 1982 and, instead, faced quantitative restrictions and a temporary import block.[5] It is also possible that foreign exorters seek VERs to gain the quota rent.

The typical VER is negotiated bilaterally, although changes and enforcement are undertaken by the exporting country. The difference to orderly marketing arrangements or voluntary restraint arrangements is that the latter agreements are modified and enforced by both parties. Orderly marketing arrangements are usually negotiated between two governments. Export forecasts and industry-to-industry arrangements involve only informal export monitoring. There is no commitment to a certain quota. Usually they operate under covert government support (Kostecki, 1987). The lack of transparency makes them sometimes hard to distinguish from national quotas or antidumping measures.

The next section explains the various procedures by which VERs can be obtained. The arguments which induce policy makers and producers to negotiate a VER are presented in Section 6.3. Unfortunately, the extremely scarce data on VERs does not allow a detailed empirical analysis on the micro or macro level. The incidence of VERs per sector and country as presented in Section 6.4, however, provides considerable support for the derived hypotheses. Section 6.5 discusses why certain industries prefer VERs to other types of protection. The chapter concludes with an outlook on the future role of VERs in the light of the "Fortress Europe" debate, the planned revision of the GATT safeguards clause and the international resistance against "grey area" measures.

6.2 The Voluntary Export Restraint Procedures

Since almost all VERs are not based on GATT regulations, there is no single legal procedure but several ways to obtain a VER. The only way VERs are negotiated in the context of EC and GATT law is through safeguards proceedings based on regulation 288/82. These

---

[5] European Communities (1982), Official Journal, L186.

can apply to the whole EC or to single member countries. In both cases, applications for safeguards measures against certain imports are forwarded to the Commission. After accepting the application, the Commission has to investigate whether the imports inflict serious injury to the industry. The injury criteria are rather vague and consist of changes in market shares, profits, employment, and prices, to name but a few. The qualification "serious", however, requires a fairly high level of injury. The injury investigation by the Commission is much shorter for national than for EC-wide cases.

If the Commission finds serious injury, there is, however, no administrative mechanism to determine the instrument and level of protection. Consultations are started between the EC and the exporting country through GATT. They are conducted by the Commission but the politicians have the final word. No negotiated solution can be reached without consent by the member governments. If the consultations do not lead to an agreement (for instance a VER), the EC can protect the injured industry and the target country can retaliate or receive compensation in other sectors. This alternative is less convenient - therefore the parties usually come to an agreement. In recent years, it has generally been a VER. In the history of GATT only one EC safeguards case was not terminated by negotiations. These VERs apply for a maximum of 3 years with a decreasing protection rate.

An important shortcoming of safeguards investigations is that the EC reports do not contain the word "safeguards". One has to know the legal basis to identify them as such. Transparency would also increase if *all* the results were published.

EC-wide agreements sometimes replace national quantitative restrictions. The only EC-wide VER which is currently in force and which is based on the safeguards regulation provides an interesting case study for a VER which starts on the national level and ends in an EC-wide restriction. In July 1987, the Italian government reported that its shoe industry was injured by Korean and Taiwanese footwear imports. A safeguards investigation was initiated in August, the same month in which France launched the same complaint. In France, national quotas on some types of shoes were already established. The Commission found increases of 14% and 11% in the combined market share of the accused producers in Italy and France respectively for the 1984-1987 period. The imports had also reduced the profitability and the employment in the domestic industries. The Commission announced a restraint agreement for shoe imports to Italy in February 1988 and to France in July 1988. These were valid until June 30th,

1990. In August 1988, the EC initiated a safeguards investigation for the whole EC affecting 1/2 billion ECU worth of shoe imports from Korea and Taiwan. In addition to the injury test, causation of the injury and the community interest were also investigated. The result was that the imports caused serious injury to EC producers. The Korean and Taiwanese governments offered a VER starting on July 1st, 1990 which was accepted by the Commission. This was later supplemented by EC-wide surveillance. The agreement is valid until the end of 1992.[6]

The extensive administrative procedure and the subsequent political negotiations between governments and the Commission through GATT render safeguards prodeedings very expensive both in terms of the cost of undertaking the procedure and of lobbying the politicians. This and the high injury standard have kept the number of VERs through safeguards to a minimum.

The Commission also negotiates all non-safeguards agreements which reach the political level. These "official", i.e. politically sanctioned, VERs are not constrained by administrative rules at all. Being without legal basis they are not voted on in the Council either. Member governments and the Council therefore exercise particularly close scrutiny during the negotiations. This, however, involves a significant amount of high-level political resources up to the ministerial level which makes it quite costly. EC-wide VERs have been negotiated by the Commission, for instance, for the agricultural sector or the steel industry. The negotiations against imports of Japanese cars have been conducted between the Commission and the Japanese government for 1 1/2 years. For most VERs, information on the underlying negotiations and investigations is minimal.

There are numerous agreements between national industries and foreign producers with the support of member governments. Most of these just involve a few letters or notes because national measures of this kind are not legal according to EC law. The EC Commission claims that it is not aware of many of them.

Unlike other protectionist instruments, the Court has not passed any rulings as regards the legal status of VERs. The legal embroilment leading to a wide array of measures and procedures is therefore likely to persist. The procedures suggest a strong political determination of VERs. Technical rules, although vague, are only important for safeguards procedings but the high costs of investigation

---

[6] The findings of the investigation, the exact coverage and the degree of protection are published in the Official Journal. See regulation 561/88 (Italy), 1857/88 (France), and 1735/90 of the Commission for the details of the VERs.

and negotiations currently deter from them. Direct negotiations without administrative rules or public scrutiny, however, proliferate. They have many advantages for the involved parties as the next section shows.

6.3 The Political Economy of Voluntary Export Restraints

Finger (1990) calls VERs the archetypal solution to trade disputes from a public choice perspective. If domestic producers seek relief from import competition, a solution is negotiated with the Commission, politicians, foreign producers and the complaining industry. The latter does not have to demonstrate, for instance, injury, economic difficulties or dumping in lengthy procedures. This gives industries with significant lobbying power the best chance of a favourable outcome in the negotiations.

Although VERs are limited to one to five year periods, renegotiation can lead to a renewal with even more restrictive terms when the policy makers can be convinced that the import surge is likely to continue. An entrenchment of benefits can therefore be expected. Entrenched protection, however, retards industry adjustment rather than promoting it, which is the stated purpose of protection for the EC Commission. Since VERs mostly disadvantage the low-cost producers, industry dynamics decrease and product cycles become longer (Kostecki, 1987).

VERs are also negotiated because they can promote the formation of cartels. The negotiations involve discussions on the business level that would not come about otherwise. These are used for market sharing deals or price fixings in oligopolistic markets. Foreign producers without a lobbying base within the EC strive for cooperation with EC producers in order to improve their counter-lobbying power and to dissipate protectionist pressure.

VERs, therefore, not only aid domestic producers but also favour established foreign exporters.[7] Quotas are usually distributed free of charge and are not auctioned. This transfers part of the protectionist rent to the foreign producers. The exporter can raise his price without paying for a quota right or a tariff and thereby increase his profitability. EC distributors of the imports may also profit from the price increase with higher profit margins.[8] The regime, however,

---

[7] Ethier (1991) discusses the economics of VERs.

[8] Kostecki (1987) reports that both Japanese producers and U.S.-distributors gained higher profit margins from the Japanese VER for car imports to the U.S.

only supports established exporters and discriminates against new market entrants from the VER-country who have problems obtaining quota rights. The established exporters oppose other regimes such as tariff protection or auctioned quotas. Exporters from countries not included in the VERs also profit from the restrictions against their competitors because they now face less competition in the foreign market. VERs are therefore preferred to other instruments and easier to negotiate in trade disputes.

In some instances, VERs are not profitable for the exporter but they are preferred to safeguards proceedings based on GATT Article XIX which may have even more detrimental effects. Developing countries, in particular, negotiate such VERs to prevent safeguards actions (Hindley, 1987).

Another advantage of VERs is that most of them are defined in terms of volume. This promotes "trading up" by exporters because they can then increase their sales in value terms without violating the restraint agreement (Feenstra, 1984). The range of Japanese car exports to the U.S., for instance, expanded from exclusively small cars in the late seventies to all sizes today.

Foreign producers may prefer VERs for still another reason. It has been observed that VERs against less developed countries frequently do not "bite" (Hughes and Krueger, 1984). Bhagwati (1987) calls this "porous protection". VERs sometimes do not help domestic producers because they are circumvented by transshipments through other countries, or because industries with low start-up costs circumvent them by shifting investments to third countries. By the time VERs include these third countries, the costs have already been recovered. VERs can also be deliberately negotiated at currently non-binding levels because domestic politicians and producers only want protection against sudden import surges.

Summarizing, domestic producers, exporters from non-participating countries and sometimes established exporters in the target country gain from VERs. The main losers are domestic consumers, but non-established exporters in the target country are also hurt. The main difference to conventional instruments such as tariffs is the compensation of foreign producers through the rent transfer.

On the political level, VERs are particularly attractive to policy makers. They can receive political support from the protected industry while political costs can be diffused. This is mainly due to the intransparent and secretive nature of the procedure (except for safeguards proceedings) which allows for low-profile measures as opposed to tariffs or antidumping. There are no administrative rules or published reports on most of the agreements. The EC can refuse to take responsibility for the trade barriers - the foreigners introduce them voluntarily. When it is convenient, it can even claim that it has no knowledge of them. It is more difficult for consumers or affected third parties to oppose VERs because sometimes they do not even hear about them.

VERs minimize the risk of retaliation because foreigners are compensated for loss of sales with higher prices. This, in turn, encourages them not to request retaliatory or compensatory measures from their government. Finger (1990) explains the political benefits to the domestic government arising from this "coup". Under the safeguards clause, GATT suggests compensation or retaliation. "If, the U.S. "paid for" new limits on imports of Japanese autos by reducing limits on imports of Japanese electronics, the U.S. economy would bear the adjustment cost of a shift of resources from electronics to autos, and the U.S. government would have the political problem of explaining why the U.S. electronics industry has to pay for the protection given to autos. The Japanese economy is in the mirror-image situation" (Finger, 1990). Retaliation would lead to similar problems. VERs provide higher prices and avoid the political problem that one industry (e.g. cars) is injured by imports and another (e.g. electronics) is injured by retaliation.

The fact that VER protection is sometimes porous, makes it attractive to politicians who must react to political pressure, but who dislike protection. VERs help them to calm their conscience by granting protection without substance. Once a VER exists, however, it is much easier to tighten the import restriction at a later date (Wolf, 1989).

VERs can be implemented quickly and they only aim at disruptive suppliers and ignore less aggressive exporters. This threat of immediate protection encourages exporters to penetrate the EC market slowly, which in turn decreases the need for future measures. The opposite can also happen as will be argued later.

Although VERs undermine the rule-oriented approach of GATT, the GATT as a bureaucracy may be equally interested in participation in negotiations (which increases its international importance and appropriations) as in rule orientation. Hence, it may promote the negotiation of "acceptable solutions". The EC Commission faces a similar trade-off. EC protectionism, for which the Commission is responsible, damages the economy. It gives the Commission an interventionist reputation. On the other hand, negotiating international agreements for the EC increases its authority - even if protectionist - at the expense of national governments who could otherwise negotiate separate agreements.

VERs, however, have some major drawbacks which make them too costly for some industries. All non-safeguards and non-MFA VERs are not explicitly covered by GATT. As mentioned, the discriminatory and political nature of VERs undermines the GATT legal system and promotes a (lobbying) power-based system of trade policies instead of a rule-based one. This destroys the foundations of the GATT (Jones, 1989). Benefits to politicians must be quite high to evade GATT and to contribute to its decline with potentially severe repercussions. In addition, negotiations on VERs often involve high-level government and administrative officials. As management resources are limited in firms, political and administrative resources on this level are also limited. Therefore industries must be quite influential politically if they want to obtain VERs.

Industries may refrain from VERs because of brand-name capital or reputation. The German chemical industry, for instance, still stands for high quality and state of the art technology. VERs, however, suggest low competitiveness, a senescent industry etc. As will be seen in the next chapter, industries which worry about their reputation prefer antidumping investigations - antidumping is officially directed against unfair trade. Dumping injures the "good" guy - and that is nothing to be ashamed of. Although this might sound dramatic, it still suits an industry that does not want to risk its high quality image with protection designed for "failing" industries.

VERs may be self-defeating for an industry for two other reasons. If only established exporters get a share of a profitable VER, this induces more exporters to enter the market as quickly as possible before the cake is eaten up. The unintended consequence is that import penetration is more extensive than without the threat of protection (Schuknecht and Stephan, 1992). Even if it does not lead to more rapid market penetration initially, the rent transfer to foreign producers increases their competitiveness. Industries oriented towards world markets may prefer other measures than VERs to prevent these adverse effects on their relative international competitiveness.

VERs induce foreign producers to invest in the EC. On the one hand this has the desired effect of creating employment in the industry, on the other hand, domestic producers will face internal instead of external competition. Foreign investments will also weaken the lobbying power of a domestic producer. The foreign investor will break up the united protectionist front of the industry. The jobs created also weaken the case for protection by the EC. Special interests can counter this threat by asking for limits on foreign investments in addition to quantitative restrictions. In other words, domestic producers will prefer to save jobs through protection instead of through foreign investments to restrict foreign lobbying power - even if the former method is less effective for preserving employment.

6.4 Empirical Evidence

The Incidence per Country

Most VERs restrict imports to the whole EC but there is still a significant number of national restraint agreements. The figures given in Table 6.1 do not give an exact estimation of protection through VERs because many agreements are not known. The table does not indicate the numerous VERs which have been negotiated with single member countries in the context of the Multi Fiber Arrangement (MFA) either. The figures confirm the findings from the previous chapter on national protection based on Article 115. France is one of the major protectionist forces in the EC. Surprisingly, also the United Kingdom, Germany and the BeNeLux countries have some residual national VER protection.

Table 6.1 Voluntary Export Restraints by the EC and its Member Countries

Total	EC	National	France	Ireland	United Kingdom	Germany	BeNeLux
69	57	12	5	1	3	1	2

30 countries have restrained their exports to the EC in 1990 as Table 6.2 indicates. Most of the target countries, however, only maintain one agreement in agriculture or textiles. Japan is by far the most important target; 21 of the EC's agreements are negotiated with Japan. Korea has 6 agreements with the EC which is close to 10% of the total. Other countries account for a maximum of three

Table 6.2 Voluntary Export Restraints per Sector and Country, 1990

VERs per sector and country	Total	Agri-cul-ture	Foot-wear	Tex-tiles (not MFA)	Steel	Mach-inery	Elec-tron-ics	Vehi-cles	Oth-er
Argentina	2	2							
Australia	2	2							
Austria	2	1			1				
Brazil	1				1				
Bulgaria	3	1		1	1				
Chile	1	1							
China	1		1						
CIS[a]	1			1					
CSFR	3	1	1		1				
Cyprus	1			1					
Egypt	1			1					
Finland	1				1				
Hungary	2	1			1				
Iceland	1	1							
Japan	21	2		1	1	6	5	2	
Korea	6	1	2				2		1
Malta	1			1					
Morocco	1			1					
N. Zealand	2	2							
Poland	2	1			1				
Romania	3	1	1		1				
Singapore	1								1
S. Africa	1	1							
Sweden	1				1				
Taiwan	2		1						1
Thailand	1								1
Tunesia	1			1					
Turkey	1			1					
USA	1				1				
Yugoslavia	2	1		1					
Total	69 (51)[b]	17 (3)	6 (4)	10	11	6	8	5	6 (4)

Source: GATT Trade Policy Review Mechanism, European Communities, March 1991.

[a] Former Soviet Union

[b] The number in brackets is provided by the GATT (1991) and does not count the agreements with single countries in agriculture, footwear etc. separately.

Table 6.3 Shares of VERs (1990) and EC Imports (1988) for Selected
Countries and Country Groups

Country or country group	Total number of cases	Share of total cases	Share of EC merchandise imports 1988
Developed countries	31	45	62
Japan	21	30	11
United States	1	1	19
Eastern Europe	14	20	8
Developing countries	24	35	30
thereof NICs	9	13	5.5
South Korea	6	9	1.8
Taiwan	2	3	2.1
Total	69[*]	100	100

* This includes 16 VERs against apples and lamb and goat meat which involve several
countries.

agreements. The targets can be found in all country groups, 45% of
the VERs include industrialized countries, 20% Eastern Europeans
and 35% developing countries. The NICs share is almost 15% of the
total (Table 6.3).

Another way to assess the relative impact of VERs on the
target countries is to compare their share of VERs with their share of
merchandise imports in the EC. Table 6.3 indicates that 30% of the
VERs involve Japan which only contributes 11% of the EC's imports.
Looking at the ratio of the two figures, Korea is hit harder. Its share
of VERs is five times as high as its import share of 1.8%. Among the
groups of countries, Eastern Europe is affected most adversely with
20% of the VERs and only 8% of EC imports. Romania,
Czechoslovakia and Bulgaria have 3 VERs each but only a minimal
share of EC imports. Developed countries, except for Japan, receive
less than their "appropriate" share of VER protection. The U.S. only
has one VER for steel but provides almost 20% of the EC's imports.

The Incidence per Sector
Table 6.2 and the appendix provide the incidence of VERs per sector (except for textiles and clothing under the MFA). Agriculture, footwear, textiles and clothing, steel, machinery, consumer electronics and vehicles are the most affected industries. While Japan is the only target of machinery and vehicle protection, Korea has two VERs in consumer electronics. The lamb and apple exporters from both developing and developed countries have VERs with the EC. Developing countries are affected by restraint agreements most frequently in the textile/clothing sector. Most VERs on iron and steel cover imports from industrialized countries and Eastern Europe. Among the footwear exporting countries, Taiwan and Korea face the most encompassing restrictions.

Currently, Japanese car imports to the EC are monitored with the understanding that the total market share should not exceed 10%. This share varies widely over the EC, ranging from nearly 0% in Italy to approximately 40% in Ireland. Car imports from Japan valued close to 8 billion ECU in 1987. Additional imports would be worth approximately 3 billion ECU, if the market share was allowed to rise to the German level of 14%. The array of current restraint agreements by Japan will be replaced by an official EC-wide VER which involves an increase in the market share to 16%, varying in each member country. Imports are supposed to be fully liberalized by the year 2000. Until then, up to half of the 16% share is to be produced in the EC.[9] This raises the stakes to more than just specific import quotas. The agreement also aims at restricting Japanese lobbying power in the EC by restricting Japanese investments. The loss of confidence in the security of investments in the EC could be more damaging than the actual trade barriers.

In the eighties, consumer electronics were more and more the target of trade protection. The Japanese and the Koreans claim that they limited their imports of video cassette recorders and microwave ovens to the EC for fear of antidumping measures (they got them anyhow in the year 1989). This indicates how "voluntary" some VERs are and how trade barriers can substitute each other.

In the early 1980s, VERs covered over two thirds of EC steel imports from outside the community to prevent the circumvention of the internal steel cartel. The importance of VERs for the steel industry, however, declined significantly. The GATT (1991) reports

---

[9] Frankfurter Allgemeine Zeitung, July 29th, 1991, 9.

ten VERs against Brazil, three EFTA countries and six Eastern European suppliers. These cover only 15% of EC steel imports.

Evidence in Support of a Political Economy Approach
The results show that only very politically influential industries can induce the EC to negotiate VERs. The agricultural, vehicle, steel, consumer electronics, textile/clothing and machinery industries are amongst the strongest lobbyists. It comes as no surprise that the less influential footwear industry, "only" facing 3 billion ECU of total imports, has to take a detour through safeguards proceedings or has to negotiate industry-to-industry arrangements (see appendix).

Whenever member countries imposed (or intended to impose) trade barriers by disregarding the Common Commercial Policy, the Commission has always been quick in fulfilling the national protectionist requests on the EC level. France speeded up the conclusion of the second MFA by threatening to impose national barriers. When France closed its video cassette recorder market by channeling all Japanese imports through Poitier, the Commission also negotiated a VER. French and Southern European car producers lobbied extensively for an EC-wide VER with Japan, which some countries resisted and which the Commission then negotiated. The EC Commission wants to keep at least control over the process and VERs are a handy device. GATT also seems to be affected by the behavioural pattern of bureaucracy. All VERs under the Multi Fiber Arrangement have been accepted by GATT and almost all safeguards proceedings have also resulted in a negotiated solution.[10]

The EC dissipates the political costs of VERs in several ways. The Commission refuses to publish or to provide any useful information on existing VERs. It blames the foreigners or the GATT negotiations for protection, and in four cases (microwave ovens from Korea, certain textiles, ball bearings, and metal flatware from Japan) it denies any knowledge of the VER. The fact that there is no complete list of existing VERs also indicates that the EC and its industries are successful in keeping information on VER protection to a minimum. Still, some VERs, such as the one for cars, have received considerable public attention.

VERs are a precedent for increasing protection. Trade barriers in the textiles and clothing industry started out as a series of VERs between Japan and the U.S. in the 1950s. It was extended and

---

[10] However, it is sometimes claimed that the common trade policy regime of the EC or that based on GATT could have collapsed if the Commission or GATT had not agreed to protection.

transformed into the Multi Fiber Arrangement which has been in force ever since (Wolf, 1989). In the EC, voluntary export restraints under the MFA became more and more restrictive.[11] In the steel industry, VERs also proved to be long-lived. The first step towards creating the EC's web of VERs was made in 1977. The Japanese VER limiting commercial vehicle exports to the UK has been in force since 1975.

Messerlin (1990) provides evidence of how antidumping proceedings are used for cartelization in the chemical industry. Similar incidents are most likely in the negotiation of VERs. For instance, when the EC steel cartel was formed, foreign exporters became subject to VERs and had to join this cartel. They had to charge a certain minimum price, otherwise the EC would have imposed an antidumping duty (Hindley, 1980).

Evidence can be found that established exporters favour VERs. Many of them involve Japanese producers who are well-established in the consumer electronics and car sectors. They face little competition from other non-EC producers which means that the quota rent is not dissipated by imported substitutes. They may even profit from VERs through quota rents more than from free trade. Hamilton (1988) estimates that Hong Kong, Taiwan and South Korean exporters of clothing to the EC gained 200 million U.S. Dollars during the years 1982 and 1983 from VERs. Exporting firms also engage visibly in trading up. The Japanese, for example, have widened their range of car exports to the EC from small to medium-sized cars (de Melo and Messerlin, 1988).

VER protection is sometimes porous. The German VER on cars has so far never been binding (de Melo and Messerlin, 1988). The first MFA did not effectively restrict imports, which led to the more restrictive MFA II. This shows that VERs may indeed be initiated by politicians who do not want protection to be effective. But as Wolf (1989) wittily notes on this subject: "The road to hell is paved with good intentions."

World market orientation and reputation may prevent the chemical industry from negotiating VERs. In other sectors, EC exports are of decreasing importance; steel, agriculture, textiles/clothing, footwear and consumer electronics are either uncompetitive or declining industries. They do not have a reputation to lose from seeking VERs. The negotiation of VERs in export

---

[11] Just recently, Hamilton (1991) reports decreased levels of protection for MFA regulated trade.

intensive sectors such as machinery or cars casts some doubts on this hypothesis. Products in these sectors, however, are so varied that competitive producers in the EC, e.g. Mercedes, need not fear loss of reputation when there is a VER on Japanese car imports.

So far no studies have been published which analyse the effect of quota rents on the long-term trade performance of affected exporters. The other question is, whether the expected rent induces foreigners to penetrate the EC market more rapidly than without anticipated protection in order to secure a large share of a VER. Winters (1990) reports that import surveillance resulted in *increased* exports to the EC by producers of certain products in anticipation of quantitative restrictions. The effect of foreign investments on the relative lobbying power of domestic producers has been recognized. The negotiation of the car VER with Japan for the nineties restricts not only imports but also Japanese investments in the EC. This suggests that EC producers in fact lobby for a restriction of foreign lobbying power.

6.5 Why Some Industries Prefer Voluntary Export Restraints

As the previous section illustrated, industries which are influential enough to get protection without support from the bureaucratic system and its formal procedures prefer VERs. It is not necessary to show injury, economic difficulties or dumping which some producers might have difficulties in proving. Lengthy administrative procedures on top of the political bargaining process are also avoided. The other main advantage lies in the lack of transparency. This is important when the costs of protection are high so that the politicians and the industries fear publicity and opposition.

VERs usually only fix restrictions for general product categories, for example cars or steel. These arguments suggest that large producers of relatively homogenous products are most suitable for VER protection (with the exception of the MFA). Generally, antidumping can serve as a relatively close substitute for a VER; it is, for instance, often chosen to replace national VERs in preparation for "Europe 1992".

6.6 Conclusion: VERs, GATT and "Europe 1992"

VERs are popular as a negotiated solution to trade disputes with politicians, and domestic and foreign producers. The dubious legality with respect to GATT and the limited availability of high level negotiators make this instrument suitable for special interests which have the political influence to achieve speedy protection without going through a lengthy legislative or administrative procedure. Recourse to VERs decreases the importance of rule-oriented GATT-consistency and raises the importance of lobbying power for obtaining protection. In most cases, however, VERs have been ineffective in saving jobs and very costly to consumers.

The prospects for the future importance of VERs are somewhat uncertain. The abolition of VERs induces national industries to seek compensation on the EC level. The political nature of VERs makes them suitable for accommodating shifting protectionist pressure - the EC car industry being a case in point. In the ongoing Uruguay Round, however, the contracting parties are renegotiating the application of the safeguards clause based on Article XIX, GATT. This includes a ban on the open negotiation of new VERs by governments.

It is planned to allow safeguards measures without retaliation or compensatory liberalization in other sectors. The new safeguards standards, however, will not make this kind of protection easy. The injury standards will be strict and a review is required after three years. There is also a sunset clause of four years as a maximum for any measure. Some industries which formerly attempted to negotiate VERs might therefore take advantage of the new safeguards regulation (or shift their protectionist requests to antidumping). On the other hand, it is conceivable that industry-to-industry agreements and similar inofficial VERs will be the prevalent alternative means of protection.[12] They have the advantage that they are even less transparent than the current type of mostly semi-official but at least publicly known VERs. Banning VERs is certainly a step in the "right" direction from a legal point of view; the future will show whether the new rules really encourage abstention from new VERs altogether. Existing VERs will be grandfathered, and this will secure their importance for a long time to come.

---

[12] GATT's lack of enforcement provisions makes it difficult to prevent the "clever" use of alternative means (Jones, 1989).

Appendix: Voluntary Export Restraints and Similar Restraint
Arrangements in the EC, as of Mid-1990

Voluntary export restraints in the EC			
Targets	Initiator	Products	Type
Agriculture:			
All suppliers[a]	EC	sheep/goats	VER[b]
Argentina, Australia, Chile, New Zealand, South Africa	EC	dessert apples	IRA[c]
Korea	EC	frozen squid	IRA
Footwear:			
Korea, Taiwan	EC	footwear, no slippers	VER
China	France	slippers + sandales	IRA
Korea	Ireland	footwear	IRA
CSFR, Romania	UK	footwear	IRA
Textiles outside MFA:			
Bulgaria	EC	MFA textiles/cloth.	VER
Soviet Union	EC	MFA textiles/cloth.	VER
Japan	EC	textiles/clothing	IRA[d]
Cyprus	EC	textiles/clothing	IRA
Egypt	EC	textiles/clothing	IRA
Malta	EC	textiles/clothing	IRA
Morocco	EC	textiles/clothing	IRA
Tunisia	EC	textiles/clothing	IRA
Turkey	EC	textiles/clothing	IRA
Yugoslavia	EC	textiles/clothing	VER
Steel/steel products:			
Austria	EC	steel	IRA
Brazil	EC	pig iron + steel	VER
Bulgaria	EC	steel	VER
CSFR	EC	steel	VER
Finland	EC	steel	IRA
Hungary	EC	steel	VER
Japan	EC	steel	IRA
Poland	EC	steel	VER
Romania	EC	steel	VER
Sweden	EC	steel	IRA
USA	EC	steel/steel products	VER

Machinery:			
Japan	EC	machine tools	VER
Japan	EC	machining centres	VER
Japan	EC	NC lathes	VER
Japan	EC	forklift trucks	VER
Japan	EC	ball bearings	IRA[d]
Japan	France	NC lathes, machining centres	VER
Electrical and electronic household equipment:			
Japan	EC	color TV sets	VER
Japan	EC	color TV tubes	VER
Japan	EC	video tape recorders	VER
Korea	EC	microwave ovens	IRA[d]
Korea	EC	video tape recorders	VER
Japan	Germany	color TV sets	IRA
Japan	France	TV tubes	IRA
Japan	EC	video tape recorders	IRA
Vehicles:			
Japan	EC	passenger cars	VER
Japan	EC	commercial vehicles	VER
Japan	EC	motorcycles	VER
Japan	UK	passenger cars commercial, four-wheel-drive vehicles	IRA
Japan	Belgium	automobiles	IRA
Other products:			
Japan	EC	metal flatware	IRA[d]
Korea	BeNeLux	metal flatware	IRA[d]
Singapore, Taiwan, Thailand	France	umbrellas	IRA
Japan	UK	pottery	IRA

Source: GATT Trade Policy Review Mechanism, European Communities, 1991.

[a] Argentina, Australia, Austria, Bulgaria, CSFR, Hungary, Iceland, New Zealand, Poland, Romania, Yugoslavia (Kostecki, 1987)

[b] VER = all formal restraint arrangements, i.e. VERs, Orderly Marketing Arrangements, Community Export Monitoring and Formal Restraint Arrangements

[c] IRA = all informal restraint arrangements, i.e. export forecasts, export ceilings, informal restraint arrangements, industry to industry arrangements, autolimitations, reference prices or price fixings, export cartels, export moderation

[d] The EC Commission or national government is not aware of these restraints

Chapter 7

ANTIDUMPING

7.1 Introduction

Antidumping laws constitute the third very potent instrument of protectionism used in the European Community.[1] During the 1980s, the EC ruled on around 900 dumping claims. The average ad valorem equivalent of antidumping measures between 1980 and 1987 was 23%, with peaks as high as 50% or more; the average tariff on manufactured goods was 5%. Imports of products subject to dumping investigations have fallen on average to half their initial level within five years after a dumping investigation (Messerlin 1989). In 1990, approximately 1.8 billion ECU worth of imports were subject to new preliminary or final antidumping measures. Over 1 billion of these were in consumer electronics. The annual costs to EC consumers have been estimated to be 1.4 billion ECU for the measures against consumer electronics alone, i.e. videos, CD players, photocopiers, video cassettes, dot-matrix printers and electronic type-writers. This shows that antidumping is not just an abstract protection device, but that it imposes a strain on everybody's budget.

The figures even underestimate the protectionist impact of antidumping because the measures have a significant harassment effect on exporters (Bhagwati, 1988). A good example is provided by the steel industry in 1978. Over 50 antidumping claims were lodged against steel exporters, many of them leading to duties. This forced exporters to charge minimum prices and to agree to voluntary export restraints to prevent more antidumping measures (Messerlin, 1989a). An antidumping claim against microwave ovens from Korea was withdrawn after the Koreans had informally agreed to restrain its

---

[1] For this reason, the EC's antidumping policy has drawn the attention of trade policy analysts. Tharakan (1988), Messerlin (1989, 1990a, 1991), Stegemann (1990), Schuknecht and Ursprung (1990), GATT (1991) and Eymann and Schuknecht (1991) discuss EC antidumping. This chapter is based mainly on A. Eymann and L. Schuknecht (1991).

exports to the EC. The GATT (1991) also reports on other voluntary export restrictions in anticipation of antidumping claims.

This chapter demonstrates the prominence of antidumping laws as an instrument of trade protection in the EC. It looks at how this instrument is applied by examining the incidence of antidumping measures per sector and country and the administrative procedures for antidumping cases. Antidumping is supposed to rectify the "unfairness" of trade, defined mainly as the finding of *dumping* and *injury*. The institutional and empirical analyses in this chapter, however, suggest the following. *What really motivates the application of antidumping measures is the prevention of injury from imports to politically influential domestic producers.* The "fairness" or "unfairness" of foreign trade practices is merely rhetoric. In the words of Finger (1991), "...antidumping is ordinary trade protection with a grand public relations programme."

The EC's antidumping regulations are not based on any economic notion of dumping but on the GATT antidumping code.[2] The specifications of the GATT code are relatively vague. They define *dumping* in three possible ways, one of them being sales below the "full" unit cost of production plus a "reasonable" profit margin. The notions of "full" and "reasonable" are not well specified, leaving considerable scope for discretionary interpretation of whether dumping has occurred in a particular instance. The definition of *injury* as a decrease in profit, employment, etc. is no more precise. In addition, injury must be inflicted on *domestic producers* of *like products* and it must be *caused* by dumping. But is a domestic company which is owned mainly by foreign share holders still domestic? What is the equivalent of Japanese semiconductors if the EC does not produce them? Is a decline in profits from an unusually high level already injury? These decisions are left to the user countries. But how meaningful is a concept of fairness if the user can apply it in almost any way he wants? If national laws do not provide the appropriate specifications, antidumping is most likely to be captured by special interests seeking protection. The institutional structures governing the determination of dumping within a nation's trade laws are, therefore, of prime importance.

---

[2] The GATT antidumping provision was preceeded by antidumping laws in several countries. In the Kennedy Round, the first supra-national antidumping code was adopted which was replaced by the Tokyo Round code. Most issues in the context of antidumping have already been discussed by de Jong (1968). For a detailed discussion of the history of antidumping see Finger (1991).

The GATT code allows countries to operate within the specifications in two different ways. The United States has taken one path, the EC the other, but both paths ultimately lead to an outcome that equates injury with unfairness and fairness with import restrictions. The United States has added precise specifications to the GATT generalities, leaving little discretion to the agencies which evaluate dumping petitions. The U.S. Congress, however, has designed the rules in a protectionist manner to cover all instances of injury.[3] The EC has taken the alternative approach of translating the GATT code into a general operational language without adding extensive detail. The administering agency, the EC Commission, is entrusted with interpreting this language. Political influence is secured through the administrators' accountability to the EC Council and to the member governments. An example may illustrate this difference. The U.S. procedure requires a profit margin of at least 8% to calculate of the foreign production costs in order to determine dumping and 8% is more than what many branches earn. The EC must apply an "appropriate" profit margin, but in some cases the "appropriate" margin is higher than in others. In other words, both the United States and the EC use antidumping measures to restrict imports. The United States formulates protectionist rules while the EC applies protectionist discretion.

7.2 Who Are the Targets of EC Antidumping Measures?

Incidence per Country Group

Antidumping is the EC's frontline defense against imports, but the distribution of these measures has by no means been equal. Japan, Eastern European countries,[4] and a few developing countries including China, Korea, Mexico, Taiwan, Turkey, and Yugoslavia, have been the object of a disproportionate share of such measures. Fourty-nine countries were involved in the 903 dumping decisions conducted during 1980-90 (Table 7.1). Almost half of these cases

---

[3] For U.S. antidumping, see Finger, Hall, and Nelson (1982), Moore (1990), Litan and Boltuck (1991) or Kaplan (1991). Finger (forthcoming 1992) provides an encompassing study of antidumping enforcement in the user countries and its effect on industries in developing countries.

[4] In this analysis, "Eastern European countries" refers to the members of the former Council of Mutual Economic Assistance, Czechoslovakia, the former Soviet Union, Hungary, Bulgaria, Romania, Poland and former East Germany.

Table 7.1 Number of EC Antidumping Cases and their Outcome per Country, 1980-90

Region/country	Rejection	Antidumping duty	Price undertaking	Number of cases
Developed countries				
Australia	0	0	1	1
Austria	2	0	3	5
Belgium	0	0	1	1
Canada	3	6	4	13
Finland	0	1	10	11
Greece	2	0	0	2
Iceland	0	1	2	3
Israel	0	0	3	3
Japan	31	85	59	175
Norway	3	1	10	14
South Africa	2	1	2	5
Spain	15	5	10	30
Sweden	4	3	18	25
Switzerland	0	0	1	1
United States	42	67	47	156
Eastern Europe				
Albania	1	0	0	1
Bulgaria	4	4	5	13
Czechoslovakia	7	7	27	41
(former) East Germany	7	9	19	35
Hungary	5	2	12	19
Poland	7	4	20	31
Romania	10	2	24	36
CIS (former Soviet Union)	10	18	16	44
Developing countries				
(excluding newly industrialized countries of Asia)				
Algeria	0	2	0	2
Argentina	1	1	1	3
Brazil	11	9	5	25
China, P. R.	4	9	12	25
Dominican Republic	1	0	0	1
Egypt	1	0	0	1
Korea, P. R.	1	0	0	1

Table 7.1 Number of EC Antidumping Cases and their Outcome per
Country, 1980-1990 (continued)

Region/country	Rejection	Antidumping duty	Price undertaking	Number of cases
Kuwait	0	1	0	1
Libya	0	1	0	1
Malaysia	1	0	1	2
Mexico	1	8	8	17
Portugal	2	0	1	3
Puerto Rico	0	3	0	3
Saudi Arabia	0	1	0	1
Surinam	1	1	0	2
Thailand	1	0	0	1
Trinidad and Tobago	1	1	0	2
Turkey	7	10	7	24
Venezuela	1	3	2	6
Virgin Islands	0	2	0	2
Yugoslavia	9	16	18	43
Zimbabwe	1	0	1	2
Newly industrialized countries (NICs)				
Hong Kong	2	7	1	10
Korea, Republic of	7	18	1	26
Singapore	2	2	3	7
Taiwan	10	7	11	28
Group totals				
Developed countries	104	170	171	445
Eastern Europe	51	46	123	220
Developing countries	65	101	72	238
thereof NICs	21	34	16	71
All countries	220	317	366	903

Note: Cases are defined as final decisions on products of single firms or countries.
Source: Computed from EC Official Journal (various issues).

(445) involved industrial countries, particularly the United States and
Japan, which accounted for two-thirds of the 445 cases. The remaining
cases were divided almost equally between Eastern European
countries (220) and developing countries (238). 30% of the cases
against developing countries involved the newly industrialized
countries of Asia (71 cases, or 8% of total cases), and in particular
Taiwan and South Korea.

A dumping investigation has three possible outcomes: rejection of the claim, the levying of an antidumping duty, or negotiation of a voluntary price increase (price undertakings) with the parties accused of dumping. Of the two restrictive outcomes - duties and price undertakings - price undertakings are more favourable to the accused party since they allow the foreign exporter to collect the protectionist rents, i.e. the price increase.[5] About one quarter of the 903 cases were rejected, 35% resulted in an antidumping duty being imposed, and 40% were resolved through price undertakings.

As a group, the share of affirmative and negative decisions for industrialized countries was close to the average for the 903 cases (Table 7.2). Eastern European countries had a larger than average share of cases resolved through price undertakings (56%), a more favourable outcome than antidumping duties. Developing countries had a higher than average share of cases in which antidumping duties were levied (43%) but also a slightly higher than average share of rejected claims (27%; 30% for the newly industrialized countries). These figures can be interpreted to suggest that imports from larger countries - industrial countries and Eastern European countries - cause more injury and therefore cases against them result in more affirmative decisions. The results also suggest that developing countries have less leverage for negotiating profitable price increases than larger countries.

Another way to assess the relative impact of antidumping measures is to compare a country's or a group's share of antidumping cases with its share of merchandise imports by the EC (Table 7.3). While 49% of cases have been initiated against industrial countries, they account for 62% of EC imports. The ratio of antidumping cases to import share, however, varies widely for individual countries. Australia and Switzerland each accounted for only 0.1% of antidumping cases while their imports constituted 1.3% and 8%, respectively, of total imports. By contrast, Japan, which accounted for 11% of EC imports, was the object of 19% of the antidumping cases.[6]

---

[5] There is an exception to this claim. In markets with rapidly falling prices, a price undertaking with constant import prices leads to continuously increasing real protectionist margins. In cases of this kind, producers may prefer the duty which allows them to stay in the market to an undertaking which results in short term rents but increasing long term protection.

[6] The relative impact of antidumping should not be generalized in evaluating the market access of certain countries to the EC. Australia faces little antidumping protection but the Common Agricultural Policy restricts agricultural exports

Table 7.2 Shares of EC Antidumping Cases and their Outcomes per
Country Group, 1980-1990

Country group	Rejection	Anti-dumping duty	Price under taking	Percentage of total cases
Developed countries	23	38	39	49
Eastern Europe	23	21	56	24
Developing countries (including NICs)	27	43	30	27
Newly industrialized countries	30	48	22	8
All countries	24	35	41	100

Note: Cases are defined as final decisions on products of single firms or countries.
Percentages are percentages of total cases for each group.
Source: Computed from data in the Official Journal of the European Communities
(various issues).

As a group, the Eastern European block was the most
adversely affected by antidumping measures relative to import share.
They accounted for 8% of EC imports but 24% of its antidumping
cases. Considered individually, Romania, Czechoslovakia, and former
East Germany had the highest share of antidumping cases relative to
import share; Czechoslovakia and East Germany also had high
percentages of cases with restrictive outcomes.

Developing countries fared relatively well as a group. They
contributed 27% of antidumping cases compared to 30% of imports.
Some individual countries, however, were subject to a
disproportionate share of antidumping measures. China, Mexico,
Turkey, Yugoslavia, and, of the newly industrialized countries, Korea
and Taiwan accounted for 70% of the antidumping measures directed
against developing countries but for only 30% of the share of EC
imports.

significantly. South Asia is not targeted by antidumping but by protection in the Multi
Fiber Arrangement.

Table 7.3 Shares of EC Antidumping Cases and EC Imports for
Selected Countries and Country Groups, 1980-1990

Country or group	Total number of cases	Share of total cases	EC import share 1988	Share with restrictive outcome
All countries	903	100	100	76
Developed countries	445	49	62	77
Eastern Europe	220	24	8	77
Developing countries (including NICs)	238	27	30	73
thereof NICs	71	8	5.5	70
Developed countries				
Australia	1	0.1	1.3	100
Japan	175	19	11	82
Switzerland	1	0.1	8	100
United States	156	17	18	73
Eastern Europe				
Czechoslovakia	41	4.5	0.5	83
(former) East Germany	35	4	0.4	80
Romania	36	4	0.5	72
Developing countries				
China, P.R.	25	3	1.8	84
Egypt	1	0.1	0.4	0
Malaysia	2	0.2	0.7	50
Mexico	17	2	0.6	94
Thailand	1	0.1	0.5	0
Turkey	24	3	1.1	71
Yugoslavia	43	5	1.5	79
Newly industrialized countries				
Hong Kong	10	1	1.6	89
Korea, Republic of	26	3	1.8	73
Singapore	7	0.8	0.8	71
Taiwan	28	3	2.1	64

Note: Cases are defined as final decisions on products of single firms or countries.
Source: Computed from data in the Official Journal of the European Communities
(various issues) and EUROASTAT, Monthly Bulletin of External Trade, 1990.

Incidence per Sector
The incidence of antidumping cases per industrial sector for 1980-1990 provides a distinct pattern of sectoral concentration (Table 7.4). The industries producing chemicals, steel and steel products, machinery, and consumer electronics were targeted in close to 70% of all antidumping claims. Imports of chemicals have been affected the most. Almost 60% of the cases against industrial countries involved chemical products, machinery, and office and computing equipment.

Cases against developing countries (except the newly industrialized countries) are concentrated in sectors often considered to have shifting comparative advantage. 57% of the cases involved steel products, basic chemicals, and synthetic fibers. Antidumping measures against steel imports protect the EC steel cartel, while measures against synthetic fiber imports add to

Table 7.4 Percentage of EC Antidumping Cases per Sector and Country Group, 1980-1990

Sector	Developed countries	Eastern Europe	Developing countries (including NICs)	NICs	Total
Chemical products[a]	37	42	40	31	39
Steel and steel products	4	4	17	1	7
Machinery	14	7	4	7	9
Office/computing machinery	8	0	0	0	4
Electrical machinery (mostly household machinery)	2	13	2	0	5
Consumer electronics	5	0	10	35	5
Other sectors	30	34	27	26	31

a For developing countries, these are mainly synthetic fibers.
Source: Computed from the Official Journal of the European Communities.

protection against textile and clothing imports negotiated in the Multi Fiber Arrangement. This pattern suggests that EC protectionism through antidumping measures prevents developing countries from profiting from their comparative advantage.

In the newly industrialized countries, high-tech firms are a frequent target of dumping investigations. More than one-third of the cases involved consumer electronics products, a sector with shifting comparative advantage and sophisticated technology requirements.

Recently, the pattern as illustrated in Table 7.4 has shifted away from chemicals and towards high-tech products (Table 7.5). In the 1982-1988 period, the chemical industry accounted for up to 80% of the antidumping decisions. In 1990, the share of chemical products subject to a preliminary or final antidumping measure was only 20% as was the share of consumer electronics. 15% involved steel products and 35% were various other products ranging from semiconductors (DRAMs) to espadrilles. The main targets in 1990 have been China, Japan and Korea. This suggests a more and more industrial policy oriented application of antidumping measures. The resurgence of antidumping claims against steel imports coincides with a reduction of VERs in the steel sector.

The relative impact of antidumping measures on different sectors can also be compared by looking at the respective import volumes affected by antidumping measures (Table 7.5). The total value of the products imported in 1989 which were hit by an antidumping measure in 1990, was 1.8 billion ECU. Of this over one billion or 60% affected consumer electronics, 300 million or 15% affected DRAMs, close to 10% steel products and 15% other products. While the imports of the four chemical products affected are only worth approximately 10 million ECU, the high-tech products (consumer electronics and DRAMs) cover 1.3 billion ECU worth of imports. The enormous difference in the import values suggests that high-tech products from Japan and the NICs are affected even more adversely than the incidence per country initially indicates.

The sectorial pattern also suggests that dumping is more prevalent in sectors with high sunk costs (steel and chemicals) and those where increased current production could lead to positive effects from "learning by doing" and a decline in future costs (consumer electronics). In both cases, marginal costs are well below the full costs of production. This can lead to the rational and non-dumping oriented business strategy of sales below the full cost of

Table 7.5 The Incidence of Preliminary and Final Duties per Sector and Country in 1990

Sector and products	Targets	Import value in million ECU, 1989
Consumer electronics (4 products)		1043
CD players	Japan, Korea	(320)
small colour TVs	Korea	(364)
cassettes	Japan, Korea, Hong Kong	(200)[a]
video cassettes	Korea, Hong Kong	(159)[a]
Computing machinery (1 product)		300
DRAMs	Japan	
Machinery (1 product)		17
ball bearings	Thailand	
Chemicals (4 products)	CSFR, CIS, Indonesia, Thailand, Korea, Taiwan, China (2x)	10
Steel (3 products)	Island, Norway, Sweden Venezuela (2x), Romania, Yugoslavia (2x), Japan, Turkey	approx. 160[b]
Other (7 products)	China (5x), Japan (2x), USA	271
Total: 20 products	17 countries	approx. 1800

a import data from 1988
b excluding imports from Romania, import data for 1 product (pipes) from 1988
Source: Computed from the EC's Official Journal and EUROSTAT, 6C, External Trade, 1988 and 1989.

production. The first type of industry applies this strategy when a recession does not allow to recover the full costs. In the second type of industry, companies expect higher future profits by increasing current sales through lower prices (Gruenspecht, 1988). The EC regulation defining dumping as sales below the full cost of production penalizes such business practices and is therefore biased against these industries.

Summarizing, the pattern of antidumping measures suggests that they are usually applied to prevent loss of domestic production to emerging competitors from both developed and developing countries.

7.3 Antidumping Procedures in the United States and the European Community

The suggestion of a politically motivated pattern of protection which emerges from the analysis of the incidence of antidumping measures per sector and country is reinforced by examining the way in which antidumping decisions are made in the EC. A comparison of EC procedures with those in the United States is informative. The contrasts between the two systems underline their one common important characteristic: both achieve protectionist ends, despite their mostly different means.[7]

The United States
In the United States, national rules specify the GATT code in a way that leaves only limited scope for bureaucratic discretion and political intervention in any one case. Protectionist interests are accommodated by the protectionist nature of the rules (Finger and Murray, 1990).

U.S. trade laws cover four distinct phases in the antidumping process: application, investigation, decision, and appeal (see Figure 7.1). Applications which fulfill certain requirements with respect to form and content automatically lead to investigations. The procedural rules governing the time frame and rights of parties involved in an investigation are clearly defined. The conditions specified for the imposition of preliminary duties, enforcement, and prevention of circumvention are unambiguous. U.S. administrators have little discretion in dumping cases. Their determination in any case must conform with detailed legislation and extensive administrative regulations (Table 7.6).

---

[7] Vermulst (1987) compares U.S. and EC practice from a legal perspective; Schuknecht and Ursprung (1990) provide a detailed institutional study of U.S. and EC practice.

Figure 7.1 The U.S. Antidumping Procedure

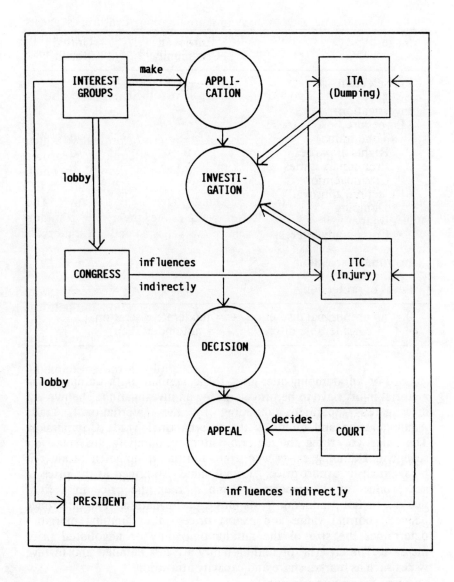

Table 7.6 Discretionary Decision Making in the EC and U.S.
Antidumping Process

Stage	European Community	United States
Pre-selection	+ +	0
Investigation Procedure		
Time frame	+	0
Rights of parties	0	0
Preliminary duties	+	0
Circumvention	+	0
Rejection/approval		
Dumping	+	0
Injury	+ +	+
Community interest	+ +	- -
Instrument selection	+ +	+ +
Level of protection	+	0

0 = no or minimal discretion, + = moderate discretion,
+ + = considerable discretion, - - = not undertaken

For antidumping measures to be applied, both dumping and material injury have to be proven during an investigation. The two are investigated separately, dumping by the International Trade Administration and injury by the International Trade Commission. The rules governing the determination of dumping are relatively stringent. Dumping exists when the "normal value" of a product is higher than its export price; "normal value" is defined as the price of the product in the exporter's home market, the price in a third market, or full production costs plus a profit margin.[8] The difference between normal value and export price - the dumping margin - determines the size of the antidumping duty or negotiated price increase. The criteria for finding injury are less detailed and involve issues such as market share and capacity utilization.

---

[8] Several studies have identified a protectionist bias in the antidumping rules (e.g. Norall 1986, Palmeter 1989, Finger, 1991). This bias increases the expected level of protection; however, it does not decide on political or technical determination.

If both dumping and injury are found, an antidumping duty equal to the dumping margin must be imposed. The accused exporter can, however, avoid the duty by agreeing to raise the price by the amount of the dumping margin. Frequently, the parties negotiate voluntary export restraints as an alternative to price undertakings.

Two other factors further decrease bureaucratic discretion and increase the likelihood that investigations will be conducted impartially. First, the protective order system allows the parties involved to inspect each other's files, thereby preventing collusion between administrators and either of the parties. Exporters accused of dumping can review the material on which the injury claim is based. Second, the Court of International Trade can remand a case to the administering agency if the court finds that the agency decided the case "...arbitrarily, capriciously, or in abuse of its discretion..." (Vermulst, 1987).

The scope for political intervention in an individual investigation is also small. Neither Congress nor the President can intervene directly in an investigation. Over the long term, however, political influence can be exerted on the process through executive nominations for the head of the International Trade Administration and members of the International Trade Commission and through legislative changes in the antidumping law.

The European Community
The EC antidumping process differs significantly from that of the United States. EC regulations translate the GATT Code into operational language, but they do not add specificity beyond the code. In deciding a case, the administering agency, the EC Commission, interprets the regulations as it deems relevant to the case. Accountability to the member governments through the Council (the forum of member governments that operates as the EC legislature) ensures that political interests will be taken into account in the application of administrative discretion.[9] This induces Stegemann (1991) to argue that antidumping is captured by EC producers. The EC rhetoric of the antidumping regulation preserving fair trade simply camouflages this fact. (The high degree of administrative discretion in the EC system compared to the U.S. system is illustrated in Table 7.6.)

---

[9] Detailed surveys of EC antidumping law are provided by Bael and Bellis (1985, 1990), Beseler and Williams (1986), Vermulst (1987), Bierwagen and Hailbronner (1988), Grolig and Bogaert (1987), and Bierwagen (1990).

The history of EC antidumping goes back to 1968, where the first antidumping regulation was passed (regulation 459/68). This laid the legal foundations for the first antidumping case in 1970. In 1979, the GATT antidumping code which was negotiated in the Tokyo Round was translated into EC law (3017/79). In 1984, injury rules were introduced (2176/84). In 1987, circumvention was regulated. In 1988, another procedural detail was added (2423/1988) which stipulated that an additional duty can be imposed if the exporter does not add the antidumping duty to the resale price, i.e. if the exporter bears the antidumping duty himself.

The EC process consists of five phases: application, pre-selection, investigation, decision, and appeal (see Figure 7.2). Applications by interested groups are forwarded to the Commission, which, in the pre-selection process, has the discretion to reject an application or initiate an investigation. The Commission first determines which applications fulfill the formal criteria and then consults the Council to decide which of these applications should lead to an investigation. Data on the pre-selection process is not published, but the rate of rejection at this stage is generally considered to be higher than 50%.[10]

The investigation is conducted by the Commission. Procedural rules allow some discretion with respect to the investigation period, imposition of temporary duties, and prevention of circumvention. The rights of the parties involved are well defined. The rules for the determination of dumping are similar in concept but not in detail to those of the United States. Most importantly, the method of calculating the dumping margin is left to the discretion of the Commission. Formal criteria for evaluating injury were added to the law only in 1984. They include such factors as changes in market share, capacity utilization, employment, and profits. These criteria also give the Commission significant discretion in the determination of injury. The Commission calculates the price increase which is necessary to provide a non-injurious import price, the so-called injury margin.

The EC has been criticized for abusing its discretion in the evaluation of dumping and injury (Hindley, 1988; Finger, 1991; Bierwagen, 1990). The critics claim that, for instance, the choice of profit margin, the cost calculations and the choice of reference

---

[10] The practice of secrecy at this stage suggests an intention to hide the pre-selection criteria. The closed nature of the pre-selection process does, however, avoid the harmful effect of an antidumping threat on imports.

Figure 7.2 The EC Antidumping Procedure

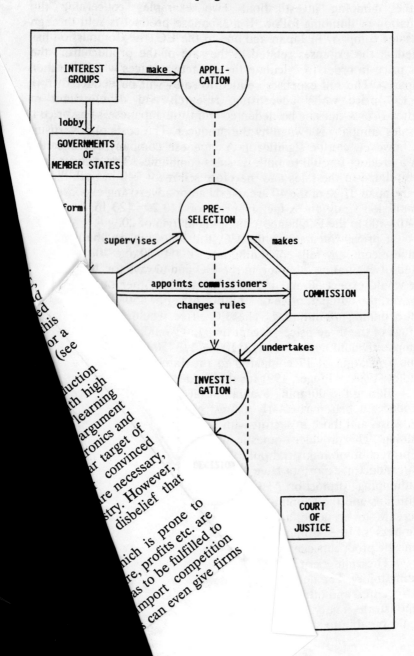

country in cases against state-trading countries favour a positive result of the dumping investigation. Two examples concerning the evaluation of dumping follow. If a Japanese product is sold through one sales company in Japan and one in the EC, the Commission has to deduct the expenses related to the sale of the product from the sales price in order to calculate the ex-factory prices which are then compared. The full expenses related to sales will be deducted from the EC price while advertising, research and development or overhead costs can not be deducted from the Japanese sales price if the sales company is owned by the producer. The costs of advertising etc., however, can be significant. A Japanese company, for instance, sells a product for 100 to both its sales companies. These incur costs of 40 related to the sales and therefore sell it for 140 in both the EC and in Japan. If 20 of the 40 are overhead or advertising expenses, the Commission finds an ex-factory price of 140-20=120 in Japan and 140-40=100 in the EC, hence a dumping margin of 20.

If prices fluctuate in the EC, the following can happen. The Japanese company sells equal amounts for 150, 50 and 100 during the period of evaluating dumping in the EC and always for 100 at home. One would expect 50 and 150 to balance each other out. In the EC however, the dumped price of 50 is not offset by 150. This would lea to the finding of dumping. The EC price would be the weight average of the three prices, except that 150 would count as 100. In example it would amount to $1/3*100 + 1/3*50 + 1/3*100 = 83,$ dumping margin of 17 compared to the Japanese price of 100 Hindley, 1988 or Finger, 1991 for these examples).

Basing the dumping evaluation on the full costs of pro introduces a bias particularly against exporters in sectors w fixed costs and those in sectors with long term benefits from by doing". This provides domestic industries with a welcome for protection on industrial policy grounds. Consumer elec semiconductor exporters have therefore become a popul antidumping protection. EC producers have so fa politicians and the Commission that industrial policies to create, for instance, a domestic semiconductor indu members of the Commission have expressed their domestic producers can ever be competitive.

The injury criteria are applied in a way w finding injury. The necessary changes in market sha not specified and often only one of these criteria h demonstrate injury. Almost everybody facing should be able to show some kind of injury. Thi an incentive to induce injury on themselves, for instance decreases in production or layoffs, in order to obtain protection.[11]

Two important factors which reduce administrative discretion during an investigation under the U.S. system are absent from the EC system. The investigation is less transparent and verifiable than in the United States, because of the lack of a protective order system giving all parties in the dispute the right to view the others' files. Also, the EC system provides only limited scope for judicial appeal. The European Court of Justice so far refuses to remand a case to the Commission on the basis of abuse of discretion.

After finding dumping and injury, the Commission is also supposed to consider issues of broader public interest, i.e. whether users and consumers of the product under investigation would be harmed by antidumping measure, before making a final decision. However, the evaluation of the so-called Community interest is not bound by any specific rules. It does not, for instance, evaluate the consumer costs incurred by protection and compare them with the benefits for producers. Consumers who mostly pay for this policy basically have no say in the matter. The Commission boldly states that consumers have no right to lower prices if they are not fair and sometimes appeals to the long-term interests of having a domestic production. In none of the 903 cases considered during the 1980s did the Commision rule against the imposition of antidumping measures on the basis of injury to users and consumers.

Hoekman and Leidy (forthcoming 1992) and Feinberg and Kaplan (1990) suggest another explanation for this observation. They argue that producers tolerate protection against imports of their inputs because they can then profit from so-called "cascading contingent protection". Antidumping protection for input producers raises costs for users through higher input prices. Downstream producers become less competitive and injury by imports increases. Injury can then make downstream producers eligible for their own antidumping protection.[12]

The Commission has considerable discretion in deciding how and by how much the price of the affected product is to be increased,

---

[11] Leidy and Hoekman (1990) show that injury to firms may be spurious. Firms have to balance the benefits from protection with the costs of self-induced injury through sub-optimal production at the margin. Although such cynical behaviour is probably not responsible for more than a few antidumping cases it nevertheless demonstrates the undesirable incentives the EC antidumping regulation may provide.

[12] Feinberg and Kaplan (1990) provide empirical evidence in support of this hypothesis for the U.S. case.

whether by price undertaking or antidumping duty. The levels of duties and price undertakings can vary between firms of the same country. Duties and undertakings are usually set at the injury margin which is often less than the full dumping margin.

Another interesting incentive arises from the fact that the current EC practice assigns the highest possible duty to all exporters which either have not cooperated in the antidumping investigation or have not yet entered the market. This means that all companies of a country threatened by antidumping claims must enter the EC market as quickly as possible, thereby increasing the speed of import penetration. This may even result in "real" dumping which, however, is not due to predatory motives. It raises the question weather EC antidumping laws do not sometimes act as pro-dumping laws (Schuknecht and Stephan, 1992).

Accountability of the Commission to the political sector is imposed through direct political scrutiny. Politicians can interfere through the Council at the two decisive stages of an antidumping procedure. They can block or promote the initiation of an investigation in the pre-selection phase and they can pressure the Commission to apply its discretionary powers in the investigation in accordance with their political objectives. The Council has to approve the Commission's findings with a qualified majority vote (fifty-four of seventy-six votes). But if the policy makers control the outcome it is likely that they will use this influence to trade protection against support from important special interests.

The Council also exerts political influence over the antidumping process in two other, less direct ways. It nominates the heads of the Commission, determines their salaries, controls their reappointments, and influences their future careers in national politics. And it can request changes in the regulations implementing the GATT code. An example is the introduction in 1984 of formal rules for determining injury. This legislative means of bringing antidumping decisions in line with political interests is, however, far less developed than in the United States.

The administrative framework of the EC antidumping process suggests that its goal is to provide a non-injurious import price to politically influential domestic producers through protection. The key to achieving this goal is administrative and political discretion rather than protectionist rules, as in the U.S. system. This, however, would mean the end of trade if applied consistently to all imports since trade in fact always involves injury to domestic producers whose sales are underbid and replaced by imports. In the following section the results of an empirical test of the determinants of antidumping decisions are presented.

7.4 An Empirical Investigation of EC Antidumping

Finger, Hall and Nelson (1982) concluded in an empirical investigation of antidumping cases in the United States that the decision to accept or reject a claim is based on the technical application of antidumping rules. We conducted an analogous test to determine whether political discretion or the application of technical/economic criteria better explains the same decisions for EC antidumping cases. From the analysis of EC administrative procedures and the incidence of antidumping cases per sector and country, it is hypothesized that political factors determine the choice between acceptance and rejection of a claim. Although, as explained later, there are some rules (details, specifications) which also influence decisions, administrators have considerable latitude to follow unstated objectives and unstated criteria. We find that the stronger domestic producers' case is for demonstrating injury and the more politicians depend on their support the better their chance is of obtaining relief from import competition through antidumping measures.

The absence of clearly specified rules governing other aspects of the antidumping process as well as the decision to accept or reject a claim suggests that, almost by definition, political factors determine how antidumping measures will be applied. The Commission has discretion to choose not only whether to accept or reject a claim, but also whether to select an application in the pre-selection stage, to levy duties or negotiate price undertakings, and to impose duties or undertakings that are lower than the dumping margin. This and the following chapter provide some evidence that undertakings may be a compensatory device for appeasing strong foreign interests through rent transfers. A thorough investigation into the motives underlying these choices is, however, impeded by a lack of published information.[13]

---

[13] Several hypotheses have been advanced to explain the choice between undertakings and duties. Hillman (1990) and Stegemann (1990) suggest that undertakings promote collusion by setting price floors. Stegemann (1991a) compares the application of undertakings between Canada and the EC. See also Tharakan (1991b) for an empirical analysis of the choice of instrument.

Econometric Modelling

For the analysis of the factors underlying the EC's decisions to accept or reject a claim, EC antidumping reports were examined for information on the specific details of each investigation.[14] Information on domestic and foreign producers was gathered and explanatory variables were selected. These are used to determine the direction of their impact on the choice between accepting or rejecting a claim.[15] A positive sign of the estimated coefficient indicates that acceptance becomes more likely as the size of that variable increases.

One-tailed t-tests were used to check whether the null hypothesis - that impact is in the opposite direction - can be rejected at the usual levels of significance (5 % and 1 %). Additionally, a goodness-of-fit index, rho^2 adjusted, reflects the explanatory quality of the estimated model specification.[16]

Description of Explanatory Variables

Explanatory variables were selected to reflect both political and technical/economic influences, as predetermined by our hypotheses. The political variables represent both national and EC pressures and international pressures; the technical variables reflect the two criteria which are supposed to govern the antidumping process, injury and dumping. (The Data Appendix Table provides details on data sources and variable types for each of the independent variables.)

Variables measuring political influences

On the *international level*, we expect a convincing threat of foreign retaliation to reduce the likelihood of an affirmative decision. Therefore, countries which absorb a large share of EC exports are expected to be confronted with fewer trade barriers. The associated

---

[14] It is suspected, however, that not only the result of an investigation but also the information provided in the reports is tailored to the political winds. Scattered information on certain attributes of some cases resulted in many "missing values" in the investigation.

[15] We use maximum likelihood estimation of a binary logit model because our data is specific to each accused firm. This estimation technique determines the acceptance probability for each accused firm rather than predicting the number of affirmative decisions per year (as would an ordinary least squares regression). The sign of the estimated coefficient for each variable reflects the direction of this impact on the probability that a claim will be accepted.

[16] This is not to be confused with the best known index R^2. Models with a goodness of fit index of 20-40% should be considered to be fairly well specified. (See also Horowitz, 1983 and Hensher and Johnson, 1981, 51).

explanatory variable contains the EC export value for each country;[17] its coefficient is expected to have a negative sign. Alternatively, a dummy variable, taking the value of one if the accused firm is U.S. based, is used. The retaliation threat from the U.S. is expected to be strong because the U.S. is the most important buyer of EC products and has retaliated against other types of EC protection during the period in question. On the other hand, the U.S. is a major user of antidumping. The expected sign of this variable is therefore also negative.[18]

The impact of various EC-based interest groups is reflected by the set of *domestic political variables*. Value added and number of employees per sector are used as indicators of lobbying power. Industrial sectors with high employment and high value added are expected to be particularly effective lobbyists for affirmative and highly protectionist decisions (see Finger, Hall and Nelson 1982). Positive signs of the coefficients can be expected.

Two variables reflect the degree of organization and unanimity among petitioners for an antidumping measure. Associations are the officially recognized and inclusively organized representatives of EC industries. They also have the necessary experience and contacts to affect EC policy. We expect decisions to be more protectionist when an application has been forwarded by an association. The coefficient for this dummy variable is expected to be positive. When individual EC firms in the petitioning industry explicitly refuse to cooperate or object to an application, a considerable weakening of the petitioners' case can be expected. When the antidumping report indicates resistance from an EC competitor, the respective dummy variable takes a value of zero; its coefficient is expected to be positive.

EC antidumping reports also contain various industrial policy arguments, such as the need to avoid "dependence on foreigners" or the "social or political importance" of the petitioning industry. The corresponding variable indicates direct or indirect intervention by an EC government in the process. A positive impact on the probability of an affirmative decision is expected when a government intervenes.

Finally, a dummy variable is included to clarify the effects of the institutional change initiated by the EC Council in the last quarter of 1984, establishing formal rules for injury determination. We expect

---

[17] The variable is lagged by one year to reflect the situation during the period covered by the investigation. Data for 1989 were not available, therefore, 1988 values were used instead.

[18] Since antidumping is based on the GATT antidumping code which does not allow retaliation, the coefficient of these two variables could also be insignificant.

the implementation of these rules to result in a tightening up of the procedure after 1984 and so in an increase in the number of rejections relative to acceptances for the years 1985-1990. The variable takes the value of one for the period 1980-1984; its coefficient is expected to have a positive sign.

Variables measuring technical influence
The degree to which technical factors are applied in the determination of dumping is examined using the two variables selected for this purpose by Finger, Hall and Nelson (1982) in their U.S. study. They argue that high average wages in a sector indicate high human capital intensity and can serve as a proxy for domestic cost advantage. The protectionist bias in the EC decision-making mechanism increases the probability of affirmative findings in cases of cost disadvantage, especially when the Commission uses production costs to determine normal value. The expected sign of the coefficient for this variable is negative.[19]

Product differentiation within a single antidumping application is approximated by the number of NIMEXE positions (statistical data categories) per case. Finger, Hall, and Nelson suggest that the coefficient of the variable should be negative since the pricing concept for dumping is relatively precise and can be more readily applied to a closely defined product than to an aggregate of products.

For injury determination, the influence of technical and economic criteria is reflected by variables for industry layoffs, changes in market share (for EC and foreign firms), and decreased profits. These factors are cited in the list of administrative criteria to be applied by the EC Commission. As already mentioned, the vague formulation of the rules allows for considerable discretion, so injury may be interpreted in ways that stray from the original intention behind the new rules. We include a dummy variable with a value of one when the antidumping reports indicate layoffs by petitioners and predict a positive sign for the coefficient. The coefficient of the variable for changes in the exporter's market share is expected to be positive because increases in foreign market shares should lead to more affirmative decisions. Increases in the market share of EC producers should affect decisions adversely; the coefficient is expected to be negative. Decreases in profits are represented by a dummy

---

[19] High wages can also be the result of monopsony power of unions. The prediction would then be the opposite.

variable with a value of one; the expected sign of the coefficient is positive.

Results

The results of the estimation indicate the strong influence of several injury proxies and political influence variables on the decision to accept or reject a claim (Table 7.7). One clear message is that injury counts. The injury proxies - layoffs, decreased profits, and loss of EC market share by EC producers - prove to be the relevant technical variables which contribute to a positive decision in an antidumping case. The better a domestic producer is capable of demonstrating injury, the better his chances are of winning relief from import competition. Boltuck and Litan (1990), Kaplan (1991), Finger and Murray (1990), to mention only a few, conclude that injury is also most important in the U.S. antidumping investigations.

In addition, the political influence of domestic industries, unified in their request for antidumping measures, affects the chances of an affirmative outcome.[20] Large industry size and active government support - indicators of the political importance of the EC producers - improve the chances of winning a case. The results show that the explanatory value of the model specification which combines both political and technical criteria is highest (estimation (3) in Table 7.7).

The EC system, like that of the U.S., is dominated by domestic and not international politics. The insignificance of the retaliation variables suggests that the administrators are not particularly concerned with the threat of foreign retaliation. This finding is consistent with the fact that GATT-conform protection such as antidumping should not lead to (threats of) retaliation. The domestic character of antidumping is further confirmed by the insignificance of the coefficient of the only injury variable which evaluates the accused parties' success in penetrating the EC market. The EC Commission does not appear to examine closely whether the target of antidumping applications and the cause of injury (an increased market share) are identical. EC producers are more concerned with changes in their own market share than with relative changes among foreigners' shares. Another interpretation of this finding is that firms (or countries) which can effectively penetrate the EC market and increase their market share rapidly are also more effective in political counterlobbying.

---

[20] The importance of a unified stance by domestic industries is mentioned by Herander and Pupp (1990) and Stegemann (1990).

Table 7.7 Acceptance versus Rejection in EC Antidumping Cases

| Dependent variable: acceptance = 1, rejection = 0 | | | | |
Political and technical influence factors	Expected direction of impact	Estimations (1)	(2)	(3)
Constant		-3.0 (-4.28)	-1.3 (-2.11)	-3.0 (-2.08)
Political influences:				
EC exports to country	-	-0.02 (-0.34)		
Applications against U.S. firms	-			-0.43 (-1.18)
Domestic Value added	+	3.1 ** (3.38)		11.9 ** (2.89)
Number of employees	+	0.05 ** (3.72)		0.14 ** (5.50)
Association as petitioner	+	0.07 (0.28)		-0.30 (-0.76)
No refusal of support by EC firms	+	1.8 ** (3.2)		1.9 * (1.76)
Industrial policy argument (government intervention)	+	1.3 ** (3.98)		2.6 ** (4.65)
Change of administrative rules (end of 1984)	+	0.74 (3.30)		0.85 ** (2.33)
Technical influences Dumping Average wage	-		7.1 (2.36)	-27.2 * (-1.89)
Number of products affected	-	0.08 (1.33)		
Injury Change of EC market share	-		-0.03 (-1.58)	-0.07 ** (-2.53)
Change of foreign market share	+		0.001 (0.07)	-0.04 -2.04
Layoffs in EC industry	+		1.0 ** (3.3)	1.2 ** (3.17)
Decrease in EC industry's profits	+		1.5 ** (5.84)	1.3 ** (4.52)
Rho^2 adjusted		0.08	0.15	0.31
Number of observations		615	564	577

Note: *(**) indicates rejection of H0 at the 5 (1) percent level of significance.

Despite the importance of industry associations in EC lobbying, the coefficient of this variable was not significant. The pre-selection stage may be biased in favour of cases initiated by associations because the latter may be able to push very weak cases through this stage. As a result of this, there may be more rejections in the final stage.

Another interesting result concerns the change in rules governing injury determination. The estimation shows that the Commission granted less relief after the formal injury rules were implemented. In other words, the new rules are less protectionist than the unwritten interpretation of injury which was previously applied. This contrasts with the experience of the United States, where changes in the rules have made them increasingly protectionist and facilitated affirmative determinations (see Finger and Murray, 1990). This result is consistent with the liberalizing effect of institutional changes in the application of Article 115 and for the completion of the Single European Market.

7.5 Why Some Industries Prefer Antidumping

The EC rhetoric intends to dissipate the political costs of antidumping measures. Since antidumping preserves fair trade, as the EC claims, it is directed against the "bad guys" who attempt to injure the EC industries by unfair means. The rules of the trade game require measures against such tactics. Users and consumers who are damaged in the short term by antidumping measures will ultimately be grateful to the Commission for its efforts. This logic has been put forward particularly in recent years to justify the highly protectionist cases covering large amounts of imports in the high-tech industries. High fixed costs in the steel and chemicals industry have facilitated antidumping claims by these industries in comparison to others.

Another general advantage of antidumping measures is the high degree of protection granted. The tariff equivalent of 23% on average is 50% higher than the equivalent of 15% of voluntary export restraints.

Part of the administrative and negotiation costs of antidumping cases can be passed on to the Commission which pays for its own investigation efforts, identifies the "problem children" among the foreigners and arranges the negotiations. The Commission also helps to provide valuable information about the foreign competitors such as their approximate production costs and capacities. This helps the EC producers to assess their relative standing and to anticipate future competition.

The Commission also provides protection for very specific product categories and prevents the circumvention of measures. This makes antidumping more suitable for detailed protection in markets which are less transparent and more limited than the markets covered by VERs. Imports of broad product categories, for instance steel or cars, are frequently limited by VERs while specific imports, such as particular pipes, are the aim of antidumping claims.

Petitioners can also take advantage of the flexibility of the final measure. An antidumping claim can lead to either a duty or an undertaking. EC producers prefer the imposition of a duty if they want to prevent foreign producers increasing their profitability with the help of quota rents. If the purpose of antidumping claims is to facilitate cartellization, the applicants prefer the negotiation of undertakings as a floor price for the cartel (Hillman, 1990, Stegemann, 1990). Counterlobbying against protection from foreigners can also lead to undertakings to compensate the foreign producers for loss of sales with higher prices.

A disadvantage of antidumping to EC producers is that dumping of imports has to be ascertained. Even with the lenient EC standards this is not always possible. Lobbying costs of easily 100,000 ECU per case suggest that a significant market must be at stake to make an antidumping claim worthwhile. The relative transparency of antidumping measures as compared to VERs or Article 115 measures raises public awareness. The EC has more and more difficulty in selling its antidumping story to the public.

7.6 Conclusion: The Future Role of Antidumping

In the European Community, as in the United States, "injury" is what antidumping is about. However, antidumping laws are a flexible tool for preventing imports from displacing domestic production in politically influential industries in particular. The vehicle for achieving this is not protectionist rules, as in the United States, but protectionist discretion. The stated purpose of antidumping - to maintain fair trade - is just rhetoric to justify industrial policies and to camouflage the bias towards influential special interests.

The empirical results have implications for EC trade policy after 1992. Protectionist interests will demand compensation for the abolition of national protectionist barriers. EC antidumping measures offer them considerable scope for achieving their goals since such measures are to a large extent determined by political discretion. Antidumping measures can therefore become a pinnacle of "Fortress Europe". Recent efforts to abolish the MFA and to reduce protectionism under the Common Agricultural Policy should remind the reformers that antidumping is flexible enough to accommodate additional shifting protectionist pressure from these areas.

The results also suggest certain strategic considerations for the trade policy of developing countries. It has been argued that antidumping measures affecting developing countries are concentrated in industries with shifting comparative advantage and that such protection is more likely in sectors with strong, politically influential interest groups. If that is indeed the case, then it is not sufficient that developing countries simply follow an export-oriented trade strategy; they also need to concentrate on sectors with weak political influence in developed countries.

Data Appendix Table: Independent Variables Considered for
Inclusion in Estimations

Independent variable	Variable type	Data source
Political variables:		
International variables		
Total EC exports to country	Continuous	OECD Foreign
accused, lagged one period	(in 10^6 ECU)	Trade Statistics
Application against	Dummy	EC Official
U.S. firms		Journal, Ser. L
Domestic variables		
Value added by petitioning	Continuous	UNIDO
EC industry, period (t-1)	(in 10^5 ECU)	Database
10^{-4}* number of employees	Continuous	UNIDO
in petitioning industry in		Database
period (t-1)		
Association as petitioner	Dummy	EC Official
		Journal, Ser. L
No refusal of support by	Dummy	EC Official
EC firms		Journal, Ser. L
Intervention of EC member	Dummy	EC Official
governments (industrial		Journal, Ser. L
policy argument)		
Final decision before change	Dummy	EC Official
of administrative rules		Journal, Ser. L
Technical variables:		
Dumping		
Average wage (including	Continuous	UNIDO
salaries) in petitioning	(in 10^5 ECU)	Database
industry lagged one period		
Number of products affected	Continuous	EC Official
(by NIMEXE positions)		Journal, Ser. L
Injury		
Absolute change of EC	Continuous	EC Official
market share		Journal, Ser. L
Absolute change of foreign	Continuous	EC Official
market share		Journal, Ser. L
Layoffs in petitioning	Dummy	EC Official
EC industry		Journal, Ser. L
Decrease in EC industry's	Dummy	EC Official
profits / increase in losses		Journal, Ser. L

Note: All ECU values have been deflated to 1980 values. Dummy variables take the
value of one for the category described. Sources of information on exchange rates and
price indices: Deutsche Bundesbank (1990) and EUROSTAT (1989).

Chapter 8

ANTIDUMPING AGAINST CENTRAL AND EASTERN EUROPE

8.1 Introduction

The Central and Eastern European economies, i.e. those of Poland, Hungary, Czechoslovakia, Romania, Bulgaria, former East Germany and the Comunity of Independent States, the CIS or former Soviet Union, (referred to as Eastern European countries in this chapter) seek transition from socialism. This entails a change in the domestic economic system, but also integration with Western market economies through international trade. Access to Western markets is important, firstly, because of the collapse of the system of trade and payments between the former members of the Council of Mutual Economic Assistance (CMEA) which has disrupted traditional trading patterns. Secondly, it is important because of the former CMEA countries' recurrent hard currency shortage and the need to meet debt service obligations. Exports are also the means of financing the technology transfer required by the former socialist countries.

The EC claims to support the process of transition in Eastern Europe. The EC has committed itself in an association treaty to abolish tariffs and quotas towards Hungary, Poland and the CSFR.[1] This chapter studies the conditions of market access for Eastern European goods to the EC during the eighties. The empirical results reported demonstrate that the Eastern European countries were faced with protectionist barriers when they tried to export to the West. Such barriers in terms of tariffs and standard trade restrictions tended not to be overt. Exports, however, faced considerable trade protection through voluntary export restraints and, within the GATT framework, through antidumping.

---

[1] Assistance has also been provided through the Phare programme and by the OECD members in the areas of training and financial infrastructure. The Commission (1991) emphasizes the importance of access to Western markets for Eastern Europe.

The question is whether the promise of market access is credible or whether the transition from socialism will be impeded by antidumping measures. The association treaty does not suspend the application of antidumping laws to the signatory parties. The Commission, however, sees the need to suspend antidumping and safeguards proceedings against Eastern Europe to reduce uncertainty about future market access for investors (Commission, 1991). Unfortunately, this claim was made by the Directorate General for Economic and Fiscal Affairs and not by the Directorate General for External Relations which administers antidumping.

To evaluate the protectionist potential of antidumping laws it must be clarified whether the determination of dumping is technical or political. While technical or administrative protection is meant to evaluate trade practices impartially through the use of technical rules and objective standards, political determination favours those producers who can most effectively lobby policy makers for protection. Politically motivated protection particularly disadvantages the most efficient import-competitors which, in the case of Eastern Europe, will be those producers most successfully adjusting to Western markets.

By the 1980s some progress had been made in Eastern Europe with the introduction of markets. Hungary had abandoned central planning in 1968 and introduced reforms to decentralize the economy. Poland also decentralized decision making in industrial enterprises and both Poland and Hungary began privatizing - in the form of spontaneous privatization.[2] Eastern European goods, however, suffered from quality deficiencies because production targets in firms were quantity and not quality-oriented. This problem had not been resolved by past reforms. Although the Eastern European "soft" goods were prinicipally suitable for trade between CMEA countries, efforts to penetrate EC markets were nevertheless made in the 1980s. The question which this paper addresses is whether these efforts were resisted by the EC, or whether the EC policy was supportive of Western export orientation of the CMEA economies.

The CMEA economies could have been particularly susceptible to "dumping" because of hard currency needs and because notions of production costs were not well developed - the state supplied the inputs. However, the "softness" of CMEA goods should

---

[2] Spontaneous privatization basically means the sale of a firm through its management without involving a privatization agency.

have prevented antidumping claims by EC firms, since "soft" goods are not directly competitive with higher quality Western goods.

The analysis also empirically investigates the implications of the "soft/hard" good distinction. Did efforts to export to the West require substantial price discounts to compensate for "softness"; and if so, did this evoke antidumping procedures? Were exports that were less "soft" or more consistent with Western quality standards targeted because of claims of injury to EC producers? If both "soft" and less "soft" goods were targeted by protectionist policies, is this the precedent for the continued EC response to Eastern European exports as these countries seek to make the transition from socialism?

The results indicate that in the past, *both "soft" and less "soft" goods from Eastern Europe faced trade barriers in accordance with political criteria*. So past EC trade policies towards Eastern European goods were not consistent with Eastern European objectives of Western market penetration to facilitate the course of transition. If the political criteria which were prevalent in the 1980s continue to dominate EC antidumping decisions and since antidumping is the prime instrument of EC protectionism towards Eastern Europe, then EC trade policies will not be conducive to the Eastern European transition from socialism.

Section 8.2 briefly reviews the institutional features of the EC antidumping procedure with emphasis on the particularities of Eastern European cases. In Section 8.3, the CMEA trading and pricing behaviour of the 1980s is discussed. Section 8.4 deals with the role of undertakings in the antidumping cases. Empirical evidence is provided in Section 8.5. The chapter concludes with implications for the Eastern European economies in the transition from socialism.

8.2 The Institutional Nature of EC Antidumping Procedures

The EC antidumping procedure has five phases: application, preselection, investigation, decision, and appeal.[3] Applications for opening an antidumping investigation are forwarded to the Commission. The Commission can reject an application or initiate an investigation at its own discretion at the preselection stage after consulting the Council. Approximately half of the applications do not pass this first hurdle. The investigation is conducted by the

---

[3] The reader familiar with the institutional nature of antidumping procedure in the EC can skip this section.

Commission. The existence of both dumping and injury must be proved in order to evoke an antidumping measure.

Since in the case of state-trading countries, domestic production costs are unknown or not computable, dumping is said to exist if the price of an imported product within the EC is lower than the ("constructed") production costs of a similar product in a comparable market economy. The criteria used for the selection of the comparable market economy and the whole concept of comparable countries has been subject to criticism. EC producers suggest a first country candidate and mostly succeed in pushing it through (Jacobs, 1989, Tharakan, 1991). There is a bias towards high cost producers, countries with subsidiaries of EC producers or even members of EC cartels (Messerlin, 1990a). The concept is flawed because a comparable stage of development does not mean comparable costs and the indicators such as per capita GDP are unreliable in Eastern Europe (Jacobs, 1989). The dumping reports do not indicate whether the constructed production costs are adjusted for quality differences. Injury is evaluated on the basis of a change in profits, employment, and market shares. The formal criteria for the evaluation of dumping and injury are vague and leave significant discretion to the Commission.

Political scrutiny also takes place at this stage: the findings of the investigation have to be approved by the Council with a qualified majority (54 out of 76 votes). Indirect political control is exerted through the nomination of the Commissioners, their reappointments, salaries and national careers.

Previous empirical tests (Eymann and Schuknecht, 1991) of the political discretion hypothesis have found that the EC uses antidumping procedures to prevent "injury" from imports to politically influential domestic producers.[4] This behaviour should also, on the basis of consistency, apply to Eastern European countries. The "softness" of their products, however, suggests that price discounts and therefore dumping margins would be high but injury relatively low. The ease with which dumping can be proved and the lax injury standards would give EC firms an incentive to initiate antidumping investigations against CMEA imports.

"Softness" is less important for homogenous products which are "quality insensitive". It is easier to penetrate Western markets with these products. The EC producers, facing more injury from such

---

[4] In the U.S., the antidumping procedure is technically determined (Finger, Hall and Nelson, 1982). The protectionist bias in the U.S. lies in the rules rather than in the procedure as in the EC (Finger and Murray, 1991).

imports, will also respond with antidumping claims. The resulting paradox is that "soft" goods (which can only be sold at high price discounts) and less "soft" goods should *both* invite antidumping investigations.

8.3 CMEA Trading and Pricing Behaviour

CMEA trade was conducted via Foreign Trade Organizations (FTOs) which monopolized external commercial relations. Each FTO was responsible for conducting the trade of a certain category of products. FTOs were assisted by trade representations in other countries in conducting trade and generating information on the particular market situation. The State Committee for Foreign Relations advised the FTOs on trade with LDCs and the other CMEA countries. Representation of companies producing exportables was limited which often led to informational inefficiency (Schrenk, 1990). Figure 8.1 provides the institutional structure of CMEA trade.[5]

The FTOs were obliged to fulfill the foreign trade plan drafted by the Ministry of Foreign Trade, the State Planning Committees, and the Ministry of Finance. All three institutions were subordinate to the Council of Ministers. The aim of the plan was to balance foreign trade and to coordinate it with the domestic economic plan. Two constraints resulted for the FTOs. They had to achieve a balance of payment and fulfill the foreign trade plan.

Frictions arose from the fact that companies and FTOs were geared to intra-CMEA trade, while Eastern European politicians set additional hard currency targets to promote industrialization or to meet their financial obligations to the West. Firms' production targets were quantity orientated. The lack of quality orientation was reinforced by the firms' "right to sales", which helped to maintain full employment. The resulting "softness" of exportables led to the FTOs orientating their trade towards the CMEA. In addition, the former Soviet Union was willing to trade "hard" goods (oil, raw materials) for "soft" goods on favourable terms of trade. The resulting rents to governments and firms consolidated intra-CMEA trade links (Hillman and Schnytzer, 1990).

Pricing in intra-CMEA trade was based on the moving average of world market prices for the past five years converted into

---

[5] The chart represents the Soviet system. It is compiled from Tischenko (1985) and Aerssen (1969). The system of the other CMEA countries worked in a similar way.

Figure 8.1 Foreign Trade Practice in the Former Soviet Union

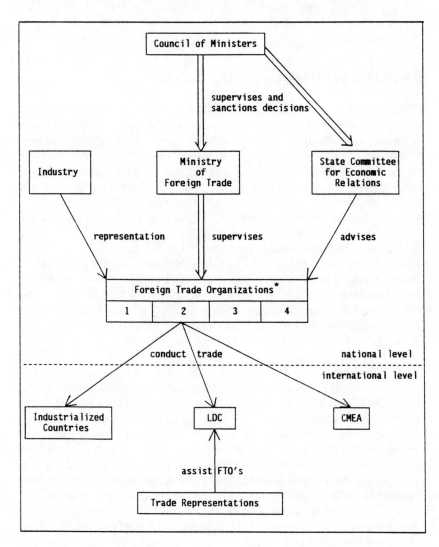

* operational realization of Foreign Trade Plan

transferable rubles. These price guidelines and the actual exchange price were often unrelated because trade had to approximately adhere to the five-year-plan targets and had to result in "...a planned bilateral zero net balance between the negotiating countries" (Hillman and Schnytzer, 1990). Furthermore, CMEA exchange prices and domestic prices often differed. To minimize problems resulting from this inconsistency, FTOs and firms interacted at domestic prices. Windfall profits and losses from the price difference were neutralized by "price equalization" skimming profits and compensating FTOs for losses. This reduced the incentive to base trade on relative prices. Trade surpluses between CMEA countries in transferable rubles were involuntary trade credits of no value because the surplus country could not purchase other products from the surplus.

CMEA "soft" goods were very suitable for intra-CMEA trade. FTOs, however, were under strong political pressure to export to the West. The politicians wanted to modernize their economy and speed up industrialization (e.g. Poland in the seventies). The balance of payment constraint resulted in hard currency targets for exports to the West. In the short term, it could be bridged by credits, but ultimately debt repayment obligations also forced the FTOs to generate hard currency. Premiums for plan fulfillment and "advantageous" sales or purchases provided further incentives to the FTOs to export to the West. The problem that arose for the CMEA countries was to sell "soft" CMEA products in quality conscious and competitive Western markets.

What do these findings imply for the FTO's pricing behaviour for exports to Western markets? Costs of production were unknown and could not be used to determine pricing. FTOs knew that they had "soft" goods on their hands. They had to choose a price for EC sales which compensated for quality differences, knowing full well that exports were vulnerable to antidumping provisions because of the price difference.[6] Antidumping claims should therefore be prevalent against all former CMEA countries.

FTOs were under even more pressure to generate hard currency with "soft" goods in times of balance of payment problems. The rigidity of foreign trade plans increased the likelihood of balance of payment problems with market economies. Changing world market prices led to unexpected imbalances in the foreign exchange account. Tischenko (1985) reports such a situation for the former Soviet Union

---

[6] See Falvey (1989) for a detailed discussion and a survey of the literature on the effect of quality uncertainty and the effect of product reputation on the pricing behaviour in export markets and possible consequences for trade policy making.

in the early eighties. As early as 1966, Wylczynski observed that CMEA members resorted to dumping surplus production in order to generate hard currency (Wilczynski, 1966).

If countries could bridge balance of payment problems with Western credits, the budget constraint for hard currency became soft. Eastern European FTOs then only had to "dump" when the country faced a debt crisis and the hard currency constraint became binding again. Fluctuations in dumping claims would then be correlated with the countries' balance of payment and debt crises. Hungarian firms, however, had autonomy in conducting trade. Coincidence of dumping and currency shortages in Hungary is therefore not anticipated.

8.4 The Role of Undertakings

As a means of antidumping protection, the Commission can levy a duty or propose an undertaking, i.e. a voluntary price increase by the foreign producer. The undertaking transfers part of the protectionist rent to the exporter in the same way as a voluntary export restraint. No rules constrain the choice between duties and undertakings. The latter are negotiated and require the consent of all parties involved, the Commission and the domestic and foreign producers. If Eastern European exporters reduce the price discount for low quality through an undertaking, the scope for injury from these imports decreases.

EC producers appear not to have been concerned by the fact that undertakings transfer protectionist rent to the exporting country. The instrument of protection did not affect the competitiveness of CMEA exports. While rents from voluntary price increases accrue directly to the exporting firms of market economies and can increase their overall competitiveness, in CMEA countries additional foreign exchange did not go to the exporting industry but to the state. Finding a large share of undertakings compared to duties would be consistent with the "soft" characterization of CMEA products and the lack of concern by EC producers about the rent transfer.

CMEA FTOs preferred undertakings to tariffs because they allowed the FTOs to capture part of the protectionist rents. On the other hand, an undertaking involved higher costs for lawyers and negotiations with the Commission and EC producers. Undertakings are therefore expected to be the predominant but not the exclusive instrument of protection against Eastern Europe under antidumping.

Undertakings can also serve as a collusion device between domestic and foreign producers (Hillman, 1990; Stegemann, 1990).

Therefore, undertakings could have been the result of price fixings between EC producers and FTOs.[7] Collusive arrangements of this kind could even help FTOs to obtain premiums for "advantageous sales or purchases" and to meet or exceed foreign revenue targets. Evidence in favour of the collusion hypothesis is provided by Messerlin (1990a). Cases where foreign producers are targeted by antidumping claims and their EC counterparts are involved in anti-cartel cases for the same products are called "twin cases". Messerlin argues that the antidumping regulation is captured by EC industries to enforce their cartels. CMEA countries were involved in between 35% and 55% of all "twin cases" which almost always led to an undertaking to prevent disrupture of the cartel.

8.5 Empirical Evidence

Antidumping was the most prominent instrument of trade protection against Eastern Europe during the 1980s. Over 20% of the total of over 900 decisions involved former East Germany (GDR), Czechoslovakia (CSFR), Poland, Hungary, the former Soviet Union (CIS), Romania, and Bulgaria (Table 8.1), although these only provided 8% of the EC's imports from non-EC countries. The average ad valorem equivalent of protective measures is 32.5% for affirmative decisions - compared to an average of 23% for all cases - leading to an average decline of import quantities by 36% within three years (Messerlin, 1989). Eastern Europe was therefore the country group treated most disadvantageously by antidumping measures.

Table 8.1 The Incidence of Antidumping Claims per Country

	Bulgaria	GDR	Poland	Rumania	CIS	CSFR	Hungary	Total
cases	11	32	25	29	35	38	18	188

[7] Tharakan (1991) argues that the Commission - as a fairness-oriented regulator - compensated the Eastern European producers for the procedural bias against them with undertakings. Another argument without political economy backing refers to the observation that the more lenient measure is more often negotiated with countries which do not have consistent trade surpluses with the EC.

Although these figures do not indicate which CMEA countries were treated most unfavourably by antidumping, Tovias and Laird (1991) find that Hungary faced much higher trade protection than the rest of Eastern Europe. The average 1983 tariff level was 6.8% for Hungary and 2.7% for all of Eastern Europe. In 1988, over 35% of the Hungarian exports to the EC were subject to non-tariff barriers compared to 21.4% for the whole of Eastern Europe. Since Hungary was the most Western oriented CMEA member, this could be a precedent for what will happen to Eastern European countries with outward orientation in the future.[8]

EC Antidumping Enforcement towards Eastern Europe
The above analysis of the administrative procedure in the EC suggests that antidumping decisions are politically determined. The test by Eymann and Schuknecht (1991) for all EC antidumping decisions, which is presented in the previous chapter, is applied here to the cases against Eastern Europe for the 1980-1990 period. The econometric modelling and the variables are briefly reviewed; however, readers interested in the detailed model and variable explanations should consult Chapter 7.4.

The empirical results for Eastern Europe support the political determination hypothesis and are consistent with the findings for all cases. The better EC producers can demonstrate injury, and the more politicians depend on their support, the better their chance is of obtaining relief from import competition through antidumping measures.

The endogenous variable takes the value of one in the case of the antidumping claim being accepted and zero when a claim is rejected. The independent variables chosen for the estimations encompass political and technical variables. The results of these estimations, i.e. estimated coefficients of the respective variables, reflect the direction of this impact on the probability of a case being accepted. The goodness of fit index, Rho^2 adjusted, indicates the explanatory quality of the estimated model specification.

Variables of the political track hypothesis
The variable list reflects the impact of interest groups on the decision-making process. Value added and number of employees per sector represent differences in the lobbying power dependent on the size of the industry.

---

[8] Far Eastern exporters also faced a surge of protectionism as a response to export orientation.

The following two variables refer to the degree of organization and unanimity among petitioners for an antidumping measure. Decisions are likely to be more protectionist when an application has been forwarded by an association which is the officially recognized and inclusively organized representative of an EC industry. When single EC firms in the petitioning industry explicitly refuse to cooperate with (or object to) an application, a considerable weakening of the petitioners' case can be expected.

Another variable incorporates the industrial policy arguments such as "dependence on foreigners", or "social and political importance", indicated in the antidumping reports of the EC. A dummy variable is included to clarify the effects of the institutional change in the last quarter of 1984 initiated by the EC Council. It is hypothesized that the implementation of formal rules for the injury evaluation led to a tightening of the procedure.

Variables of the technical track hypothesis
The degree of technical dumping determination is examined with the same variables used in the previous chapter. Low average wages in a sector indicate low human capital intensity which increases the probability of an affirmative decision.

The administrative injury determination is illustrated by layoffs, changes in foreign or domestic market share and profits. The occurence of injury should also increase the probability of an affirmative decision. Table 8.2 indicates the expected signs in support of the political or technical determination hypothesis.

Results
The estimation results for CMEA cases as presented in estimation 2.1 (Table 8.2) refer firstly to two of the injury proxies, i.e. layoffs and changes in EC market share,[9] and secondly to most of the political variables, i.e. industry size and a unified front within the petitioning industry. The message from this is that political discretion rather than technical rules is the vehicle for antidumping protection. Antidumping measures provide relief from injury for politically influential EC producers. The goodness of fit index of 0.47 is particularly high for CMEA countries, indicating a fairly well specified model when political and technical track variables are combined.

---

[9] The coefficient of the average wage variable is not robust in different model specifications and therefore not included in this list.

Table 8.2 Acceptance versus Rejection in Antidumping Cases against Former CMEA members, 1980-1990

Variables		Estimations	
	(expected sign)	(2.1) Eastern Europe	(2.2) all cases
Constant		0.00 (0.00)	-3.1 (-2.08)
Political influences:			
Value added in industry	(+)	68.4** (3.05)	11.9** (2.89)
No of employees	(+)	0.02** (2.26)	0.14** (5.50)
Applicant is association	(+)	2.63* (1.77)	-0.30 (-0.76)
No refusal of cooperation by EC firms	(+)	3.66* (1.61)	1.90* (1.76)
Industrial policy arguments	(+)	10.06 (1.17)	2.60** (4.65)
Institutional change 1984/85	(+)	1.38 (1.3)	0.85** (2.33)
Technical influences:			
Average industry wage	(-)	-204.3^w** (-2.78)	-27.2^w* (-1.89)
Petitioner suffered layoffs	(+)	2.95* (2.06)	1.2** (3.17)
Change in market share by EC producers	(-)	-0.17* (-2.17)	-0.07** (-2.53)
Change in market share by foreign producers	(+)	-0.14 (-1.99)	-0.04 (-2.04)
Drop of EC industry's profits	(+)	0.45 (0.48)	1.3** (4.52)
Rho^2 adjusted		0.47	0.31
Number of observations		123	577

Coefficients reflect the variables' impact on the probability of acceptance, the expected direction is shown in second column. *(**): rejection of H_0 at 5% (1%) level; w: the coefficient is not stable in different model specifications.

Comparing the results for CMEA cases and the overall sample (estimation 2.2), it is worthwhile noting that the means for the dumping determination are fairly similar across country groups. Industry size and cooperation within the petitioning industry as well as injury through layoffs and changes in market share are significant determinants of antidumping decisions in both cases. Relief against injury from imports, however, seems to be less important in cases against CMEA economies. The coefficients of the injury variables are either less significant or, in the case of profits, insignificant.[10] This finding conforms with the previously discussed "soft-hard" goods distinction. Injury motivates antidumping claims but CMEA "soft" goods do less harm than other imports.

The insignificance of government intervention can be explained with the same argument as mentioned above. "Soft" CMEA goods do not inflict enough damage to necessitate government intervention.

Evidence on the Eastern European Trade Practise
Exports from the former CMEA countries were "soft" goods and they did "injure" EC producers but to a lesser extent than other countries' exports. The figures in Table 8.3 indicate that in 42% of the CMEA dumping cases the Commission found dumping margins in excess of 30% which compares to 16% of the decisions against other countries. This finding can be interpreted as a significant price discount for quality differences. At the same time, injury inflicted by CMEA goods was relatively small. The market share of EC producers decreased by more than 5% in only 10% of the cases which compares to the same proportion of injury in 27% of the decisions against other countries.

If dumping was the main cause of injury, high dumping margins and high injury margins should correlate. The expected result would be an accumulation of cases in the categories printed in bold letters in Table 8.4. This predicted pattern, however, is not consistent with the presented data. Decreases in the market share of EC producers of over 10% are in fact concentrated in cases with dumping margins over 30%. On the other hand, in 52% of antidumping claims with dumping margins over 30%, the EC market share did not decline. For lower dumping margins between 10% and 30% and under 10% the figures should be higher but they are in fact only 45% and 11% respectively.

---

[10] The value of the coefficient is not relevant for the comparison of the relative impact of variables in logit models.

Table 8.3 Dumping and Injury in CMEA Cases Compared to Other Cases

	% of cases	CMEA	Other	Observations
Dumping margin	less than 10%	8	35	877
	10 - 30%	23	28	
	more than 30%	42	16	
	no information	21	27	
Decrease in EC market share	more than 5%	10	27	881
	0 - 5%	15	15	
	increase	49	43	
	no information	26	16	

Table 8.4 The Correlation between Dumping Margin and Injury in CMEA Cases

Decrease in the EC market share, % of cases	More than 10%	Between 10% and over 0%	No decrease	No infor- mation
Dumping margin				
less than 10%	0	28	**11**	61
10 - 30%	2	**27**	45	26
more than 30%	**19**	9	52	20
no information	7	9	57	27
total	10	15	48	27

This indicates more injury in spite of lower dumping margins. These ambiguous findings suggest that it is not always the dumping margins that determine the degree of injury in CMEA cases.

Claims against CMEA products are concentrated in areas with low average wages and low technical sophistication (Table 8.5). The 1980 average wage was lower than 15000 ECU in 36% of the CMEA cases which compares to 20% for other cases. CMEA antidumping claims mostly concern basic chemicals and household machinery

Table 8.5 Average Industry Wages

	% of cases	CMEA	Other	Observations
Average wage per industry, 1980, ECU	< 15 000	36%	20%	424
	15 000 - 20 000	43%	47%	
	> 20 000	21%	33%	

(55%) while only 7% of the cases involve other machinery or consumer electronics (Table 8.6). These figures compare to 39% and 27% respectively for industrialized countries. These findings can be interpreted to suggest that the FTOs indeed tried to export relatively homogenous and technologically basic products to minimize the "soft-hard" good conflict. They suggest that imports from Eastern Europe were more competitive in these sectors and, because they caused more injury, attracted antidumping claims.

Table 8.6 The Incidence of CMEA Antidumping Cases per Sector

Sectors	Chemical products	Steel + steel products	Machi nery	Electrical machinery	Other
Cases %	42	4	7	13	34

Dumping and Hard Currency Shortage

CMEA governments set hard currency targets for their FTOs. Earning hard currency was particularly important in times of debt and/or balance of payment crises. The number of antidumping claims was likely to increase when such crises occured and FTOs tried to raise exports to the West.

If the number of dumping cases is correlated with CMEA trade deficits or changes in currency reserves, the hard currency shortage hypothesis would be confirmed.[11] Since the volume of "emergency" dumping is insufficient to reverse the trade balance, the expected sign for both coefficients is negative. If trade deficits were debt-financed, dumping cases should correlate with debt crises and debt rescheduling agreements.

The pricing strategy should lead to a basic number of antidumping claims independent of debt problems. A significant constant term is therefore anticipated.

The following equations are tested:

$$cases = aC + b_1(\text{trade deficits/currency reserves})$$
$$cases = aC + b_1(\text{trade deficits/currency reserves})$$
$$+ b_2(\text{debt reschedulings})$$

Results

The findings of the estimations in Table 8.7 confirm the relevance of the pricing strategy and of debt reschedulings for the prevalence of antidumping measures. The existence of a basic number of antidumping cases is illustrated by the constant term which has a significant coefficient for the estimations for all CMEA countries, Romania, and (not indicated) for Hungary, the former GDR, and Bulgaria.

In a debt crisis, countries resorted to dumping in addition to asking for debt relief from creditor banks. This is true for the total CMEA sample as well as for the individual countries as illustrated by estimation 7.1 (all CMEA countries)[12] and 7.2 (only Romania). The results for Poland are similar to Romania.

---

[11] Data on trade balances is taken from the OECD trade statistics; data on currency reserves was only available for Hungary and Romania and was taken from the IMF Financial Statistics. The respective variable contains the growth rates of reserves to avoid problems of deflation.

[12] When estimating (3.1) without the former Soviet Union and the CSFR (which did not accumulate excessive debt), the results were very similar except for much improved DW statistics.

Table 8.7 Determinants of CMEA "Dumping" - The Hard Currency Shortage Hypothesis

OLS: Dependent variable is number of antidumping cases against CMEA countries Sample: 1970-1989					
Variables		Estimations			
	(expected sign)	(7.1) all CMEA	(7.2) Romania	(7.3) former Soviet Union[a]	(7.4) CSFR[a]
Constant		7.81_{**} (2.79)	2.00_{**} (3.25)	1.19 (1.47)	-0.26 (-0.29)
Trade balance	(-)	0.0009 (0.59)		-0.0008 (-1.97)	-0.008_{**} (-3.3)
Currency reserves	(-)		-1.32 (-1.54)		
Total debt reschedulings	(+)	12.03_{**} (4.98)	3.44_{**} (2.48)		
R²-adjusted		0.57	0.23	0.13	0.34
Durbin Watson		1.49	2.39	1.19	1.92
F-statistic		13.59	3.13	3.88	10.67
No of observations		20	15	20	20

*(**): rejection of H0 at 10%(5%) level
[a] No debt reschedulings

The coefficient of the trade balance variable is only significant for those countries which faced a strict balance of payment constraint and which did not reschedule debt, i.e. the former Soviet Union (7.3) and Czechoslovakia (7.4). The fact that the former Soviet Union and the CSFR did not accumulate excessive foreign debt is also illustrated by the small discount on their debt traded in secondary markets during the eighties. Discounts were very high for Poland and Romania.

Data on currency reserves was not available except for Romania and Hungary. The result for Romania (7.2) indicates that a decline in reserves may have influenced the trading agency's decision to dump. The level of significance, however, is low. For Hungary, as hypothesized, dumping and changes in currency reserves do not correlate. As mentioned previously, the case of Hungary is distinct from the other former CMEA countries. Although both Hungary and Poland accumulated significant debt, Hungary did not default. Hungarian dumping did not correlate with balance of payment problems either. The debt constraint was less dominant and the Hungarian government's grip on export activities was weaker, which produced less politically induced dumping.

Undertakings in EC-CMEA Trade
Section 8.4 suggested that the interaction of "soft" and "hard" goods in Western markets, the rent transfer into the foreign exchange pool instead of to firms, and the potential for collusion should lead to a large share of undertakings. Table 8.8 supports this hypothesis: 73% of the CMEA affirmative decisions resulted in a voluntary price increase. Less than half of the other affirmative decisions involved undertakings.

CMEA countries also obtained relatively low levels of protection. 66% of CMEA traders obtained measures at less than the full dumping margin while this figure only amounts to 52% for other countries. This finding supports the "soft" good hypothesis. Since the dumping margin reflected the price discount to compensate for "softness", injury from these imports could be ameliorated by a relatively small voluntary price increase. The overall share of acceptances, however, did not differ from other cases.

Table 8.8 Share of Acceptances, Undertakings and Reduced Levels of Protection

	CMEA	Other	Observations
% of acceptances of total decisions	77	75	880
% of undertakings of affirmative decisions	73	47	663
% of affirmative decisions with reduced dumping margin	66	52	591

The collusion hypothesis can be tested by arguing that an increase in the number of firms and products involved in an antidumping claim reduces the potential for collusion because of the free-riding incentives in cartels. A unified front in the EC's petitioning industry raises the potential for collusion for the same reason. A test of the choice between price undertakings and duties in antidumping decisions with two sets of variables indicating the potential for collusion, i.e. the degree of organization and agreement and the number of firms and countries involved, however, did not yield significant results.

Collusion is more likely in markets where Eastern European and Western products are close substitutes. If high dumping margins result from price discounts for particularly "soft" goods, and low dumping margins from less "softness", collusion through undertakings is more likely in cases with low dumping margins. The empirical evidence in Table 8.9 supports the latter hypothesis. 94% of the of the affirmative decisions with margins of less than 10% result in an undertaking. The corresponding figure for cases with margins over 30% is a 59% share of undertakings.[13] Messerlin's evidence on collusion also supports this claim (Messerlin, 1990a). The products involved in "twin" antitrust and antidumping investigations such as basic chemicals are not quality sensitive.

Table 8.9 The Correlation between Dumping Margin and Instrument in CMEA Cases

% of affirmative decisions		Duty	Undertaking
Dumping margin	less than 10%	6	94
	10 - 30%	25	75
	more than 30%	41	59
	no information	8	92
	total	27	73

[13] Interestingly, 36 affirmative decisions, 92% or 33 of which end in an undertaking, do not indicate a dumping margin. This finding illustrates the Commission's latitude in how to decide and what to report. The practice of non-reporting facilitates disguising the real motive underlying antidumping decisions.

8.5 Conclusion: Implications for the Transition from Socialism

The former CMEA countries were frequently the target of protectionism in their attempts to access Western markets during the eighties. Antidumping measures, in particular undertakings, were the most important means of protecting EC producers against "soft" goods exported at considerable price discounts as well as against less "soft" products. The root of the problem is that antidumping is implemented to provide relief from import competition to politically influential EC producers and that it is not designed to enforce commercial standards of fairness.

The politicized application of antidumping poses a dilemma for Eastern European governments which want to ease their economies' transition from socialism to capitalism by promoting exports to the West. If the antidumping practise of the 1980s is continued, firms which want to adjust to Western standards and produce high-quality products for export might not think it worthwhile if their efforts could be undermined by antidumping protection.[14]

In the light of these findings, the process of transition should be supported by the suspension of antidumping claims against Eastern Europe. An alternative for Eastern European countries would be to join the European Economic Space. A smooth transition from socialism would save EC governments a significant amount in direct payments in order to stabilize the Eastern European economies. It is therefore also in the EC's interest to assist by providing market access.

In the same way as firms in developing countries, Eastern European firms should consider the sensitivity of exports to antidumping claims, particularly in politically influential industries. It would be better for them to concentrate on products in industries that have a weak EC producer lobby.

---

[14] This implication also holds for many developing countries where "softness" of exports is prevalent. This makes the problem more general than implied by the limited discussion in this chapter.

Chapter 9

THE SINGLE EUROPEAN MARKET

9.1 Introduction

The European Community envisages the completion of its Single Market by the end of 1992. Before the current liberalization programme started in the mid-eighties, the unsatisfactory state of the internal market had been lamented and the benefits of internal liberalization had been propagated. In 1985, the EC Commission published the White Paper arguing that the completion of the Single European Market is necessary for EC industries to remain competitive. "Disunity" in the EC would lead to a decline vis-à-vis the U.S. and Japan. The assessment of existing barriers to trade found significant scope for internal liberalization and identified three major barriers: physical barriers, such as administrative costs related to border crossings, technical barriers, e.g. quantitative restrictions and regulations, and fiscal barriers consisting of export subsidies, tax exemptions etc.

   The highly publicized Cecchini Report by the EC Commission (1988)[1] estimates that the completion of the Single European Market will result in an extra GDP growth of 2.5% to 6.5% plus potential medium and long-term dynamic gains. Other estimates by Baldwin (1989) have been even higher. Among the beneficial effects, factor price equalization, technology transfer, utilization of scale economies and more product variety are expected. Smith and Venables (1988) estimate the "costs of non-Europe" by looking at industries with economies of scale. They find that significant welfare gains will accrue because larger markets reduce production costs and, more importantly, price differentiation within the EC.[2] Non-member countries including developing countries will also profit from the

---

[1] A detailed version is edited by Emerson (1988).
[2] Winters (1991a) surveys the literature on the welfare and trade effects of "Europe 1992".

larger market as long as a "Fortress Europe" does not arise (Findlay, 1990).

The Single European Act of 1987 launched the project to complete the Single European Market. In this document, the member countries of the EC agreed on an agenda of completion and a change in the voting rule for trade policy issues. These factors give the project credibility because single member countries cannot veto trade liberalization any more and have to consent on all open issues before the end of 1992 (Holmes, 1991).

It is widely assumed within and outside academia that efficiency gains were the driving force of "Europe 1992". This view is also supported by the standard integration literature (Viner, 1950, Johnson, 1962, Balassa, 1961, El-Agraa, 1988). However, it contrasts with the fact that any free trade negotiation, be it within the GATT or bilateral, results in significant haggling and often outright failure. Rent-seeking protectionist forces almost always prove to be too strong to allow for full liberalization of trade between countries. In the EC, two previous attempts at trade integration fell short of a single market. Failure of trade liberalization programms seems to be the rule despite the efficiency gains.

The ongoing attempt to complete the Single European Market should, however, succeed. Even very controversial issues such as indirect taxation have been successfully tackled. The relevant question is then *why trade integration in the EC is possible now despite protectionist special interests* which have prevented wealth-enhancing trade integration in other circumstances.

The standard integration literature assumes that benevolent governments pursue trade liberalization in order to maximize their countries' welfare. It ignores the existence of distributional conflicts over liberalization of this kind. This chapter argues that rent-seeking motivated *interest in protection* within the EC *has significantly decreased* over the past decades because distributional conflicts between factor owners and between industries have become less pronounced. This has cleared the way for internal liberalization.[3]

The Common Market project also tackles the intricacies of implementing such far-reaching reforms. It is tailored to compensate those who stand to lose from integration. The *change in the EC's institutional governance structure* in the Single European Act gave it credibility. The emergence of the Court as a reliable judiciary favouring internal free trade in its rulings and the EC competition law

---

[3] See Schuknecht (1991a) for a preliminary discussion.

preventing internal monopolization also ensure that undesirable results from the Single European Market are avoided.

Alternatively, it has been argued that politicians did not favour the Single European Market for the purpose of liberalization but to reduce competition between governments or industries and to promote redistribution through centralization. This hypothesis, however, is largely dismissed.

This chapter goes further than the previous ones by *endogenizing the choice of institutions*. The institutional analysis is illustrated by empirical evidence. The next section provides an overview of the history of trade integration. Section 9.3 discusses the hypothesis that integration serves the collusion of governments and industries. Section 9.4 examines the interests of the political actors in the EC's internal trade regime. These interests are strongly influenced by the contents of the EC's Single European Act whose constitutional elements are discussed in Section 9.5. The concluding section evaluates the dynamic process towards free trade within the EC.

9.2 The History of Integration

The Treaty of Rome (1957) laid the foundations for the Common Commercial Policy of the European Community. Between 1957 and 1968, the Common Customs Tariff was implemented, trade barriers between member countries were reduced, and the share of trade between member countries increased rapidly relative to their total trade. However, the Single European Market was not completed as intended in the Treaty of Rome. On the contrary, the process of integration stalled from the mid-seventies to early eigthies. Countries erected new national barriers towards member and non-member countries. European politics were characterized as suffering from "Eurosclerosis". The Common Commercial Policy was threatened by widespread national disregard.

The question arose whether the tendencies of disintegration and decline in trade were due to monetary uncertainty between member countries after the collapse of the Bretton Woods system of fixed exchange rates or due to structural problems related to an incomplete Common Market (Jacquemin and Sapir, 1989). The monetary hypothesis was dismissed when monetary uncertainty decreased after the formation of the European Monetary System in 1979, but trade patterns did not change.

The blame was then put on an incomplete Common Market. Faber and Breyer (1980) argue that the Treaty of Rome did not provide the institutional means to maintain a high degree of functional (trade) integration. Two major institutional obstacles prevented the complete liberalization of trade. The EC's strategy was integration through harmonization. This required the standardization of thousands of national regulations including even technical standards. In the seventies therefore, integration through harmonization progressed more slowly than it was obstructed by countervailing measures of new national regulation.

The second obstacle was the unanimous voting rule resulting from the Luxembourg Accord. It invited countries to veto any decisions to extract a maximum of benefits (strategic bargaining). This slowed down the decision-making process to glacial speed. Any country could block free-trade legislation and frequently did so.

In the late seventies and early eighties the perception of successful policy regimes changed. Privatization and deregulation in the context of supply side policies were propagated instead of demand management and government intervention à la Keynes. This regime change and the frustration over "Eurosclerosis" which threatened all common policy making changed the tide for institutional reforms towards liberalization.

First the Court and then the Commission and the member states tackled the institutional shortcomings. As discussed earlier, the Court ruled in 1979 that national regulation does not justify trade protection against other member countries for any other reasons than those under Article 36, Treaty of Rome (public health and security). This ruling forced Germany to allow the import of Cassis de Dijon from France. From then on, the importing country had to prove that exports from other members were, for instance, a health hazard and not the other way round. This opened "...the flood-gates of competition based on differences..." (Curzon Price, 1991). It induced the EC Commission to abandon its harmonization strategy and instead to follow the principle of mutual recognition of norms between member countries. The number of issues to be tackled for completing the Single European Market immediately declined to a fraction. In the following years, the European Court of Justice upheld this principle in its rulings, and established its judiciary authority and its liberal stance on internal trade. As a consequence, national courts also increasingly began to enforce EC law. The Court then increased the credibility of the Single European Market mainly by making sure that it would be enforced.

The most important change was the ratification of the Single European Act which came into force in 1987. The preparations began in 1984, when the French position on European integration changed from propagating a Socialist Europe to a more pragmatic standpoint. The French President Mitterrand launched an initiative at the EC's Fontainebleau summit in June 1984 which entailed internal liberalization and institutional reforms for implementing the Single European Market. As a prerequisite for further negotiations, a consensus was soon reached on reduced British contributions to the EC budget, the Common Agricultural Policy and the accession of Spain and Portugal.

An intergovernmental conference to amend the Treaty of Rome based on Article 236 was held in 1985. The member countries agreed with unanimous consent to implement the necessary policies for a completion of the Single European Market before the end of 1992 (Article 8a of the Treaty of Rome). This was the first amendment of the Treaty and changed the constitution of the European Community. An agenda for completing the Single European Market before the end of 1992 with a list of 279 issues to be resolved was set. The Single European Act confirmed the new liberal strategy of mutual acceptance of norms. (De-) regulation to liberalize trade in goods and services, and the movement of labour and capital were planned for the intermediate six-year period. The package also included doubling the EC's structural funds - which goes to the marginal and poor regions in the EC - in the subsequent years.

Most importantly, the Single European Act has changed the voting rule for most 1992-related issues from unanimous consent to a qualified majority rule (fifty-four of seventy-six votes). A qualified majority is sufficient for the liberalization of tariffs, trade in services, air and sea traffic, cooperation in the sphere of foreign exchange policy, and the liberalization of capital movements.[4] Although the voting practise has not changed and decisions are still made unanimously, the threat of being overruled has reduced the incentive for single countries to obstruct decision making. Consequently, the Single European Market project is largely within its preset time-table. The advantages of the project are strongly advertised to the public and the business community under the slogan "Europe 1992".

In preparation for the Single European Market, the EC's competition law (Article 85 ff, Treaty of Rome) was extended with a

---

[4] The Single European Act does not alter the Luxembourg Accord but defines the exceptions. For a different view see Holmes (1991a).

provision for the control of mergers. So far it had only been an anti-cartel law. This new regulation aims to prevent the undesirable effects of monpolization in the Single European Market and to maintain competition. It came into force in September 1990.

9.3 Integration as Cartelization

On the political level, politicians can promote integration to prevent competition between different legal/institutional systems thereby reducing pressure for domestic reforms. It is also frequently argued that integration can facilitate the cartelization of industries beyond national boundaries. Monopoly profits would be the underlying motive for supporting an integrative policy. Neither argument is plausible to explain integration in the European Community.

Monopolization can be achieved through price fixing or mergers/acquisitions. As briefly mentioned in the history section, price fixings and cartelization are prevented on the EC level by the competition law. This is now very restrictive towards mergers/acquisitions. Mergers involving firms with a total turnover of more than 5 billion ECU (among other criteria) have to pass an inspection process. Cases with less sales volume are still handled by the national agencies. The EC law is much stricter than the previous national competition laws (if member countries have one at all), except for Great Britain and Germany. Monopolization of markets through mergers and EC-wide price fixings will therefore be more difficult than before the new clause in the competition law. In addition, many former national cartels and monopolies are likely to break up in the Single European Market. The new liberalization in public procurement will work in the same direction. Companies which were formerly spoiled by their "right to sales" to their national governments now face EC-wide competition.

So far, member countries have "competed" for their citizens who have the option to migrate to the country with the most preferred legal/institutional environment. Competition could be reduced if integration was accompanied by a comprehensive harmonization of law, norms and institutions between member countries. This strategy was pursued by the Commission until 1979. Institutional diversity, however, will prevail under the new scheme because national norms are now mutually recognized. Furthermore, the principle of subsidiarity was embedded in the interpretation of EC law, which may contribute to prevent political cartelization through centralization. Single countries can also veto further centralization.

The collusion argument also suggests looking at the Single European Market from an Olsonian perspective. Olson (1982) argues that wars or other events which destroy the old rent-seeking network of special interests can promote prosperity because more resources are invested in productive activities instead of redistribution. From this perspective, Peirce (1990) is optimistic. The project promises to break up many of the existing cartels between national governments and their "pet industries" and puts an end to rent seeking for protection on the national level. On the negative side, the project does not determine constitutional barriers to rent seeking, it leaves scope for EC-wide industrial policies, and contains an inherent bias towards producer interests in federal states.[5]

9.4 Pressure Politics and the Single European Market

Although the approval of the Single European Act required unanimous consent in the Council, not *all* politicians, bureaucrats, interest groups and voters had to agree. Only the heads of all national governments had to consent and gain approval from a majority in their national legislatures. It was therefore only necessary to gain enough support from voters, interest groups, bureaucrats and politicians to secure all national majorities. This section therefore discusses the interests of these political actors with respect to trade integration. It is shown that opposition to trade integration declined, the others sold out. Table 9.1 surveys the winners and losers from integration and the latters' compensation.

The Court of Justice
The foundations of the Single European Market were laid by the Court of Justice in its famous Cassis de Dijon ruling (649/79) which opened the German market for French blackcurrant liquor.[6] This

---

[5] About 80% of the EC's budget is spent on agriculture and structural funds. To limit redistribution and rent seeking on the EC level, Bernholz (1990) suggests including the right to secession and the prohibition of subsidies and transfers by the EC government into the constitution of a future political union.
[6] So far, there is no economic theory of the European Court of Justice. The fact that the Court took the initiative long before the EC governments picked up the idea of the Single European Market does not confirm the Landes and Posner (1975) hypothesis for the European Court of Justice, according to which the U.S. Supreme

Table 9.1 Winners and Losers from the Single European Market

	Winners	Losers	Compensation
Judicary	Court of Justice with prestige and Court of First Instance	--	--
Bureaucrats	EC Commission; national bureaucrats with complementary function	National bureaucrats replaced by Commission	Promotion to well-payed EC position
Politicians	EC and national politicians with EC career prospects	Other national	EC funds
Voters	All as consumers with cheaper and diverse products	--	--
Interest groups			
short term	Exporters	Import competitors	External protection, EC funds
long term	Labour/capital in labour/capital abundant country	Capital in labour abundant country vice versa	Social Charter

precedent was upheld in later similar cases for beer and sausage imports to Germany. The Court's situation in the 1970s brings to light the gains won by changing the course of European trade integration with its rulings. The Court, although independent, often had to balance national political interests with EC law because of its limited

Court enforces the deals U.S. congress strikes. A different interpretation of the role of the European Court is warranted. Also see Chapter 3.4 on the role of the Court.

enforcement capacities. It still had to gain judicial authority and the Cassis de Dijon case created an excellent opportunity to increase its prestige and influence.

It is certainly not a coincidence that liberalization was triggered by a case involving the export of liquor from relatively interventionist France to relatively liberal Germany. The Germans did not oppose the Court's ruling in order to keep its liberal reputation. In addition, the German producer lobby against importing this liquor was relatively weak. The French welcomed the decision - after all its producer lobby had got what it wanted. A liberal ruling for imports from Germany to France would have faced much more resistance. The frustration over the slow decision-making process in the Council also helped the Court to succeed in its ruling.

This pioneering decision has already paid for the Court. Over the past decade, the widespread acceptance of the supremacy of EC law over national law has emerged and has increased the Court's prestige significantly. It has also been honoured with a Court of First Instance.

Bureaucrats
Niskanen (1971) assumes that bureaucratic self-interest lies in increased funds, jobs, status etc. which is best represented by an interest in budgetary expansion. Assuming such a derived utility function, EC bureaucrats (i.e. the EC Commission) clearly gain from the Single European Market project and the related expansion in jobs, responsibility, salaries and status. In the light of the early 1980s' "Eurosclerosis", the advantages for the Commission become even more obvious. The Common Market project reversed the negative attitude towards the EC and its bureaucracy. The Commission won support by successfully drafting the rules and regulations for "Europe 1992". The initiators of the project, Jacques Delors and Lord Arthur Cockfield, have already made history.

On the other hand, national bureaucratic agencies, especially the economic ministries, antitrust agencies, and eventually monetary authorities will lose responsibility when they are substituted by EC agencies. The Commission's salary structure, however, will compensate some officials (at least higher and more mobile ones) with well-paid jobs in Brussels. In recent years, for instance, many positions in the Commission have been filled by delegates from national ministries. This compensation might dissipate resistance from national administrations.

National bureaucrats also profit from the full delegation of trade policy authority to the EC. Kuhn (1991) provides a number of instances in which centralization rather complements than substitutes national bureaucracies. The availability of new jobs on the EC level increases demand and thus raises their market value. Their skills are also required to administer the new EC regulations and the increased structural funds. Bureaucratic discretion increases with the administration of unspecified EC regulation and its exemptions. Furthermore, they can delegate the "dirty work" (for instance protection) to the EC and keep a "clean" (e.g. liberal) slate (Vaubel, 1986).

Politicians
Trade integration is more likely to be pursued when it is also to the personal advantage of policy makers. Politicians have some personal discretion because pressure groups do not yet have complete control over politicians in EC issues. One personal advantage from trade integration can be career prospects in the EC or, in other words, political "trading up".

The prospects for attractive future political appointments in Brussels differ. Politicians from smaller countries are less likely to determine future EC politics. On the other hand, French, English and German politicians are most likely to shape future EC policies. The role of France, for instance, documents this unequal balance of countries and politicians in the political process. After autarcic socialist policies failed in the early eigthies, the French government decided to expand French influence on the supranational level and promoted integration in the EC (Moravcsik, 1991).

Viane (1991) points out that European politicians are interested in getting lobbyists off their back. Again, transferring the "dirty work" to the supranational level gives them more discretion and resources to pursue other interests. Since European politics are still influenced on the national level, this argument is only partially valid. European farmers for instance, who make up the most successful interest group considering their size and economic importance, are now bothering both the EC Commission and various national governments and their ministries.

Countries in the geographical center of the EC will profit from job creation through their central location or by hosting EC government agencies. Additional jobs translate into more support for policy makers. The BeNeLux countries and France are currently in this position. Politicians from the geographical margin of the EC can not profit in this way.

In the light of these arguments, the EC's structural and regional funds can be interpreted as a compensation scheme for politicians who stand to lose from integration. The structural funds are supposed to increase from 7 billion ECU in 1987 to 14 billion ECU in 1993. Most of these funds are allocated to geographically marginal and/or poorer countries (Portugal, Spain, Greece, Ireland, Southern Italy). These funds allow politicians to take up support-enhancing measures for their constituencies. They compensate for discretion lost due to the Single European Market. Ultimately, however, the Single European Market has to be popular with voters and interest groups. The next two sub-sections discuss to what extent politicians were motivated by voter and interest group support in agreeing on the Single European Act and "Europe 1992".

Voters
Voters as consumers are the unambiguous winners from trade-enhancing integration. The public choice literature, however, argues that trade policy is only one issue in the policy platform of candidates. Voter interests in trade policy therefore do not determine these platforms. In reality, however, it is a different story. Politicians invest heavily in voter information on "Europe 1992" and most politicians make this a vote-winning issue in national elections. The explanation for this paradox may lie in the stakes of the project. The Single European Act laid the foundations for a major liberalization programme promising significant gains to the EC consumer. It was also the starting point of the political and monetary union because the idea of a European Union and the EC as a functioning government has regained credibility. "Europe 1992" will therefore influence the way people live together in Europe for the next decades. Trade policy for once is therefore important enough to dominate the policy platforms. The Single European Market promised votes and politicians supported it almost unanimously. As mentioned, the French government for instance decided to move towards integration when it found its economy faltering and its popularity waning after the failure of autarkic policies.

Voter support is particularly important for politicians in times of economic booms when special interest protection is not so pressing (Peltzman, 1976). The timing of the Single European Act during a boom can be seen as a lucky coincidence or a support-maximizing move by politicians in the light of this argument. In any case, the economic boom facilitated liberalization.

Interest Groups
Various sources identify organized interest groups as the driving force behind the Common Market Project. Curzon Price (1991) and Moravscik (1991) mention the European Round Table comprising 40 of the most important EC and EFTA business leaders as a major supporter of "Europe 1992" and the institutional changes in the Single European Act.[7]

The interests of pressure groups in trade policy have a strong effect on politics because politicians depend on support from these groups. It is argued here, that opposition to internal free trade decreased significantly over the past decades because distributional conflicts over trade policy have become less important. It should also be noted that the EC now possesses a wide array of protectionist instruments to compensate real or self-claimed losers from trade integration. In addition, the EC's structural and regional funds might also help producers to cope with increased internal competition.

Interdependence within the EC
The more countries trade with each other the more they lose interest in protection seeking because protection would cause economic disruptions. Many national producers, for instance, are dependent on supplies from other EC member countries. Requesting protection might damage their suppliers or lead to retaliation which could backfire against the protectionist industry. Interdepence can even increase support for liberalization since more companies engage in international trade and therefore profit from reducing residual protection.

Trade, and in particular trade between member countries, grew faster over the past 30 years than GDP (Table 9.2). Nominal GDP rose from 160 billion ECU to over 4 trillion ECU between 1958 and 1989. Trade increased almost twice as fast from 23 billion ECU to over one trillion ECU in the same period. The share of intra-industry trade rose from 30% to close to 60%, illustrating the increase in interdependence between member countries.

---

[7] Unfortunately, the Round Table also strongly supports industrial policies which Curzon Price (1991) identifies as a much bigger danger for the European market economies than "Fortress Europe".

Table 9.2 GDP, Trade and Interdependence in the EC

	Year	Nominal GDP (in billion ECU)	Total imports	Intra-EC trade as percentage of total imports	GDP
EC 6	1958	160	23	30.4	4.4
	1959	168	24	33.2	4.8
	1960	188	30	33.3	5.3
	1961	210	32	37.5	5.7
	1962	232	36	36.0	5.6
	1963	255	40	40.0	6.3
	1964	282	45	40.0	6.4
	1965	307	49	40.8	6.5
	1966	329	54	42.6	7.0
	1967	348	55	43.6	6.9
	1968	379	62	45.2	7.4
	1969	422	76	47.4	8.5
	1970	477	88	48.9	9.0
	1971	528	99	49.5	9.3
	1972	595 *	109	51.4	9.4
EC 9	1973	870 *	168	53.0	10.2
	1974	986	235	46.8	11.2
	1975	1109	228	48.2	9.9
	1976	1269	271	48.3	10.1
	1977	1409	336	50.0	11.9
	1978	1562 *	362	50.8	11.8
	1979	1754 *	439	50.6	12.7
EC 10	1980	2089	528	48.1	12.2
	1981	2286	582	47.6	12.1
	1982	2489	630	49.0	12.4
EC 12	1983	2879	708	51.6	12.7
	1984	3110	813	51.4	13.4
	1985	3340	875	53.4	14.0
	1986	3536	796	57.8	13.0
	1987	3721	829	58.7	13.1
	1988	4008	931	58.1	13.5
	1989	4349	1074	58.1	14.3

*slight inconsistency in EC data on GDP and imports between this year and the previous one.
Source: EUROSTAT (various issues) Monthly Bulletin of External Trade, Series 6b, Volkswirtschaftliche Gesamtrechnungen ESVG.

Interdependence, however, can best be illustrated by comparing the size of intra-EC trade with the EC's GDP. The ratio indicates what percentage of GDP is earned through trade with other member countries. Column 5 in Table 9.2 shows that this share rose more than threefold between 1958 and 1989 from 4.4% to 14.4%. Every seventh ECU is now directly earned by trade between member countries.

Long-Term Interests in Integration
Long-term interests in free trade or protection are identified in a Heckscher-Ohlin framework. The stylized setting of Heckscher-Ohlin consists of two factors, labour and capital, and two goods in two countries. Distributional conflicts over trade policy choices arise between factor owners when countries determine their trade policy. The scarce factor is interested in protection and the abundant factor wins from free trade. A conflict over trade liberalization between countries is more pronounced the more factor prices differ between them. The more wages differ within the EC, for instance, the stronger is the downward pressure on wages in high-wage countries and the stronger is the resistance against such changes. Consequently, attempts towards trade integration in the EC face less opposition the less factor prices diverge. A *convergence of factor prices* can be observed in the EC for the past 30 years which is one of the reasons why opposition to integration has decreased.[8]

Although the dividing line between protectionist and free trade interests usually does not separate capitalists and labour, there is some relevance to this perspective. Recent attempts by unions of high-wage countries to impose a wage and social security floor in the EC Social Charter reveal the fear of the work force in high wage countries of lower wages or job losses. During the European Council meeting in Maastricht in December 1991, all countries except for Great Britain signed the Social Charter. This agreement could become a compensation device for the unions in high-wage countries by increasing relative labour costs in the low-wage countries.[9]

---

[8] Mokhtari and Rassekh (1989) and Gremmen (1985) find that trade openness is the main factor leading to factor price equalization. This convergence in turn was therefore due to internal liberalization during the sixties.
[9] Migration of labour also indicates the subjective evaluation of wage differences when moving costs are considered. If wage differentials decline, migration between EC members should also decrease. Migration is therefore also an indicator for real wage equalization and consequently decreasing opposition to integration. Statistics on

Factor price equalization is analyzed in several studies by looking at 1) real labour costs and 2) wages in purchasing power standards. Companies consider labour costs when deciding on employment. Differences in labour costs therefore affect trade policy interests of labour representations. On the other hand, union members care more for their purchasing power. The smaller the differences in purchasing power the less the workers in labour-scarce countries like Germany or BeNeLux fear a relative decline in their living standards through the Single European Market. Both indicators are therefore used to trace relative factor price developments in the EC since 1957.

Tovias (1982) reports on variation in EC labour costs in manufacturing for the 1957-77 period. He finds decreasing coefficients of variation, which indicate the relative dispersion of labour costs, for the 1957 (0.12) to 1968 (0.08) period and increasing coefficients afterwards (Table 9.3). Table 9.4, compiled from the EC Stastical Revue, confirms this trend for the 1975 to 1981 period, but indicates a marked decrease in labour cost variation for the 1981-84 period.

While the results for labour costs are ambiguous, Table 9.5 shows that hourly earnings for total industry in purchasing power standards converged over the 1972-1986 period for the first nine EC members. The coefficient of variation decreased from 0.19 in 1971 to 0.07 in 1986. The downward trend in living standard variation also suggests reduced potential for conflict over trade policy between the member countries' labour representations.

Apart from the Tovias study, the overall results for the long-term interests of factor owners in the EC support the hypothesis of a trend towards less resistance to trade integration.

Short-Term Interests in Integration
The observation that support of trade integration by interest groups promoted the Single European Market project is related to the finding of increased intra-industry trade within the EC. Marvel and Ray (1987) argue that intra-industry trade results in less protection seeking by import competing producers than inter-industry trade because import competitors have to face resistance not only from consumers but also from exporters within the industry.

---

migration within the EC, however, are not available because registration of citizens is not practiced in most EC countries.

Returns to capital would also be worthwhile studying in this context. Relevant studies, however, do not exist. Since capital mobility has increased significantly since World War II, returns to capital have probably converged over the past decades.

Table 9.3 Labour Costs in the Manufacturing Industry, 1957-1977

Years	Standard deviation of labour costs	Coefficient of variation[1]
1957	45.51	0.1198
1958	42.20	0.1071
1959	30.79	0.0776
1961	(58.95)	(0.1268)
1962	(57.01)	(0.1096)
1963	(47.43)	(0.0832)
1964	53.44	0.0871
1965	56.00	0.0851
1966	62.70	0.0873
1967	63.87	0.0829
1968	66.15	0.0805
1969	83.43	0.0917
1970	123.03	0.1158
1971	161.05	0.1301
1972	192.83	0.1345
1973	270.01	0.1538
1974	380.39	0.1804
1975	391.20	0.1577
1976	49.66	0.1849
1977	614.84	0.1907

[1] The coefficient of variation is the ratio of the standard deviation and the mean of labour costs within the EC.
Source: Tovias (1982)

In the short term, the owners of specific factors such as fixed capital in import-competing branches have an interest in seeking protection to gain rents. The standard endogenous trade policy models, however, only apply to inter-industry trade because they tacitly assume that import competitors and exporters do not coexist within the same industry. In other words, the dividing line between protectionists and free-traders lies between industries; import-competing industries only face resistance by consumers and possibly other exporting industries when lobbying for protection.

With intra-industry trade of differentiated products, industries comprise both import-competing and exporting producers. When an

Table 9.4 Labour Costs in the Processing Industry[1], Selected Years

	1975	1981	1984
Belgium	5.88	12.16	13.16
Denmark	5.74	9.54	11.79
Germany	5.75	10.96	14.17
France	4.69	9.82	12.28
Ireland	2.66	5.99	8.50
Italy	4.26	7.34	10.37
Luxembourg	5.93	10.29	11.58
Netherlands	6.46	10.77	13.64
Great Britain	2.95	7.32	8.84
Mean	4.92	9.35	11.59
Standard deviation	3.89	9.59	8.84
Coefficient of variation[2]	0.79	1.03	0.76

[1] per hour in ECU
[2] For a definition see Table 9.3.
Source: EUROSTAT, Revue Rassegna, 1977-86, p.135 and 1971-80, p.147.

industry then applies for protection, the target country can threaten to retaliate directly against the protecting industry's exports. Those producers which export therefore resist trade protection. The unified front of an industry in favour of protection breaks down. This leads to less protection seeking than in inter-industry trade. In inter-industry trade, retaliation never hits the protecting industry but becomes an externality for others because direct retaliation is not possible.

National vehicle producers in the EC, for instance, are exporters and import-competitors of differentiated products. Volkswagen could gain rents from import restrictions against French cars in Germany but it also exports cars to France. If Volkswagen achieved protection, the French could retaliate directly against German car imports and protection would backfire on Volkswagen. Free trade should therefore in principle be the best policy.[10]

---

[10] There is an exception to this rule. If the two companies could exert domestic monopoly power by reducing mutual competition, the right to export could be traded by the two companies against the benefits from domestic monopoly power.

Table 9.5 Labour Costs in the EC in Purchasing Power Standards, (Processing Industry), 1971-1986

Year	Mean	Standard deviation of labour costs	Coefficient of variation[1]
1971	1.46	0.28	0.19
1972	1.74	0.27	0.16
1973	1.94	0.36	0.19
1974	2.36	0.47	0.18
1975	2.82	0.45	0.16
1976	3.19	0.51	0.16
1977	3.58	0.65	0.18
1978	3.96	0.63	0.16
1979	4.46	0.78	0.17
1980	5.02	0.75	0.15
1981	5.65	0.89	0.16
1982	6.17	0.83	0.13
1983	6.69	0.84	0.13
1984	7.01	0.78	0.11
1985	7.81	0.85	0.11
1986	8.47	0.62	0.07

[1] For a definition see Table 9.3
Source: EUROSTAT, Revue Rassegna, 1977-86, p.130 and 1971-80, p.142.

Cars from Japan, however, are more under threat from EC trade barriers. Japan cannot retaliate directly against the European car industry because car exports to Japan are relatively small. It would have to retaliate against other industries which would not hurt EC car producers. However, even the front of European car producers against Japan is not unified. German car producers with a large stake in the Japanese car market opposed the recent Japanese restraint agreement with the EC while Italian and French producers could not get enough protection.

Repercussions on the foreign economy through protection can also backfire on the domestic producer. If German protectionism hurts the French economy, the demand for German cars in France, for instance, would decline, thus damaging the German producers. In other words, interdependence through intra-industry trade raises the costs of supporting protectionist policies.

This leads to the hypothesis that a shift from inter-industry to intra-industry trade also results in a relative political shift towards trade liberalization because protectionist pressure declines. The following evidence shows that in fact, *intra-industry trade increased significantly within the EC relative to inter-industry trade* over the past 30 years. This has reduced opposition to "Europe 1992". There are simply not many organized interests within the EC anymore which would profit from internal protection.

Globerman and Dean (1990) and Pelkmans (1984) survey the empirical studies.[11] Balassa (1975) and Grubel and Lloyd (1975) were the first to investigate the development of intra-industry trade in the EC. Both studies find a 30% increase in the share of intra-industry trade. Balassa's results (Table 9.6) show an unambiguous increase in the relative share of intra-industry trade over the investigated period 1958-1970 except for trade between the Netherlands and Italy. The value of the intra-industry trade indicator for trade between the Netherlands and France for instance increases from 0.65 to 0.80. Grubel and Lloyd (1975) also find a growing share of intra-industry trade in manufacturing products for the 1959-1967 period for almost all product categories.

Sazanami and Hamaguchi (1978) show that intra-industry trade grew rapidly in the 1962-1972 period. Its absolute share within the EC increased above average in Germany, Italy and the Netherlands while in France and Belgium/Luxemburg it lagged. Drabek and Greenway (1984) show that intra-industry trade increased in the 1964-77 period (Table 9.7). The respective index for manufacturing products rose from 64 to 68. They find that the share of intra-industry trade between EC member countries is higher than between other developed countries - a result first brought up by Grubel and Lloyd (1975).

Glejser (1983) investigates the 1973-1979 period and finds a deceleration in the increase of intra-industry trade compared to the 1960s. Comparing the changes of the 1970-1980 and 1975-1985 period, Globerman and Dean (1990) conclude that the trend towards higher shares in intra-industry trade levelled off in the late seventies. This

---

[11] Trade theorists distinguish between Aquino (1978) type indices which look at import and export patterns, and indices which look at trade overlaps based on the pioneering work by Grubel and Lloyd (1975). Althought theoretically distinct, the indices yield empirically similar results (Silber and Broll, 1990). The type of index used in the empirical studies is therefore irrelevant for the argument of this chapter.

Table 9.6 Intra-Industry Trade between Selected EC Member
Countries, 1958-70*

	Year	Belgium	France	Germany	Italy	Netherlands
Belgium	1958	-	0.576	0.433	0.403	0.539
	1963	-	0.719	0.595	0.485	0.682
	1970	-	0.763	0.755	0.604	0.789
France	1958	0.576	-	0.643	0.528	0.651
	1963	0.719	-	0.760	0.716	0.782
	1970	0.763	-	0.869	0.788	0.800
Germany	1958	0.433	0.643	-	0.416	0.566
	1963	0.595	0.760	-	0.592	0.682
	1970	0.755	0.869	-	0.792	0.821
Italy	1958	0.403	0.528	0.416	-	0.549
	1963	0.485	0.716	0.592	-	0.688
	1970	0.604	0.788	0.792	-	0.657
Netherlands	1958	0.539	0.651	0.566	0.549	-
	1963	0.682	0.782	0.682	0.688	-
	1970	0.789	0.800	0.821	0.657	-

*Rank correlation coefficients for the structure of intra-EC exports of manufactured goods, for a definition see Balassa (1975). Source: Balassa (1975).

detailed survey of the empirical literature illustrates the significant increase in intra-industry trade over the past three decades suggesting a decline in opposition to trade integration.

The literature also shows that intra-industry trade is more pronounced between EC members compared to other industrialized countries or compared to developing countries. This suggests a reason why trade integration with other industrialized countries is less developed than within the EC. It explains why the EFTA/European Economic Space has been formed with some European countries and no similar agreement has been made with the U.S. or Japan. The success of trade liberalization between developed nations compared to the prevalence of trade barriers in north-south trade also becomes more understandable from this point of view (Culem and Lindberg, 1986). The argument applies to other free trade agreements as well. Globerman and Dean (1990) provide evidence of increasing shares of intra-industry trade preceding the recent U.S.-Canadian Free Trade Agreement and the Closer Economic Relations Pact between Australia and New Zealand.

Table 9.7 Intra-Industry Trade within the EC, 1964-77*

SITC group	EC average	
	1964	1977
5	63	67
6	61	68
7	64	70
8	67	67
5-8	64	68

*Unweighted Bj-indices by SITC division for EC countries, for a definition see Grubel and Lloyd (1975)
Source: Drabek and Greenaway (1984).

Summarizing, opposition to internal free trade has decreased across the board of political interests. Interdependence has reached significant proportions. The distributional conflicts between sectors and between factors have become less pronounced. Furthermore support for trade integration has been strengthened by the particular packaging of the Single European Act whose compensatory elements changed the politicians' and bureaucrats' incentives to favour the Single European Market.

9.5 The Constitutional Economics of the Single European Market

The project for the Single European Market is credible - this differentiates it from previous attempts to create a single market within the EC (Holmes, 1991). What then makes "Europe 1992" credible and why is it being implemented at all? Again, a reference to allocative efficiency gains is not the key to answering this question. The previous section established that the Commission as the initiator, the European Court of Justice as the enforcement agency and the politicians as intermediaries for the realization of voter and pressure group interests all profit from the Single European Market. Special interest support has also increased. However, only when major *changes in the trade policy rules* were brought about did liberalization become possible.

Let us consider the situation during the seventies again: internal trade liberalization was the goal of the founding fathers of the Treaty of Rome but the institutions proved to be inadequate. Decision making was slow and costly because of the unanimous voting rule. The number of policy issues was artificially inflated by the Commission's strategy of liberalization through harmonization. The judiciary was too weak to resolve conflicts on trade between member countries and the EC against national protection.

The 1979 Cassis de Dijon ruling constituted a major step towards liberalization in the EC for two reasons: it ended the "cat and mouse game" between the harmonizing Commission and the protectionist national regulators. The Commission then supported this ruling by pursuing liberalization through the "mutual acceptance of norms". Secondly, the ruling started a process which resulted in increased authority of the EC's judiciary and the enforcement of EC law by national courts. These changes significantly reduced the problems of enforcing and implementing liberalization which are so prevalent in GATT.[12]

The main issues to be tackled were then the deficiency of the voting rule, the lack of an agenda and a credible commitment. The Single European Act provided the solution. In this the Commission drafted a policy package that was feasible and credible. The Single European Act *changed the voting rule* to a qualified majority rule and thereby speeded up the decision-making process. Credibility was further increased by the availability of a *concrete agenda*: the project's 279 issues suddenly looked manageable and were delegated to the responsible bureaucrats and politicians. The countries *committed* themselves explicitly in the Treaty of Rome to actually implement the Single European Market before the end of 1992 - which is the strongest legal bound possible. This set the process of completing the Single European Market rolling without actually determining the details in advance. The combination of precommitment and open issues was crucial for finding a consensus among governments; otherwise they would have negotiated forever and ever (Holmes, 1991a).

The project is implemented over a six year period. This adjustment period has several major advantages for the involved

---

[12] Both organizations take advantage of the fact that politicians are more willing to trade concessions on the supranational level (Moser, 1990, Vanberg, 1991) but only the EC can now profit from effective enforcement on the national level. Tumlir suggests enforcing GATT rules also on the national level. For a survey of Tumlir's work on the international trade order see Hauser, Moser, Planta and Schmid (1988).

parties and can be considered a clever move by the Commission because it facilitates implementation. Six years is enough time for industries to adjust to the changed situation and eventually to negotiate compensatory external protection. Political costs from adjustment are therefore minimized. Since businesses anticipate "Europe 1992" some of the growth effects and resulting political benefits are also anticipated. While the benefits can already be reaped, the agreement commits future governments and burdens them with remaining adjustment costs. Time is also necessary to draft the regulations.

At first glance, the commitment by the present governments does not look like it is renegotiation-proof. Future politicians may agree to postpone the project or to abandon it. However, the precommitment through the Single European Act gives companies an incentive to invest in the Single European Market. Once these investments are undertaken, new special interests are created which pressure for implementation of the Common Market in order to secure the returns to their investments (Holmes, 1991). In other words, the precommitment creates vested interests in integration. Rent seeking will force future governments to stick to the deal struck by their predecessors. Further plans have been made for a political union and the first draft of a constitution for a liberal Europe has already been proposed (Bernholz, 1990).

9.6 Conclusion: The Dynamics of Trade Integration

Efficiency gains were a necessary condition for the realization of "Europe 1992" but were not sufficient. They have always been present potentially - not only in the mid-eighties. The relevant question is why protectionist forces did not prevent "Europe 1992". The change in the policy rules, less distributional conflicts and a compensation scheme have decreased opposition to internal free trade so that efficiency gains could be realized.

The course of trade integration in the EC has an another important implication for those lamenting the decline of the world trade order. Balassa and Bauwens (1987) argue and show that liberalization causes more intra-industry trade. This has happened in the EC, where a first move to trade liberalization between 1957 and 1968 was followed by wage and factor price approximation as well as increasing intra-industry trade. If, as argued, intra-industry trade and factor price equalization weaken the opposition to freer trade, these developments are conducive to further trade liberalization as for instance in the completion of the Single European Market. In the EC, there has then been a dynamic process towards freer trade which has more than offset the rent-seeking dynamics towards protection.

Chapter 10

CONCLUSION

This study provides an institutional and empirical analysis of external protectionism and internal liberalization in the European Community. It explains policy choices within given institutions and the change in these institutions by examining the EC's political decision-making process. Although EC trade protection should theoretically be classified as administered protection it is in fact highly politicized. This is because EC bureaucrats have considerable discretion in administering and negotiating trade policy but - being under close scrutiny by the EC member governments through the Council - they usually have to apply this discretion in the interest of member governments. The outcome observed in the EC is therefore similar to the outcome of political protection in the U.S.. Protection is geared to accommodate domestic producer interests. The latter claim injury by imports and lobby for relief. Those who have more political influence have a better chance of being protected against foreign competition.

This result is not due to "bad" policy making but to institutions which do not constrain policy makers sufficiently. The standards applied for the evaluation of protectionist claims - if any - are relatively vague and unspecific. There is no fair system of checks and balances between diverse trade policy interests because consumers in particular are underrepresented. This problem is aggravated by lack of transparency.

There is also a more conciliatory message in this study. EC trade policy rules are still in the process of evolving. They have changed several times over the past decade and usually for the "better". Rule changes have promoted liberalization and transparency in the preparation for "Europe 1992" and in the antidumping regulation. Broader policy interests (i.e. in free trade) have in the past had a better chance of being considered on the rule making (constitutional) level than in every-day policy making.

Considerable institutional and empirical evidence supports the politicized protection hypothesis of this study. The evidence is not undisputed in every instance, but it all points in the same direction. Detailed case studies, or an analysis of the other instruments and the

193

international agreements of the EC could be added to the study. Some
evidence on substitutability and supplementation in the EC trade
policy network is summarized later, but this discussion does not
exhaust the subject.

This study thoroughly investigates those issues "where the action is".
This puts the burden of proof on those who want to tell a different
story. They now have to show that voluntary export restraints are
social policy motivated or that antidumping is in fact geared to
preventing unfair trade. It is not claimed here that strict trade policy
rules solve all the problems. Nevertheless, opponents to a rule-
orientated approach now have to show when political discretion leads
to preferable results.

10.1 Summary of EC Trade Policy Making

Following the introduction, Chapter 2 of this study introduces the
theory of endogenous protection. The availability of rents motivates
organized special interests to seek barriers against foreign imports.
Policy makers give in to such requests in order to enhance their
support. Since no interest group has an incentive to abstain from rent
seeking, a Prisoners' Dilemma may result. The Dilemma, however,
has its origins on a national and not - as some trade theorists suggest -
on an international level. The first part also presents the logical
distinction between policy choices within rules and choices between
rules. Rules govern exchanges in the political market. Rules which
constrain the protectionist options of policy makers are suggested as a
remedy for the intra-national Prisoners' Dilemma.

Chapters 3 and 4 survey EC policy making and the available
trade policy instruments. The main actors are the Council, the
Commission and the Court, which are influenced by national
governments and interest groups. A complex system of checks and
balances has evolved over the past 30 years. The most relevant
features of trade policy making are the Commission's discretion in
administering EC policies and the Council's strong political scrutiny
over the Commission. The Commission drafts and negotiates all trade
policy decisions, but has to gain approval from the Council for most of
them. The Court has frequently intervened in the application of policy
rules. It promotes internal liberalization and also prevents excessive
expansion of external protection. The institutional framework for
external protection consists of an array of GATT-conform and "grey
area" measures. The survey of policy instruments provides empirical

evidence and the institutional framework in which these instruments
are applied.

Chapters 5 to 8 discuss the application of the most important
trade policy instruments, i.e. national protection based on Article 115,
voluntary export restraints and EC antidumping measures. This
protection is politicized to varying degrees. In all cases, industries
normally have a better chance of gaining relief from import
competition the more politicians depend on their support. The
analysis also shows that discretion can accommodate bureaucratic
interests in expansion.

The country groups targeted by protection are not all affected
to the same degree. Article 115 measures are mainly applied against
developing countries including the newly industrialized countries of
East Asia (NICs). The latter countries, as well as Japan, the U.S. and
Eastern Europe are the main targets of antidumping investigations. A
major share of the voluntary export restraints is negotiated with
Japan, the NICs and Eastern Europe. Comparing these countries'
import shares and their share of overall protection, it becomes
obvious that they have been treated the most unfavourably during the
1980s.

The instruments are not equally suitable for all EC industries.
Institutional particularities affect the degree of political discretion, the
transparency, the duration and the costs of proceedings, the required
cohesion of an industry, the effects of protection on industry
reputation and the precision with which certain products can be
targeted. This results in a certain pattern when considering which
industries apply for which trade policy measure.

It is worthwhile presenting this pattern here (Table 10.1). The
chemical industry specializes exclusively in antidumping claims. This
is also the main instrument of consumer electronics producers, who,
however, also frequently take recourse to Article 115 and VERs. The
textile and clothing sector enforces its deals under the Multi Fiber
Arrangement mainly in connection with Article 115 and additional
VERs. The vehicle and the shoe industry prefer voluntary export
restraints but also apply some Article 115 measures. The steel
industry is mainly protected by a cartel which is supplemented by
VERs and antidumping claims.

The reason for this pattern of specialization is discussed in
more detail in the relevant chapters. One additional argument should

Table 10.1 The Specialization of Industries in Trade Barriers

	Antidumping	Article 115	VERs
Chemicals	+ +	0	0 *
Clothing/textiles	0	+ +	+
Consumer electronics	+	+	+
Machinery	+	0	+
Shoes	0	+	+ +
Steel	+	0	+
Vehicles	0	+	+ +
+ + = strong recourse, + = moderate recourse, 0 = no or minor recourse			

* additional to VERs under the Multi Fiber Arrangement

be mentioned here. The pattern also suggests that there may be gains from such specialization. Lobbying involves specific investments. In antidumping for instance, where an extensive procedure is involved, previous negotiating experience and connections in the Commission may enhance the chances of a favourable decision.

    Considering that industries and their products are not homogenous, it is not too surprising that industries seek protection through more than one instrument. In the steel industry for instance, overall imports are mostly regulated by VERs while imports of specific products such as alloys or pipes are targeted by antidumping measures. Another interesting observation can be made when looking at the products targeted by the various policy instruments. In many cases, several instruments apply to one product. In some instances the instruments supplement each other. Tariffs and antidumping duties applied to the same product, for instance, increase the protectionist margin. Article 115 enforces national quotas or VERs. However, many trade barriers must be substituted in preparation for "Europe 1992". Article 115 measures, for instance, must be replaced. VERs (or, after completion of the Uruguay Round, possibly safeguards protection) and antidumping measures are conceivable as substitutes.

    Table 10.2 surveys some products which have been targeted by more than one type of trade barrier. VERs and Article 115 measures for espadrilles (Basque summer shoes), vehicles, television sets, video cassette recorders and umbrellas supplement each other. In the

Table 10.2 Substitution and Supplementation in EC Protection

Products	Antidumping	VERs	Article 115
	years, targets, (applicants if not EC) (substitutes or supplements)		
Espadrilles (Basque summer shoes)	1990, China (substitute)	1980s, China (France) (supplements)	1980s, China (France)
Vehicles	--	Japan (EC; Britain, Belgium) (supplements) EC-wide VER (substitute)	1980s, Japan (Italy, Spain)
Ball bearings	1981, 1990, Japan + 5 countries (supplements)	Japan	--
Color television sets	1990, Korea	after 1983, Japan (supplements)	1980s, Japan, Korea (France, Spain), China (Britain)
Video cassette recorders	1989, Japan, Korea	after 1983 Japan, Korea after anti-dumping threat (supplements)	Japan, Korea (Spain)
Microwave ovens	1988, Korea, Japan, Singapore (claim withdrawn)	after 1988, Korea (substitute)	--
Umbrellas	--	Singapore, Taiwan, Thailand (France) (supplements)	1980s, Taiwan China (France, Spain)

eighties, EC-wide vehicle imports from Japan were regulated by a VER, while single countries such as Italy and Spain had their own specific national quotas enforced by Article 115. Imports of Japanese television sets and video cassette recorders were treated in a similar manner. The VERs for umbrellas and espadrilles to France were also supplemented by Article 115 measures. Antidumping measures against ball bearings from six countries (including Japan) were supplemented by a Japanese VER.

The table also suggests four substitutions of one set of measures by another. A VER by Korean microwave exporters led to the withdrawal of an antidumping claim by EC producers in 1988. Substitution in preparation for "Europe 1992" is in progress. The antidumping claims against colour television sets from Korea, against video cassette recorders from Japan and South Korea and against espadrilles from China are replacing national VERs and Article 115 measures. The same holds for the new VER on Japanese vehicle imports to the EC. These findings on supplementation and substitutability suggest that there is more than one "loophole" in the EC trade policy system.

Although the institutional framework allows a flexible handling of these instruments, substitutability is limited. Those producers, for instance, who want to find a substitute for Article 115 in preparation for the Single European Market will have problems when current protection is confined to very specific products for which the other procedures are too costly. Producers operating in national markets where the interests within the EC industry are not cohesive could also fail in obtaining compensation.

Chapter 9 of this study investigates the motives and means underlying the implementation of the Single European Market. All political actors have supported the project. It has been skillfully packaged with a manageable agenda and compensation for the major losers in politics, administration and among special interests. Distributional conflicts between industries within the EC have decreased over the past decades and this has in turn reduced opposition to internal liberalization.

The crucial difference between this attempt to create the EC's Common Market and the previous ones is the change in the policy rules. The Common Market project only became credible after the mutual recognition of national norms was introduced, after the member governments committed themselves to complete the Single Market before the end of 1992 and after the voting rule in the Council was changed to a qualified majority rule.

10.2 Policy Implications

Baldwin (1985) proposes some basic principles of good policy making for the U.S. which should also guide future reforms in EC trade policy rules. He suggests that objective standards of evaluation should be applied. The procedure should result in an impartial administration of trade policy instruments. The implementation should provide for maximum transparency. This list can be supplemented by the qualification that the chosen instrument should result in minimal distortions. The shortcomings of EC trade policies are of an institutional nature because they do not provide an incentive to follow these principles.

Baldwin's Principles of "Good" Policy Making and the EC Practice

If *standards of evaluation* for protectionist claims are applied at all, they *do not lead to an impartial evaluation* of these as the previous chapters have shown. Significant discretion allows the Commission to interpret the regulation as it deems relevant to the case. This favours well-organized special interests which can easily lobby politicians and the Commission in order to achieve a favourable interpretation. Discretion also facilitates discriminating between the targets of protection. In recent years, many antidumping claims against Far Eastern producers have also been accepted on industrial policy grounds. Unspecified regulation makes it easier for the EC to find unfair trade practices. Sometimes one has the impression that Japan and the Asian NICs are becoming the scapegoat for the economic problems of the EC.

The *procedures* do not result in an impartial evaluation of the trade policy interests because they *are geared to satisfying EC producers*. EC producers forward the claims and provide most of the relevant information. In antidumping, the investigations involve hearing foreign, user and consumer interests but organized lobbying is necessary in order for the interests to be considered. Consumers, however, are badly organized. In the words of Messerlin (1990), there is no adequate system of checks and balances in the procedures.

The policy analyses of the previous chapters also brought to light a significant *protectionist bias in the trade policy rules* which prevents an impartial evaluation of the claims. The dumping evaluation based on the full costs of production, the material injury standards for antidumping measures and the "economic difficulty" requirement for Article 115 measures, for instance, all invite protection seeking.

A *lack of transparency* also furthers unbalanced representation of policy interests. Information costs to consumers/voters depend crucially on the availability of information and also on the clarity of the applied standards. In the case of VERs and Article 115, there are no clear rules. In the case of antidumping, the rules change frequently (three times between 1984 and 1988). The results of the negotiation of VERs are not published and Article 115 measures are only published in brief statements. Antidumping reports are lengthy but the published information looks like it has been tailored to the political winds. Mistrust based on the lack of transparency is aggravated by the EC's rhetoric which seems to want to disguise the real motives and means of policy making.

The *choice of instruments does not follow the principle of minimizing distortions* either. The Commission applies mainly non-tariff barriers which are more distortive than tariffs. This practice induces especially foreign producers to strive for either a voluntary export restraint or a price undertaking which both transfer the protectionist rents into their pocket.

Suggestions for Reform
Stricter standards of evaluation should be introduced, leaving less discretion to the administrator. In the case of antidumping, for instance, Hoekman and Leidy (1990) recommend that only indicators of import penetration should serve as injury standards (although this indicator plays the least important role in the current antidumping investigation). Vaubel (1991) suggests administering antidumping based on the very strict standards in German competition law. Antidumping measures should only be applied when foreign producers have a dominant market share. A market share is "dominant" when it exceeds 33% for one firm, 50% for two to three firms and 66% for four to five firms. If VERs are regulated, discretion as present in the antidumping rules should be avoided.

The comparison of EC and U.S. antidumping has shown that rules can result in as much protection as discretion. Reducing the protectionist bias in the policy rules would also curb the application of certain instruments. Messerlin (1991), for instance, suggests abolishing the controversial constructed value method in the antidumping investigations. Policy recommendations for the stricter regulation of single instruments, however, should be considered in the context of the whole network of EC protectionism. The availability of substitutes invites the replacement of one instrument by another. This has occured with tariffs which have been largely replaced by non-tariff barriers. Various economists now regret that tariffs were the major target of previous trade negotiations because they do not violate the principles of "good" policy making as much as their substitutes do. The current negotiations on safeguards protection based on GATT Article XIX must be seen in the context of recent pressure to tighten the antidumping rules and to prohibit VERs.

The most important problem seems to be the inadequate system of checks and balances. Hillman (1989), Hoekman and Leidy (1990), Messerlin (1991) and the Eminent Persons Group (1985) stress the importance of information and suggest a cost-benefit analysis or a "protection balance sheet" which evaluates the economic effects of trade barriers. Messerlin (1991) also suggests that the introduction of counterbalancing forces in trade negotiations and investigations should be considered. These could consist of trade review institutions, for instance, which conduct annual reviews and cost-benefit analyses of this kind. Establishing the GATT trade policy review mechanism is a first step in this direction. Although it does not yet analyze the welfare and distribution effects of protection, its biannual description of the EC's trade policy developments facilitates monitoring between the contracting parties ("peer pressure") significantly. This monitoring device also gives developing countries the opportunity to scrutinize and criticize the policies of developed countries (Curzon Price, 1991a).

Messerlin (1991), Vaubel (1991), Kostecki (1987) and various other sources suggest shifting the decision-making power to more free trade-oriented agents. They recommend involving the EC's Directorate General for competition policies in antidumping decisions.

Transparency would increase significantly if the investigation and negotiation results for all trade barriers were actually published. The publications should include *all* the results and not only those favourable to the petitioning industry or those which confirm the findings of the Commission. Vaubel (1991) suggests that the votes of single member governments in antidumping decisions should be published to facilitate the identification of protectionist forces in the EC. Analogously, the positions of member governments and firms in the negotiation of VERs should be made public. As mentioned, the GATT trade policy review mechanism is a first step towards increased transparency because it provides information about certain countries' trade policies. It was found that sometimes even domestic politicians do not know about this, let alone outsiders (Courzon Price, 1991a).

Is there a protectionist safety valve allowing protection in a less distortive way than the current ones? Hoekman and Leidy (1990), for example, suggest abolishing VERs and introducing tradeable quotas for established exporters only. Such a system of emergency protection is simple and non-discriminatory. The quota rents compensate the foreign producers for loss of sales. As argued before, however, this could aggravate the injury problem because a (profitably) tradeable quota would induce exporters to penetrate the EC market more rapidly in order to secure a large share for themselves (Schuknecht and Stephan, 1992). A revival of tariffs replacing specifically non-tariff barriers should be taken into consideration.

Reform Prospects - It's a Long Way to Tipperary
The importance of the rule level of policy making at which liberalization is introduced has by now been stressed many times. Rule changes have made the Single European Market possible. This is now the corner stone of a fairly liberal and democratic order within the EC. The EC not only deserves credit for good policy making but also for selling it to all important political forces including the public.

The root of the problem of EC external protection is that it affects non-members outside the EC's legal and judiciary system. External trade policy is therefore based on GATT rules. While the rule-oriented approach to constraining protection finds widespread support and has been successfully applied within the EC, external protection proliferates. The institutional problems identified in the previous section are mostly caused by the fact that GATT does not provide sufficient external constraints. It grandfathers "old" protection from pre-EC times (some Article 115 measures). It does not regulate certain issues (most VERs and other Article 115 measures) and it cannot provide and enforce standards which would result in a strictly rule based national procedure (antidumping but also countervailing duties, subsidies, etc.).

Before tightening international trade rules the problem of enforcing them should be resolved. Only on this condition can external protection of the EC be successfully tackled. Without enforcement, rules are not credible and dubious compromises will proliferate. The previous discussion on European integration demonstrates that the Tumlir proposal (Tumlir, 1983) to enforce international rules in national courts has been applied successfully within the EC. The European Court of Justice sets the trade policy precedents for national courts. Given functioning and independent national judiciaries, the Tumlir proposal is also desirable on the international level. Along these lines, Petersmann (1991) suggests incorporating prohibitive GATT rules into domestic trade regulation.

Instead of a strengthening of the GATT rules, a decline of the international trade order has been frequently observed. This decline allowed the current antidumping regulations to emerge and the implementation of VERs to proliferate. The Uruguay Round did not really tackle this problem. Reforms, for instance, of the antidumping code are unlikely to strengthen the rule-orientated nature of GATT (van Bael, 1991). The system of international trade policy rules does not require partial reforms but an overhaul in most areas. The purpose of such an encompassing reform can only be to reestablish the constitutional foundations of the international trade order. Vested interests in the current GATT system, however, are very strong.

In addition, the tendency towards less protection is not as strong on the world level as in the EC. Here, the convergence of interests in trade integration has been identified as a major driving force of liberalization. Globally, however, there is still too much to gain from protection. Significant progress towards a more liberal international trade order and towards narrow constraints on external trade policy making by the EC can therefore not be expected in the forseeable future.

Bibliography

Abbot, Kenneth W. (1985) The Trading Nation's Dilemma: The Functions of the Law of International Trade. *Harvard International Law Journal*, Vol. 26, 501-532.

Aerssen, Jochen van (1969) *Beziehungen der Staatshandelsländer Osteuropas zu GATT und EWG*, Bonn.

Amelung, Torsten (1989) *Die Politische Ökonomie der Importsubstitution und der Handelsliberalisieung. Das Beispiel Türkei.* Kieler Studien 227, Tübingen: Mohr.

Aquino, A. (1978) Intra-Industry Trade and Inter-Industry Specialization as Concurrent Sources of International Trade in Manufactures. *Weltwirtschaftliches Archiv*, Vol. 114, 275-296.

Arrow, Kenneth J. (1951) *Social Choice and Individual Values*. New York: Wiley.

Axelrod, Robert (1984) *The Evolution of Cooperation*. New York: Basic Books Inc. Publishers.

Bael, Ivo van and **Bellis**, Jean Francois (1985) *International Trade Law and Practice of the European Community*. Bicester: CCH Editions.

Bael, Ivo van and **Bellis**, Jean Francois (1987) *Competition Law of the EEC*. Oxfordshire: CCH Edition Limited.

Bael, Ivo van and **Bellis**, Jean Francois (1990) *Anti-Dumping and other Trade Protection Laws of the EEC*, 2nd ed.. Bicester: CCH Editions.

Bael, Ivo van (1991) Improving GATT Disciplines Relating to Antidumping Measures, in **Oppermann**, Thomas and **Molsberger**, Josef (eds.) *A New GATT for the Nineties and Europe '92'*. Baden-Baden: Nomos.

Balassa, Bela (1961) Towards a Theory of Economic Integration. *Kyklos*, Vol 14, 1-17.

Balassa, Bela, (1975) Trade creation and trade diversion in the European Common Market: An appraisal of the evidence, in: **Balassa**, B. (ed.) *European Economic Integration*. Amsterdam: North-Holland.

Balassa, Bela (ed.) (1975) *European Economic Integration*. Amsterdam: North-Holland.

Balassa, Bela and **Bauwens**, Luc (1987) Intra-Industry Specialization in a Multi-Country and Multi-Industry Framework. *The Economic Journal*, Vol. 97, 923-939.

Baldwin, Richard (1988) Evaluating Strategic Trade Policies. *Außenwirtschaft*, Vol. 43, 207-230.

Baldwin, Richard (1989) The Growth Effects of 1992. *Economic Policy*, October 1989, 248-281.

Baldwin, Robert E. (1982) The Political Economy of Protectionism, in: **Bhagwati**, Jagdish (ed.) *Import Competition and Response*. Chicago: Chicago University Press, 263-292.

Baldwin, Robert E. (1985) *The Political Economy of US Import Policy*. Cambridge: MIT Press.

Baldwin, Robert E. (1988) *Trade Policy in a Changing World Economy.* Hertfordshire: Harvester Wheatsheaf.

Baldwin, Robert E., **Hamilton**, Carl B. and **Sapir**, Andre (eds.) (1988) *Issues in US-EC Trade Relations.* Chicago: University of Chicago Press.

Baldwin, Robert and **Krueger**, Anne O. (eds.) (1984) The Structure and Evolution of Recent US Trade Policy. Chicago: Chicago University Press for NBER.

Barrington, Ruth and **Cooney**, John (1984) *Inside the EEC. An Irish Guide.* Dublin: The O'Brien Press.

Bellis, Jean Francois, **Vermulst**, Edwin and **Musquar**, Philippe (1988) The New EEC Regulation on Unfair Pricing Practices in Maritime Transport: A Forerunner of the Extension of Unfair Trade concepts to Services? *Journal of World Trade*, Vol 22, 47-65.

Bellis, Jean Francois (1989) The EEC Antidumping System, in: **Jackson**, John H. and **Vermulst**, E. (eds.) *Antidumping Law and Practice.* Ann Arbor: University of Michigan Press.

Bernholz, Peter (1990) Constitutional Proposals for Europe. Basel: *Mimeo.*

Beseler, J.F. and **Williams**, A.N. (1986) *Anti-Dumping and Anti-Subsidy Law.* The European Communities. London: Sweet & Maxwell.

Bhagwati, Jagdish N. (ed.) (1982) *Import Competition and Response.* Chicago: University of Chicago Press.

Bhagwati, Jagdish N. (1987) VERs, Quid pro Quo DFI and VIEs: Political-Economy Theoretic Analysis. *International Economic Journal*, Vol.1, 1-14.

Bhagwati, Jagdish N. and **Irwin**, Douglas (1987) The Return of the Reciprocitarians: U.S. Trade Policy Today. *The World Economy*, Vol. 10, 109-130.

Bhagwati, Jagdish N. (1988) *Protectionism.* Cambridge: MIT Press.

Bhagwati, Jagdish N. (1991) *The World Trading System at Risk.* New York/London: Harvester Wheatsheaf.

Bierwagen, Rainer M. (1990) *GATT Article VI and the Protectionist Bias in Anti-Dumping Laws.* Deventer: Kluwer.

Bierwagen, Rainer M. and **Hailbronner**, Kay (1988) Input, Downstream, Upstream, Secondary, Diversionary, and Components or Subassembly Dumping. *Journal of World Trade*, Vol. 22, 27-59.

Boettcher, Erik, **Herder-Dorneich**, Philip, **Schenk**, Karl-Ernst and **Schmidtchen**, Dieter (eds.) (1990) *Jahrbuch für Neue Politische Ökonomie Volume 9.* Tübingen: Mohr.

Brander, James A. and **Spencer**, Barbara J. (1983) International R&D Rivalry and Industrial Strategy. *Review of Economic Studies*, Vol. 50, 707-722.

Brander, James A. and **Spencer**, Barbara J. (1985) Export Subsidies and International Market Share Rivalry. *Journal of Internatioanl Economics*, Vol. 18, 83-100.

Breton, A., and **Wintrobe** R. (1975) The Equilibrium Size of a Budget-Maximizing Bureau: A Note on Niskanen's Theory of Bureaucracy. *Journal of Political Economy*, Vol. 83, 195-207.

Buchanan, James M. (1975) *The Limits of Liberty. Between Anarchy and Leviathan.* Chicago: University of Chicago Press.

Buchanan, James M. (1980) Rent Seeking and Profit Seeking, in: **Buchanan**, James M. et al. (eds.) *Toward a Theory of the Rent-Seeking Society.* College Station: Texas A&M University Press.

Buchanan, James M. (1986) The Relevance of the Constitutional Strategy. *Cato Journal*, Vol. 6, No. 2, 513-517.

Buchanan, James M., **Tollison**, Robert D., and **Tullock**, Gordon (eds.) (1980) *Toward a Theory of the Rent-Seeking Society.* College Station: Texas A&M University Press.

Buchanan, James M. and **Tullock**, Gordon (1962) *The Calculus of Consent.* Ann Arbour: The University of Michigan Press.

Cassing, James H. and **Hillman**, Arye L. (1985) Political Influence Motives and the Choice between Tariffs and Quotas. *Journal of International Economics*, Vol. 19, 279-290.

Cassing, James H., **McKeown**, Timothy J. and **Ochs**, Jack (1986) The Political Economy of the Tariff Cycle. *American Political Science Review*, Vol. 80, 843-862.

Cecchini, Paolo (1988) The Cecchini Report. 1992. The Benefits of a Single Market, Brussels.

Cline, William R. (1990) Textiles, in: **Schott**, Jeffrey J. (ed.) *Completing the Uruguay Round.* Washington D.C.: Institute for International Economics.

de Clerq, Willy (1988) Fair Practise, not Protectionism. *Financial Times* (London), Monday, 21 November 1988, p.21.

Commission of the European Communities (1982) *The Competitiveness of the Community Industry*, Luxembourg.

Commission of the European Communities (1985) *White Paper of the Commission*, Luxembourg.

Commission of the European Communities (1989) *Organigramme de la Commission des Communautés Européennes*, Luxembourg.

Commission of the European Communities (1990) *Industrial Policy in an Open and Competitive Environment*, Brussels.

Commission of the European Communities (1991) *European Economy. The Path of Reform in Central and Eastern Europe*, Special edition No 2, Luxembourg.

Corden, W.M. (1974) *Trade Policy and Economic Welfare.* Oxford: Oxford University Press.

Crandall, R.W. (1980) The Economics of the Current Steel Crisis in OECD Member Countries, in: *Steel in the 80s: Paris Symposium February 1980.* Paris: OECD.

Culem, Claudy and **Lundberg**, Lars (1986) The Product Pattern of Intra-Industry Trade: Stability among Countries and over Time. *Weltwirtschaftliches Archiv*, Vol. 122, 113-130.

Curzon Price, Victoria (1991) The Threat of "Fortress Europe" from the Development of Social and Industrial Policies at a European Level. *Außenwirtschaft/The Swiss Review of International Economics*, Vol. 46, 119-138.

Curzon Price, Victoria (1991a) GATT's New Trade Policy Review Mechanism. *The World Economy*, Vol. 14, 227-238.
Dam, Kenneth W. (1970) *The GATT Law and International Economic Organization*. Chicago and London: University of Chicago Press.
De Jong, H.W. (1968) The Significance of Dumping in International Trade, *Journal of World Trade*, Vol. 2, 162-188.
De Melo, Jaime and **Messerlin**, Patrick (1988) Price, Quality and Welfare Effects of European VERs on Japanese Autos, *European Economic Review*, Vol. 32 (7), 1527-1546.
Destler, I.M. (1986) *American Trade Politics*. Washington D.C.: Institute for International Economics.
Deutsche Bundesbank (1990) *Statistische Beihefte zu den Monatsberichten der Deutschen Bundesbank*, Series 5, No. 2.
Dicke, Detlev and **Petersmann**, Ernst-Ulrich (eds.) (1988) *Foreign Trade in the Present and a New International Economic Order*. Fribourg: University Press Fribourg.
Dollar, David and **Wolff**, Edward N. (1988) Convergence of Industry Labor Productivity among Advanced Economies, 1963-1982. *The Review of Economics and Statistics*, Vol. 70, 549-558.
Downs, Anthony (1957) *An Economic Theory of Democracy*. New York: Harper and Row.
Drabek, Zdenek and **Greenaway**, David (1984) Economic Integration and Intra-Industry Trade: The EEC and CMEA Compared. *Kyklos*, Vol. 37, 444-469.
Dudley, James W. (1989) *1992 Strategies for the Single Market*. London: Kogan Page.
Ebke, Werner F. (1985) Enforcement Techniques within the European Communities: Flying Close to the Sun with Waxen Wings. *Journal of Air Law and Commerce*, Vol. 50, 685-725.
The Economist (various issues).
El-Agraa, Ali M. (1988) *International Economic Integration*. Houndmills: Macmillan.
Emerson Michael (ed.) (1988) *The Economics of 1992. The Commission's Assessment of the Economic Effects of Completing the Internal Market*. Oxford: Oxford University Press.
Eminent Persons Group (1985) *Trade Policies for a Better Future*. Geneva: GATT.
Ethier, Wilfred J. (1982) Dumping. *Journal of Political Economy*, Vol. 90, 487-506.
Ethier, Wilfred J. (1991) The Economics and Political Economy of Managed Trade in: **Hillman**, Arye L. (ed.) *Markets and Politicians*. Boston: Kluwer, 283-306.
Europarecht (1989), Nördlingen: Beck/dtv.
Europe Institute (ed.) (1983) *Protectionism and the European Community*. Deventer: Kluwer.
European Communities (various issues) *Official Journal of the European Communities*, Brussels.

European Court of Justice (various issues) *Collection of the Court's Rulings*, Luxembourg.

European Research Associates (1981 and 1982) *EEC Protectionism*, Brussels.

EUROSTAT (1989) *Basic Statistics*, 26th ed., Brussels.

EUROSTAT (various issues) *Balance of Payments*, Yearbook, Global Data, Quarterly Data, Luxembourg.

EUROSTAT (various issues) *Basic Statistics of the Community* (various issues) Luxembourg.

EUROSTAT (1988, 1989) *External Trade*, 6c, Luxembourg.

EUROSTAT (1987) *Foreign Trade*, Statistical Yearbook, 6, Luxembourg.

EUROSTAT (various issues) *Monthly Bulletin of External Trade*, 6B, Luxembourg.

EUROSTAT (1984) *Monthly External Trade Bulletin*, Special Number 1958-81, 6, Luxembourg.

EUROSTAT (various issues), *Revue Rassegna*, Luxembourg.

EUROSTAT (various issues), *Volkswirtschaftliche Gesamtrechnungen ESVG*, Luxembourg.

Eymann, Angelika and **Schuknecht**, Ludger (1990) Antidumping Policy in the European Community: Political Discretion or Technical Determination. *University of Konstanz, Discussion Paper* No. 106.

Eymann, Angelika and **Schuknecht**, Ludger (1991) Antidumping Enforcement in the European Community, World Bank PRE Working Paper 743, forthcoming in: **Finger**, J. Michael (ed.) *If at First You Don't Succeed: How Antidumping Works and Who Gets Hurt*. Ann Arbour: University of Michigan Press.

Faber, Malte and **Breyer**, Friedrich (1980) Eine ökonomische Analyse konstitutioneller Aspekte der europäischen Integraton, in Jahrbuch für Sozialwissenschaften. Göttingen: Vandenhoeck & Ruprecht.

Falvey, Rodney E. (1989) Trade, Quality Reputations, and Commercial Policy. *International Economic Review*, Vol. 30, 607-622.

Feenstra, Robert C. (1984) Voluntary Export Restraint in U.S. Autos 1980-1981: Quality, Employment and Welfare Effects, in **Baldwin**, Robert E. and **Krueger**, Anne O. (eds.) *The Structures and Evolution of Recent U.S. Trade Policy*. Chicago: The University of Chicago Press for NBER, 298-325.

Feigenbaum, Susan, **Ortiz**, Henry and **Willett**, Thomas D. (1985) Protectionist Pressures and Aggregate Eocnomic Conditions: Comment on Takacs. *Economic Inquiry*, Vol. 23, 175-184.

Feinberg, Robert M. and **Kaplan**, Seth (1990) Fishing Downstream: The Political Economy of Effective Protection, *Mimeo*.

Findlay, Ronald (1990) The Impact of Europe 1992 on the Less Developed Countries. Paper presented at the Conference on *The European Community 1992 and the Perspective from Outside*, Basel.

Finger, J. Michael (1989) Protectionist Rules and Internationalist Degression in the Making of National Trade Policy, in: **Vosgerau**, H.-J. (ed.) *New Institutional Arrangements for the World Economy*. Berlin: Springer.

Finger, J. Michael (1990) International Discipline over Trade Restrictions: A Public Choice Approach. *Mimeo*.

Finger, J.Michael (1991) The Origins and Evolution of Antidumping Regulation, *World Bank Working Paper* 783.

Finger, J.Michael (1991a) The GATT as an International Discipline over Trade Restrictions: A Public Choice Approach, in: **Vaubel**, Roland and **Willett**, Thomas D. (eds.) *The Political Economy of International Organizations. A Puplic Choice Approach*. Boulder: Westview Press.

Finger, J. Michael (ed.) (forthcoming 1992) *If at First You Don't Succeed: How Antidumping Works and Who Gets Hurt*. Ann Arbour: University of Michigan Press.

Finger, J. Michael, **Hall**, H. Keith and **Nelson**, Douglas R. (1982) The Political Economy of Administered Protection. *The American Economic Review*, Vol. 72, 452-466.

Finger, J. Michael and **Murray** Tracy (1991) Policing Unfair Imports: The U.S. Example. *Journal of World Trade*, Vol. 24, 39-54.

Finger, J. Michael and **Nogués**, Julio (1987) International Control of Subsidies and Countervailing Duties. *The World Bank Economic Review*, Vol.1, No.4, 707-725.

Finger, Michael J. and **Olechowski**, Andrzej (1987) Trade Barriers: Who Does What to Whom? In: **Giersch**, Herbert (ed.) *Free Trade in the World Economy. Towards an Opening of Markets*. Tübingen: Mohr.

Frankfurter Allgemeine Zeitung (July 29th 1991), p.9.

Frey, Bruno (1984) *International Political Economics*. Oxford: Basil Blackwell.

Friedman, Milton and **Friedman**, Rose (1981) *Free to Choose*. New York: Avon Books.

Gard, L.M. and **Reidel**, J. (1980) Safeguard Protection of Industry in Developed Countries: An Assessement of the Implications for Developing Countries. *Weltwirtschaftliches Archiv*, Vol. 116, 471-92.

Garland, John S. (1977) *Financing Foreign Trade in Eastern Europe*. New York: Praeger Publishers.

General Agreement on Tariffs and Trade (1991) European Communities. Report by the Secretariat. *Trade Policy Review Mechanism*, Geneva.

General Agreement on Tariffs and Trade (1991a) *Basic Instruments and Selected Documents*, Supplement 37, Geneva.

Giersch, Herbert (ed.) (1987) *Free Trade in the World Economy. Towards an Opening of Markets*. Tübingen: Mohr.

Glejser, H. (1983) Intra-Industry Trade Specialization: Trend and Cycle in the EEC (1973-1979), in: **Tharakan**, P.K.M. (ed.) *Intra-Industry Trade. Empirical and Methodological Aspects*. Amsterdam: North-Holland.

Glismann, Hans H. (1989) EC 1992: Strategic and Policy Issues for the 1990s. *Kiel Working Paper* No. 387.

Globerman, Steven and **Dean**, James W. (1990) Recent Trends in Intra-Industry Trade and Their Implications for Future Trade Liberalization. *Weltwirtschaftliches Archiv*, Vol. 126, 25-49.

Goldstein, Judith L. and **Krasner**, Stephen D. (1984), Unfair Trade Practices: The Case for a Differential Response. *American Economic Review*, Vol. 74, No. 2, 282-287.

Greenaway, David and **Hindley**, Brian (1985) *What Britain Pays for Voluntary Export Restraints*. London: Trade Policy Research Centre.

Gremmen, Hans J. (1985) Testing the Factor Price Equalization Theorem in the E.C.: An Alternative Approach. *Journal of Common Market Studies*, Vol. 23, 278-286.

Grolig, Otto and **Bogaert**, Peter (1987) The Newly-Amended EEC Anti-Dumping Regulation: Black Holes in the Common Market? *Journal of World Trade*, Vol.21, 79-87.

Grubel, Herbert G. and **Lloyd**, P.J. (1975) *Intra-Industry Trade*. London: Macmillan.

Gruenspecht, Howard K. (1988) Dumping and Dynamic Competition. *Journal of International Economics*, Vol. 25, 225-248.

Haberler, G. (1936) *The Theory of International Trade with its Applications to Commercial Policy*. London: Hodge.

Hailbronner, Kay, and **Bierwagen**, Rainer M., (1989) Neuere Entwicklungen im Außenwirtschaftsrecht der Europäischen Gemeinschaften. *Neue Juristische Wochenschrift*, No. 22.

Haberler, G (1936) *The Theory of International Trade with its Applications to Commercial Policy*. London: Hodge.

Hamilton, Carl B. (1986) An Assessement of Voluntary Restraints on Hong Kong Exports to Europe and the USA. *Economica*, Vol. 53, 339-350.

Hamilton, Carl B. (1988) Restrictiveness and International Transmission of the "New" Protectionism, in: **Baldwin**, Robert E., **Hamilton**, Carl and **Sapir**, André (eds.) *Issues in US-EC Trade Relations*. Chicago and London: The University of Chicago Press.

Hamilton, Carl B. (1991) European Community External Protection and 1992. Voluntary Export Restraints Applied to Pacific Asia. *European Economic Review*, Vol.35, 378-387.

Hamilton, Collin and **Whalley**, John (1990) Safeguards, in: **Schott**, Jeffrey J. (ed.) *Completing the Uruguay Round*. Washington D.C.: Institute for International Economics.

Harberger, A.C. (1959) Using the Resources at Hand more Effectively. *American Economic Review*, Vol. 49, 134-146.

Harris, Richard G. (1985) Why Voluntary Export Restraints are Voluntary. *Canadian Economic Journal*, Vol. 18, 799-809.

Hartley, T.C. (1981) *The Foundations of European Community Law. An Introduction to the Constitutional and Administrative Law of the European Community*. Oxford: Clarendon Press.

Hathaway, Dale E.(1990) Agriculture, in: **Schott**, Jeffrey J. (ed.) *Completing the Uruguay Round*. Washington D.C.: Institute for International Economics.

Hauser, Heinz (1986) Domestic Policy Foundation and Domestic Policy Function of International Trade Rules, in: **Hauser**, Heinz (ed.) *Protectionism and Structural Adjustment*. Gruesch: Rüegger, 9-22.

Hauser, Heinz (ed.) (1986a) *Protectionism and Structural Adjustment*. Gruesch: Rüegger.

Hauser, Heinz (1988) Foreign Trade Policy and the Function of the Rules for Trade Policy Making, in: **Dicke**, Detlev et al. (eds.) *Foreign Trade in the Present and a New International Economic Order*. Fribourg: University Press Fribourg, 18-38.

Hauser, Heinz, **Moser**, Peter, **Planta**, Renaud and **Schmid**, Ruedi (1988) Der Beitrag von Jan Tumlir zur Entwicklung einer ökonomischen Verfassungstheorie internationaler Handelsregeln. *ORDO*, Vol. 39, 219-237.

Hayes, Dermont and **Schmitz**, Andrew (1988) The Price and Welfare Implications of Current Conflicts Between the Agricultural Policies of the United States and the European Community, in: **Baldwin**, Robert E. et al. (eds.) *Issues in US-EC Trade Relations*. Chicago: University of Chicago Press.

Heitger, Bernhard (1987) Import Protection and Export Performance - Their Impact on Economic Growth. *Weltwirtschaftliches Archiv*, Vol. 123, 249-261.

Henig, S. (1971) *External Relations of the European Community*. London: Chatham House and PEP.

Hensher, David A. and **Lester** W. Johnson (1981) *Applied Discrete-Choice Modelling*. London: Croom Helm.

Herander, Mark G. and **Pupp**, Roger L. (1991) Firm Participation in Steel Industry Lobbying. *Economic Inquiry*, Vol. 29, 134-147.

Hill, B.E. (1984) *The Common Agriculture Policy: Past Present and Future*. London: Methuen.

Hillman, Arye L. (1989) *The Political Economy of Protection*. Chur: Harwood Academic Publishers.

Hillman, Arye L. (1990) Protection as the Regulation of International Industry. *Public Choice*, Vol. 67, 101-110.

Hillman, Arye L. (ed.) (1991), *Markets and Politicians*. Boston: Kluwer.

Hillman, Arye L. and **Katz**, Eliakim (1984) Risk-Averse Rent Seekers and the Social Cost of Monopoly Power. *Economic Journal*, Vol. 94, 104-110.

Hillman, Arye L. and **Schnytzer**, Adi (1990) Creating the Reform-Resistant Dependent Economy. The CMEA International Trading Relationship. *The World Bank PRE Working Paper* No. 505.

Hillman, Arye L. and **Ursprung**, Heinrich W. (1988) Domestic Politics, Foreign Interests, and International Trade Policy. *The American Economic Review*, Vol. 78, 729-745.

Hindley, Brian (1980) Voluntary Export Restraints and GATT's Main Escape Clause. *The World Economy*, Vol. 3, 313-42.

Hindley, Brian (1987) GATT Safeguards and Voluntary Export Restraints: What are the Interests of the Developing Countries? *The World Bank Economic Review*, Vol. 1, 689-705.

Hindley, Brian (1988) Dumping and the Far East Trade of the European Community. *The World Economy*, Vol. 11, 445-463.

Hine, R.C. (1985) *The Political Economy of European Trade*. Brighton: Wheatsheaf.

Hoekman, Bernard M. and **Leidy**, Michael P. (1990) Policy Responses to Shifting Comparative Advantage: Designing a System of Emergency Protection. *Kyklos*, Vol. 43, 25-51.

Hoekman, Bernard M. and **Leidy**, Michael P. (1991) Antidumping for Services? In: **Tharakan**, P.K.M. (ed.) *Policy Implications of Antidumping Measures*. Amsterdam: North-Holland.

Hoekman, Bernard M. and **Leidy**, Michael P. (Forthcoming 1992) Cascading Contingent Protection. *European Economic Review*.

Holmes, Peter (1991) Europe 1992: From the Common to the Single Market, in: **Hillman**, Arye L. (ed.) *Markets and Politicians*. Boston: Kluwer.

Holmes, Peter (1991a) Trade, Competition and Technology Policy in the EC: Can they be Reconciled? An Initial View. University of Sussex: *Mimeo*.

Horowitz, Joel L. (1983) Statistical Comparison of Non-Nested Probabilistic Discrete Choice Models. *Transportation Science*, Vol. 17, 319-350.

Hufbauer, Gary Clyde (1990) Subsidies, in: **Schott**, Jeffrey J. (ed.) *Completing the Uruguay Round*. Washington D.C.: Institute for International Economics.

Hughes, Helen and **Krueger**, Anne (1984) Effects of Protection in Developed Countries on Developing Countries, in: **Baldwin**, Robert et al. (eds.) The Structure and Evolution of Recent US Trade Policy. Chicago: Chicago University Press for NBER.

Institute for Contemporary Studies (eds.) (1979) *Tariffs, Quotas, and Trade: The Politics of Protectionism*, San Francisco

International Monetary Fund (1988) Issues and Developments in International Trade Policy. *Occasional Paper* No. 63.

International Monetary Fund (various issues) *International Financial Statistics*, Washington D.C..

Jackson, John H. (1969) *World Trade and the Law of GATT: A Legal Analysis of the General Agreement on Tariffs and Trade*. Indianapolis: Bobbs-Merill Company.

Jackson, John H. (1989) *The World Trading System. Law and Policy of International Economic Relations*. Cambridge: MIT Press.

Jacquemin, Alexis and **Sapir**, André (1989) *The European Internal Market. Trade and Competition*. Oxford: Oxford University Press.

Jacquemin, Alexis and **Sapir**, André (1990) Competition and Imports in the European Market. *CEPR Discussion Paper* No. 474, London.

Jacquemin, Alexis and **Sapir**, André (1991) Europe Post-1992: Internal and External Liberalization. *American Economic Review*, Vol. 81, 166-170.

Jacobs, Francis (1989) Antidumping procedures with regard to imports from Eastern Europe, in: **Maresceau**, Marc (ed.) *The Political and Legal Framework of Trade Relations Between the European Community and Eastern Europe*. Dordrecht: Martinus Nijhoff Publishers.

Johnson, H.G. (1962) The Economic Theory of Customs Unions, in: *Money, Trade and Economic Growth*. Cambridge: Harvard University Press.

Jones, Kent (1989) Voluntary Export Restraints: Political Economy, History and the Role of the GATT. *Journal of World Trade*, Vol. 23, 125-140.

Kalantzopoulos, Orsalia (1985) *The Costs of Voluntary Export Restraints*, Washington.

Kaplan, Seth (1991) Injury and Causation in USITC Antidumping Determinations: Five Recent Views, in: **Tharakan**, P.K.M. (ed) *Policy Implications of Antidumping Measures*. Amsterdam: North Holland.

Kindleberger, Charles P. (1986) International Public Goods without International Government. *American Economic Review*, Vol. 76, 1-13.

Köves, André (1985) *The CMEA Countries in the World Economy. Turning Inwards or Turning Outwards*. Budapest: Akadémiai Kiadó.

Kostecki, Michel (1987) Export-Restraint Arrangements and Trade Liberalization. *The World Economy*, Vol. 10, 425-453.

Kreinin, Mordechai E. (1974) *Trade Relations of the EC: An Empirical Investigation*. New York: Praeger Publishers.

Krueger, Anne O. (1974) The Political Economy of the Rent-Seeking Society. *American Economic Review*, Vol. 64, 291-303.

Krugman, Paul R. (1987) Is Free Trade Passé? *Economic Perspectives*, Vol. 1, 131-144.

Kuhn, Britta (1991) Vereinheitlichung der Arbeitszeitregulierungen in Europa. Universität Mannheim: *Mimeo*.

Landes, William M. and **Posner**, Richard A. (1975) The Independent Judiciary in an Interest Group Perspective. *Journal of Law and Economics*, Vol. 18, 875-902.

Lehmbruch, Gerhard (1986) Interest Groups, Government, and the Politics of Protectionism, in: **Hauser**, Heinz (ed.) *Protectionism and Structural Adjustment*. Grüsch: Rüegger, 111-140.

Leidy, Michael P. and **Hoekman**, Bernhard M. (1991) Spurious Injury as Indirect Rent Seeking: Free Trade under the Prospect of Protection. *Economics and Politics*, Vol. 3, 111-137.

Litan, Robert E., and **Boltuck**, Richard D. (1991) *Administration of Trade Remedy Laws*. Washington, D.C.: Brookings.

Magee, Stephen P. (1980) Three Simple Tests of the Stolper-Samuelson Theorem, in **Oppenheimer**, Peter (ed.) *Issues in International Economics*. Stocksfield: Oriel Press, 138-153.

Magee, Stephen P., **Brock**, William A., and **Young**, Leslie (1989) *Black Hole Tariffs and Endogenous Policy Theory. Political Economy in General Equilibrium*. New York: Cambridge University Press.

Maresceau, Marc (1989) *The Political and Legal Framework of Trade Relations Between the European Community and Eastern Europe.* Dordrecht: Martinus Nijhoff Publishers.

Marvel, Howard P. and **Ray**, Edward John (1983) The Kennedy Round: Evidence on the Regulation of International Trade in the United States. *American Economic Review*, Vol.73, 190-197.

Marvel, Howard P. and **Ray**, Edward John (1987) Intraindustry Trade: Sources and Effects on Protection. *Journal of Political Economy*, Vol.95, 1278-1291.

McKelvey, R.D. (1976) Intransitivities in Multidimensional Voting Models and Some Implications for Agenda Control. *Journal of Economic Theory*, Vol. 12, 472-482.

Mennes, L.B.M. and **Kol**, Jacob (eds.) (1988) *European Trade Policies and the Developed World.* London: Croom Helm.

Messerlin, Patrick A. (1981) The Political Economy of Protectionism: The Bureaucratic Case. *Weltwirtschaftliches Archiv*, Vol. 117, 469-496.

Messerlin, Patrick A. (1989) The EC Antidumping Regulations: A first Economic Appraisal, 1980-85. *Weltwirtschaftliches Archiv*, Vol. 125, 563-587.

Messerlin, Patrick A. (1989a) GATT-Inconsistent Outcomes of GATT-Consistent Laws: The Long-Term Evolution of the EC Antidumping Law. The World Bank: *Mimeo*.

Messerlin, Patrick A. (1990) Antidumping, in **Schott**, Jeffrey J. (ed.) *Completing the Uruguay Round.* Washington D.C.: Institute for International Economics.

Messerlin, Patrick A. (1990a) Antidumping Regulations or Procartel Law? The EC Chemical Cases. *The World Economy*, Vol.13, 465-92.

Messerlin, Patrick A. (1991) The Uruguay Negotiations on Antidumping Enforcement: Some Basic Issues, in: **Tharakan**, P.K.M. (ed.) *Policy Implications of Antidumping Measures.* Amsterdam: North-Holland.

Mokhtari, Manouchehr and **Rassekh**, Farhad (1989) The Tendency Towards Factor Price Equalization among OECD Countries. *The Review of Economics and Statistics*, Vol. 71, 636-642.

Moore, Michael O. (1990) Rules or Politics?: An Empirical Analysis of ITC Antidumping Decisions. *Economic Discussion·Paper*, George Washington University, D-9005.

Moravcsik, Andrew (1991) Negotiating the Single European Act: National Interests and Conventional Statecraft in the European Community. *International Organization*, Vol. 45, 19-56.

Moser, Peter (1989) Toward an Open World Order: A Constitutional Economic Approach. *Cato Journal*, Vol. 9, No. 1, 133-147.

Moser, Peter (1990) *The Political Economy of the GATT.* Grüsch: Rüegger.

Moser, Peter (1991) The Domestic Politics of International Trade Negotiations: The Ambiguity of Reciprocity. *Working Paper*, University of St. Gallen.

National Consumer Council (1990) Textiles and Clothes. *Working Paper* No. 2, London.

Nelson, Douglas R. (1981) The Political Structure of the New Protectionism. *World Bank Staff Working Paper*, No. 471, Washington D.C..

Neme, Colette, (1988) 1992 et la Clause de l'Article 115: A Quand une Politique Commerciale Commune? *Revue du Marché Commun*, No. 322.

Niskanen, William A. (1971) *Bureaucracy and Representative Government*. Chicago: Rand McNelly.

Noguès, Julio J., **Olechowski**, Andrzej, and **Winters**, L. Alan (1986) The Extent of Nontariff Barriers to Imports of Industrial Countries. *World Bank Staff Working Papers*, No. 789.

Norall, Christopher (1986) New Trends in Anti-dumping Practice in Brussels. *World Economy*, Vol. 9, No. 1, 97-110.

Nugent, Neill (1989) *The Government and Politics of the European Community*. London: Macmillan.

OECD (various issues) *OECD Statistics of Foreign Trade, Monthly Bulletins*, Paris.

OECD (1983) *Textile and Clothing Industries*, Paris.

Official Journal of the European Communities (various issues), Brussels.

Olson, Mancur (1965) *The Logic of Collective Action. Public Goods and the Theory of Groups*. Cambridge: Harvard University Press.

Olson, Mancur (1982) *The Rise and Decline of Nations*. New Haven: Yale University Press.

Oppermann, Thomas and **Molsberger**, Josef (eds.) (1991) *A New GATT for the Nineties and Europe '92'*. Baden-Baden: Nomos.

Oppenheimer, Peter (ed.) (1980) *Issues in International Economics*. Stocksfield: Oriel Press.

Palmeter, N.D. (1989) The Capture of the Anti-Dumping Law. *Yale Journal of International Law*, Vol. 14, No. 1., 182-198.

Pearce, J. (1983) Export Credit: The Implication of the 1982 Revision for Developing Countries, in: **Stevens**, C. (ed.) *The EC and the Third World: a Survey*. London: Hodder & Stoughton, in Association with ODI and IDS.

Peirce, William S. (1990) After 1992. The European Community and the Redistribution of Rents. Case Western Reserve University: *Mimeo*.

Peirce, William S. (1991) Agenda Setter, Legislature, or Bureaucracy? The Commission of the European Community. Paper prepared for the *Public Choice Society Meeting*, New Orleans.

Pelkmans, Jacques (1984) *Market Integration in the European Community*. The Hague: Kluwer.

Peltzman, Samuel (1976) Toward a More General Theory of Regulation. *Journal of Law and Economics*, Vol. 19, 211-240.

Petersmann, Ernst-Ulrich (1986) Trade Policy as a Constitutional Problem. On the "Domestic Policy Functions" of International Trade Rules, in: **Hauser**, Heinz, (ed.) *Protectionism and Structural Adjustment*. Grüsch: Rüegger, 243-277.

Petersmann, Ernst-Ulrich (1988) Strengthening the Domestic Legal Framework of the GATT Multilateral Trade System: Possibilities and Problems of Making GATT Rules Effective in Domestic Legal Systems, in: **Petersmann**, Ernst-Ulrich et al. (eds.) *The New GATT Round of Multilateral Trade Negotiations: Legal and Economic Problems.* Deventer: Kluwer, 33-113.

Petersmann, Ernst-Ulrich and **Hilf**, Meinhard (eds.) (1988a) *The New GATT Round of Multilateral Trade Negotiations: Legal and Economic Problems.* Deventer: Kluwer.

Petersmann, Ernst- Ulrich (1991) Improvements to the Functioning of the GATT System Including Dispute Settlement, in **Oppermann**, Thomas and **Molsberger**, Josef (eds.) *A New GATT for the Nineties and Europe '92'.* Baden-Baden: Nomos.

Ricardo, David (1973/1817) *The Principles of Political Economy and Taxation.* London: Everyman's Library.

Roessler, Frieder (1985) The Scope, Limits and Function of the GATT Legal System. *The World Economy*, Vol. 8, 287-298.

Roessler, Frieder (1986) Competition and Trade Policies. The Constitutional Function of International Economic Law, in: **Hauser**, Heinz (ed.) *Protectionism and Structural Adjustment.* Grüsch: Rüegger, 305-312.

Romer, Thomas and **Rosenthal**, Howard (1979) Political Resource Allocation, Controlled Agendas, and the Status Quo. *Public Choice*, Vol. 33, No. 4, 27-43.

Rowley, Charles K. and **Tollison**, Robert D. (1986) Rent-Seeking and Trade Protection, in: **Hauser**, Heinz (ed.) *Protectionism and Structural Adjustment.* Grüsch: Rüegger, 141-166.

Rowley, Charles K., **Tollison**, Robert D. and **Tullock**, Gordon (1988) *The Political Economy of Rent-Seeking.* Boston/Dordrecht: Kluwer.

Sazanami, V. and **Hamaguchi**, N. (1978) Intra-Industry Trade in the EEC; 1962-1972. *Keyo Economic Studies*, 53-68.

Schmidtchen, Dieter and **Schmidt-Trenz**, Jörg (1990) The Division of Labour is Limited by the Extent of the Law - A Constitutional Economics Approach to International Private Law. *Constitutional Political Economy*, Vol. 1, No. 3, 49-72.

Schott, Jeffrey J. (ed.) (1990) *Completing the Uruguay Round.* Washington D.C.: Institute for International Economics.

Schrenk, Martin (1990) The CMEA System of Trade and Payments: Today and Tomorrow. *The World Bank, Strategic Planning and Review*, Discussion Paper No. 5.

Schuknecht, Ludger (1990) Protectionism an Intra-National Prisoners' Dilemma. *Außenwirtschaft/The Swiss Review of International Relations*, Vol. 45, 39-55.

Schuknecht, Ludger (1991) The Political Economy of EC Protectionism: National Protection Based on Art. 115, Treaty of Rome. *Public Choice*, Vol.72, 37-50.

Schuknecht, Ludger (1991a) The Political Economy of Current European Integration, in: **Vosgerau**, H.J. (ed.) *European Integration in the World Economy*. Berlin: Springer.

Schuknecht, Ludger (1992) "Europe 1992" - Economic Efficiency or Pressure Politics? Universität Konstanz: *Mimeo*.

Schuknecht, Ludger and **Stephan**, Joerg (1992), The EC Pro-Dumping Laws. Universität Konstanz: *Mimeo*.

Schuknecht, Ludger and **Ursprung**, Heinrich W. (1990) Die Anti-Dumping Politik der EG und der USA: Ein Vergleich aus der Sicht der Neuen Politischen Ökonomie, in: **Boettcher**, Erik, **Herder-Dorneich**, Philip, **Schenk**, Karl-Ernst and **Schmidtchen**, Dieter (eds.) *Jahrbuch für Neue Politische Ökonomie Volume 9*. Tübingen: Mohr.

Senti, Richard (1986) *GATT-Allgemeines Zoll- und Handelsabkommen als System der Welthandlungsordnung*. Zürich: Schulthess Polygraphischer Verlag.

Senti, Richard (1989) *EG, EFTA, Binnenmarkt: Organisation, Funktionsweise, Perspektiven*. Zürich: Institut für Wirtschaftsforschung.

Shapley, L.S. and **Shubik**, M. (1954) A Method for Evaluating the Distribution of Power in a Committee System. *American Political Science Review*, Vol. 48, 787-792.

Shughart II, William F. and **Tollison**, Robert D. (1985) The Cyclical Character of Regulatory Activity. *Public Choice*, Vol. 45, 303-311.

Siebert, Horst (1988) Strategische Handelspolitik, Theoretische Ansätze und Wirtschaftspolitische Empfehlungen. *Außenwirtschaft*, Vol. 43, 549-584.

Silber, Jacques and **Broll**, Udo (1990) Trade Overlap and Trade Pattern Indices of Intra-Industry Trade: Theoretical Distinctions versus Empirical Similarities. *University of Konstanz Discussion Papers*, No. 107.

Smith, Adam (1776/1976) *An Inquiry into the Nature and Causes of the Wealth of Nations*. Indianapolis: Liberty Classics.

Smith, Alasdair (1989) The Market for Cars in the Enlarged European Community. *Centre for Economic Policy Research Discussion Paper Series*, No. 360, London.

Smith, Alasdair and **Venables**, Anthony (1988) The Costs of Non-Europe. An Assessment Based on a Formal Model of Imperfect Competiton and Economies of Scale. *Commission of the European Communities Internal Paper*, Brussels.

Stegemann, Klaus (1990) EC Anti-Dumping Policy: are Price Undertakings a Legal Substitute for Illegal Price Fixing? *Weltwirtschaftliches Archiv*, Vol. 126, 268-298.

Stegemann, Klaus (1991) The International Regulation of Dumping: Protection Made to Easy. Queen's University, Canada: *Mimeo*.

Stegemann, Klaus (1991a) Settlement of Anti-Dumping Cases by Price Undertaking: Is the E.C. More Liberal than Canada? In: **Tharakan**, P.K.M. (ed.) *Policy Implications of Antidumping Measures*. Amsterdam: North-Holland.

Stein, Arthur A. (1982) Coordination and Collaboration: Regimes in an Anarchic World. *International Organization*, Vol. 36, 299-324.

Stevens, C. (ed.) (1983) *The EC and the Third World: a Survey*. London: Hodder & Stoughton, in Association with ODI and IDS.

Stigler, George J. (1971) The Theory of Economic Regulation. *Bell Journal of Economics and Management Science* (The Rand Journal of Economics), Vol. 1, 1-21.

Takacs, Wendy E. (1981) Pressures for Protectionism: an Empirical Analysis. *Economic Inquiry*, Vol. 19, 687-693.

Takacs, Wendy E., **Winters**, L. Alan (1990) Labour Adjustment Costs and British Footwear Protection. *Centre for Economic Policy Research Discussion Paper Series*, No. 376, London.

Tharakan, P.K.M. (ed.) (1983) *Intra-Industry Trade. Empirical and Methodological Aspects*. Amsterdam: North-Holland.

Tharakan, P.K.M. (1988) The Sector-Country Incidence of Anti-Dumping and Countervailing Duty Cases in the European Communities, in: **Mennes**, L.B.M. et al. (eds.) *European Trade Policies and the Developed World*, 99-142. London: Croom Helm.

Tharakan, P.K.M. (1991) East European State Trading Countries and Antidumping Undertakings, in: **Tharakan**, P.K.M. (ed.) *Policy Implications of Antidumping Measures*. Amsterdam: North-Holland.

Tharakan, P.K.M. (ed.) (1991a) *Policy Implications of Antidumping Measures*. Amsterdam: North-Holland.

Tharakan, P.K.M. (1991b) The Political Economy of Anti-Dumping Undertakings in the European Communities. *European Economic Review*, Vol. 35, 1341-1359.

Tischenko, O. (1985) Trade Policies of the USSR and other Socialist Countries of Eastern Europe: Modalities and Mechanisms. *UNCTAD Paper* TD/B/1032.

Tovias, Alfred (1977) *Tariff Preferences in Mediterranean Diplomacy*. London: Macmillan.

Tovias, Alfred (1982) Testing Factor Price Equalization in the EEC. *Journal of Common Market Studies*, Vol. 20, No.4, 375-388.

Tullock, Gordon (1967/1980) The Welfare Costs of Tariffs, Monopolies, and Theft, in: **Buchanan**, James M. et al. (eds.) *Towards a Theory of the Rent-Seeking Society*. College Station: Texas A&M University Press, 16-36.

Tumlir, Jan (1983) International Economic Order and Democratic Constitutionalism. *ORDO*, Vol. 34, 73-81.

UNCTAD (1987) *Protectionism and Structural Adjustment*. Trade and Development Board, TD/B/1126/Add.1.

United Nations (various issues) *Industrial Statistics Yearbook*, Vol. 2, New York.

United Nations (1991) Population and Vital Statistic Report. *Statistical Papers*, Series A, Vol. 63, No.3.

Ursprung, Heinrich W. (1987) Die Einfuehrung politischer Elemente in die Theorie der internationalen Handelspolitik: Einige neuere Ergebnisse. *Geld und Währung*, Monetary Affairs, Vol. 3, 28-44.

Ursprung, Heinrich W. (1990) Public Goods, Rent Dissipation and Candidate Competition. *Economics and Politics*, Vol. 2, 115-132.

Vanberg, Viktor (1991) A Constitutional Political Economy Perspective on International Trade. Paper prepared for the *Annual Meeting of the International Agricultural Trade Research Consortium*, San Diego.

Vanberg, Viktor and Buchanan, James M. (1989) Interests and Theories in Constitutional Choice. *Journal of Theoretical Politics*, Vol. 1, 49-62.

Vaubel, Roland (1986) A Public Choice Approach to International Organization. *Public Choice*, Vol. 51, 39-57.

Vaubel, Roland (1991) The Antidumping Policy of the European Community: A Critique and Two Proposals, in Oppermann, Thomas and Molsberger, Josef (eds.) *A New GATT for the Nineties and Europe '92'*. Baden-Baden: Nomos.

Vaubel, Roland and Willett, Thomas D. (eds.) (1991) *The Political Economy of International Organization: A Public Choice Approach*. Boulder: Westview Publishers.

Vermulst, E.A. (1987) *Antidumping Law and Practice in the United States and the European Communities: A Comparative Analysis*. Amsterdam: North-Holland.

Verreydt, Eric and Waelbrock, Jean (1982) European Community Protection against Manufactured Imports from Developing Countries: A Case Study in the Political Economy of Protection, in: Bhagwati, Jagdish N. (ed.) *Import Competition and Response*. Chicago: University of Chicago Press.

Viane, Jean-Marie (1991) Comments on Ludger Schuknecht: The Political Economy of Current European Integration, in: Vosgerau, H.-J. (ed.) *European Integration in the World Economy*. Berlin: Springer.

Viner, Jacob (1923/1966) *Dumping: A Problem in International Trade*. New York: Kelley.

Viner, Jacob (1950) *The Customs Union Issue*. New York: Carnegie Endowment for International Peace.

Vosgerau, H.-J. (ed.) (1989) *New Institutional Arrangements for the World Economy*. Berlin: Springer.

Vosgerau, H.-J. (ed.) (1992) *European Integration in the World Economy*. Berlin: Springer

Weck-Hannemann, Hannelore (1990) Protectionism in Direct Democracy. *Journal of Institutional and Theoretical Economics*, Vol. 146, 389-418.

Weck-Hannemann, Hannelore (1992) *Politische Ökonomie des Protektionismus: Eine institutionelle und empirische Analyse*. Frankfurt/New York: Campus.

Wilczynski, J. (1966) Dumping and Central Planning. *Journal of Political Economy*, Vol. 74, 250-264.

Wildavsky, Aaron (1964) *The Politics of the Budgetary Process*. Boston: Little, Brown & Comp.

Winters, L. Alan (1988) Completing the European Internal Market. Some Notes on Trade Policy. *European Economic Review*, Vol 32, 1477-1499.

Winters, L. Alan (1990) Import Surveillance as a Strategic Trade Policy. *Centre for Economic Policy Research Discussion Paper Series*, No. 404, London.

Winters, L. Alan (1991) *International Economics*, (4th ed.). London: Harper Collins.

Winters, L. Alan (1991a) International Trade and '1992'. An Overview. *European Economic Review*, Vol. 35, 367-377.

Wolf, Martin (1989) Why Voluntary Export Restraints? A Historical analysis. *The World Economy*, Vol. 12, Nr. 3, 273-292.

Young, Leslie and **Magee**, Stephen P. (1983), A Prisoner's Dilemma Theory of Endogenous Tariffs. Austin, Texas: *Mimeo*.

Young, Leslie and **Magee**, Stephen P. (1986), Endogenous Protection, Factor Returns and Resource Allocation. *Review of Economic Studies*, Vol. 53, 407-419.

Author Index

Abbot 26, 28
Aerssen 153
Amelung 7
Aquino 187
Arrow 16
Axelrod 29
Bael 34, 133, 203
Balassa 170, 187, 188, 191
Baldwin 7, 15, 16, 32, 96, 169, 199
Barrington 50
Bauwens 191
Bellis 34, 58, 133
Bernholz 37, 175, 191
Bhagwati 2, 3, 28, 105, 119
Bierwagen 84, 85, 133, 134
Bogaert 133
Boltuck 121, 143
Brander 14, 16
Breton 23, 86
Breyer 172
Brock 12, 17, 22, 26
Broll 187
Buchanan 17, 26, 29
Cassing 20, 22
Cecchini 2, 34, 169
Cline 67
Commission 33, 62, 101, 149
Corden 57
Cooney 50
Culem 188
Curzon Price 65, 172, 180, 201
Dams 35
De Clerq 1, 2
De Jong 120
De Melo 100, 113
Dean 187, 188
Destler 7
Downs 21
Drabek 187, 189
Dudley 31, 34
Ebke 50
El-Agraa 170
Emerson 169
Eminent Persons Group 201
Ethier 104

Eymann 24, 119, 152, 158
Faber 172
Falvey 155
Feenstra 21, 105
Feigenbaum 88
Feinberg 137
Findlay 170
Finger 24, 28, 60, 85, 99, 104, 106, 120f, 130, 132, 134, 136, 139, 141ff, 145, 152
Frey 17
Friedman 28
Glejser 187
Globerman 187f
Goldstein 15
Greenaway 3, 100, 189
Gremmen 182
Grolig 133
Grubel 187, 189
Gruenspecht 129
Hailbronner 85, 133
Hall 121, 152
Hamaguchi 187
Hamilton 61, 75, 97, 100, 113
Harberger 18, 19
Harris 21
Hartley 50
Hathaway 67
Hauser 17, 28, 190
Heitger 3
Henig 33
Hensher 140
Herander 143
Hill 67·
Hillman 12, 17, 19, 21ff, 87, 99, 139, 146, 153, 155, 156, 201
Hindley 3, 100, 105, 113, 134, 136
Hine 31ff, 37, 45, 69, 74
Hoekman 58, 137, 200, 201
Holmes 44, 170, 173, 189ff
Horrowitz 140
Hufbauer 60
Hughes 105
Irwin 28
Jackson 35
Jacobs 152

Jacquemin 35, 171
Johnson 140, 170
Jones 107, 115
Kalantzopoulos 3, 100
Kaplan 121, 137, 143
Katz 19
Kindleberger 27
Kostecki 4, 99, 100, 101, 104, 117, 201
Krueger 17, 105
Krugman 15f, 28
Kuhn 178
Landes 50, 175
Leidy 58, 137, 200f
Litan 121, 143
Lloyd 187, 189
Magee 12, 17, 19, 22, 25f
Marvel 183
McKelvey 41
McKeown 20
Messerlin 4, 23f, 100, 113, 119, 133, 152, 157, 167, 199ff
Mokhtari 182
Moore 24, 121
Moravcsik 178
Moser 7, 21f, 24, 27f, 32, 35, 190
Murray 130, 143, 145, 152
Musquar 58
Nelson 24, 85, 121, 139, 141f, 152
Neme 85
Niskanen 23, 86, 177
Nogues 60
Norall 132
Nugent 31, 38, 44f, 48, 52
Ochs 20
Olechowski 3, 99
Olson 21, 24, 175
Peirce 41
Palmeter 132
Pelkmans 187
Peltzman 22f, 85, 179
Petersmann 27, 28, 203
Planta 190
Posner 50, 175
Pupp 143
Rassekh 182
Ray 32, 183
Ricardo 9, 20

Roessler 28, 35
Romer 41
Rosenthal 41
Rowley 17f, 23
Sapir 35, 171
Sazanami 187
Schmid 190
Schmidt-Trenz 28
Schmidtchen 28
Schrenk 153
Schuknecht 24, 26, 75, 107, 119, 130, 138, 152, 158, 170, 202
Senti 35, 69
Shapley 47
Shubik 47
Shughart 85, 88
Siebert 15
Silber 187
Smith 10, 169
Spencer 14, 16
Stegemann 36, 119, 133, 139, 143, 146, 156
Stein 15
Stephan 107, 138, 202
Stigler 22f, 85
Takacs 85, 88, 100
Tharakan 119, 139, 152, 157
Tischenko 153, 155
Tollison 17f, 23, 85, 88
Tovias 158, 183f
Tullock 19, 23, 29, 100
Tumlir 28, 202
Ursprung 17, 19, 21, 23f, 99, 119, 130
Vanberg 28, 190
Vaubel 31, 50, 178, 200f
Venables 169
Vermulst 58, 130, 133
Viner 20, 22, 170
Weck-Hannemann 7, 23
Whalley 61
Wilczynski 156
Wildavsky 86
Willett 31
Winters 3, 75, 100, 114, 169
Wintrobe 23, 86
Wolf 106, 113
Young 12, 17, 22, 25f

Subject Index

Adjustment cost 106
Administered protection 5, 23f, 54, 74, 82, 99, 193
Agenda 39, 40f, 170, 173, 190, 198
Anticipation of protection 114
Antidumping 57ff, 119ff, 149ff, 195ff
    against Eastern Europe 149ff
    code 58, 69
    country incidence 121ff
    EC procedure 59, 133ff
    empirical evidence 139ff
        Eastern Europe 157ff
    sector incidence 127ff
    U.S. procedure 130ff
Article 115 64ff, 73ff, 195ff
    bureaucratic interests 91, 94
    country incidence 76ff
    empirical evidence 87ff
    and "Europe 1992" 96ff
    measures 64, 73
    procedure 65, 82ff
    sector incidence 78ff
Association to EC 38, 52, 68, 70
Association, Industry 144ff, 159
Automobile industry 56, 63, 79ff, 97ff, 111ff, 146, 159, 185, 195ff
Balance of payment 12, 33, 153ff, 164ff
Belgium 38, 47, 71, 117, 122, 185ff, 197
BeNeLux 64, 77f, 108, 117, 178, 183
Bureaucracy 27, 90, 106, 112, 177
Cartelization 66, 113, 174f
Cassis de Dijon 34, 51, 70, 172-177, 190
Cecchini 70, 169
Checks and balances 5, 31, 48f, 193f, 199ff
Chemical industry 107, 113, 127f, 163, 195
Circumvention 74, 111, 130ff, 146
Clothing industry 62ff, 74ff, 86, 97, 100, 111-116, 128, 195f
Codification ratchet 36
Commissioner 1, 39, 42f, 68
Common Agricultural Policy 67, 147, 173

Common Commercial Policy 32ff, 65, 73f, 85, 96, 112, 171
Common Customs Tariff 32ff, 56f, 171
Community interest 103, 132, 137
Comparative advantage 6, 9f, 21, 127f, 147
Compensation 7, 16f, 57, 65, 97, 102ff, 115, 146, 175ff, 191, 198
Competition policy, EC 2, 34, 44,170ff, 200
Competitiveness 21, 33, 68, 107, 156
Consumer electronics 3, 63ff, 73, 78ff, 97ff, 111ff, 119, 127ff, 136, 163, 195f
Consumers 1-5, 21f, 28, 35, 67, 85, 100ff, 115ff, 137, 145, 176ff, 193, 199f
COREPER 39, 45ff
Cost-benefit analysis 201
Countervailing Duties 59f, 202
Credibility 4, 7, 27, 34, 170ff, 179, 190
Customs Union 32ff, 56
Cyclical factors 23, 85ff
Declining industries 20ff, 33, 65, 77, 113
Delors, Jacques 2, 42, 177
Denmark 33, 38, 47f, 62ff, 77f, 185
Developing countries, 38ff, 53, 62ff, 75ff, 105, 110f, 121ff, 147, 168f, 188, 195, 201
Dillon Round 32
Directorate General 44, 82, 150, 201
Discretion 5ff, 27, 54ff, 74, 82ff, 96, 121, 130ff, 151f, 159, 178f, 193ff
Dispute settlement 36, 61
Distributional conflicts 29, 170, 180ff, 198
Duty 59
Economic and Social Committee 40, 52
Economic difficulties 73, 82ff, 89, 104, 114
Economies of scale 5, 9f, 14f, 169
EC import volume 3
EFTA 33f, 53, 68, 112, 180, 188
Entrenchment of protection 104
Escape clause 64, 73

"Europe 1992" 7, 28, 34f, 47f, 56, 114f, 170ff, 193ff
European Court of Justice 34ff, 42ff, 70, 82, 137, 172, 189, 202
European Economic Space 34, 68f, 168, 188
European Parliament 38, 44
Export credits 43, 54, 66
Export-oriented strategies 147, 168
Fairness 1f, 5, 59, 87, 99, 120f, 168
Footwear industry 3, 21, 56, 63, 99, 100ff, 109ff
"Fortress Europe" 35, 61, 75, 96ff, 101, 147, 170
France 38ff, 61ff, 71ff, 93, 97, 101f, 108ff, 172, 177ff, 197f
Foreign Trade Organizations 153, 155
GATT 27ff, 54ff, 74, 95ff, 120f, 130ff, 138, 143, 149, 170, 190ff
    Articles VI: 58
    XI: 36, 62
    XIX: 36, 60f, 105, 201
    Trade Policy Review Mechanism 54, 109, 117, 201
Germany 34ff, 47, 62ff, 70, 77f, 108, 117, 122ff, 149, 157, 172ff, 183ff
Grandfathered protection 36, 55, 64, 74, 115
Great Britain 33ff, 62ff, 67, 77f, 81, 108, 174, 182, 185
Greece 38, 47, 74, 77f, 122, 179
"Grey area" measures 36, 62ff, 74
Harassment 119
Hard currency shortage 149, 164, 165
Heckscher-Ohlin 19f
High-tech industries 35, 68, 128, 145
Import penetration 71, 107, 138, 200
Import-competing industries 20, 23, 101, 184
Industrial policies 42, 54, 62ff, 73, 77, 136, 146, 175
Infant industry 36
Institutional analysis 8, 59, 85, 171
Institutional framework 4ff, 23ff, 31, 54, 75, 82, 194ff
Inter-industry trade 10, 183ff
Interdependence 31, 38, 180ff, 187ff

Internal barriers 61, 70f, 97
Intra-industry trade 10, 180, 183ff
Prisoners' Dilemma, intra-national 13, 17, 24, 29
Ireland 33, 38, 47, 64, 73ff, 111, 116, 179, 185
Italy 33, 38, 47, 64, 71, 73ff, 102, 111, 179, 185ff, 197f
Japan 33, 53ff, 68f, 74ff, 100, 108ff, 121ff, 136, 169, 186ff
Judicial authority 177
Kennedy Round 32f, 36
Labour cost variation 183
Layoffs 84, 137, 142ff, 148, 159ff
Learning by doing 128, 136
Liberalization 28, 33f, 42, 50, 56, 69, 96f, 115, 169ff, 193f, 198ff
Lomé 57, 68f
Luxembourg 38, 41, 46ff, 172, 185
Managed Trade 65f
Multi Fiber Arrangement 60ff, 73ff, 86ff, 99f, 107ff, 128, 147, 195f
Mutual acceptance of norms 7, 173, 190
Council of Mutual Economic Assistance 6, 149ff
Natural monopoly 9, 14f
Netherlands 38, 42, 47f, 62, 185ff
New Commercial Policy Instrument 61f
Newly industrialized countries 33, 53, 74, 78, 122ff, 195
Non-tariff barriers 2f, 32ff, 53, 158, 200ff
Optimum tariff 14
Political accountability 54, 59, 84
Political support 22, 28, 85, 105
Political union 37, 44, 191
Politicized protection 3ff 31, 54, 84, 99, 168, 193ff
Porous protection 105
Portugal 38, 47, 77ff, 123, 173, 179
Preferential treatment 33ff, 56f, 68ff
Preselection 59, 82ff, 91, 151
Price equalization 155
Product differentiation 10, 16, 53, 142
Protectionist margin 196

Public choice 4, 9, 13, 31, 85, 96, 104, 179
Public good 27
Public procurement 37, 71, 174
Publicity 7, 74f, 95f, 114
Qualified majority 7, 29, 47, 138, 152, 173, 190, 198
Recession 23, 33, 67, 129
Reciprocity 28, 36
Redistribution 10, 13, 17, 22ff, 89, 171, 175
Rent dissipation 20
Rent seeking 13, 17ff, 89, 175, 191, 194
Quota rents 100, 113f, 146, 202
Repeated games 29
Retaliation 12, 16, 20, 60ff, 106, 115, 140ff, 180, 185
Rhetoric, EC 1ff, 51, 59, 120, 133, 145f, 200
Ricardo-Viner 20
Rule changes 7, 96, 193, 202
Safeguards 36, 55, 60ff, 99ff, 112ff, 150, 196, 201
Scrutiny by politicians 6, 23, 44, 48, 57, 65ff, 70, 74, 84, 95, 103f, 138, 152, 193f
Single European Act 7, 34, 47, 170ff, 179f, 189ff
Single European Market: see "Europe 1992"
"Soft" goods 6, 150ff
Spain 38, 47, 60, 64, 73, 77ff, 122, 173, 179, 197f
Specific factors 20, 184
Steel industry 52, 63ff, 99ff, 109ff, 119, 127ff, 145f, 163, 195f
Strategic trade policies 15f
Structural funds 173, 178f
Subsidiariness 37, 50
Substitutes 97, 113, 167, 178, 196ff
Sunset clause 115
Surveillance 60, 64, 73ff, 103, 114
Tariff equivalent 145
Tariffs 3, 12ff, 31ff, 53ff, 68, 105f, 149, 156, 173, 196, 200ff
Technical rules 2, 24, 82, 103, 150, 159
Tokyo Round 57f, 134
Transaction costs 16

Transition from socialism 6, 149ff, 168
Transparency 5, 48, 51, 58f, 64, 74, 87, 101f, 114, 146, 193ff, 199ff
Treaty of Rome 2f, 32ff, 50, 57, 62ff, 73, 171ff, 190
Articles 8a: 70, 173
       36: 37, 70, 76, 94, 172, 181, 186
       113: 32, 70
       137: 38
       145: 44
       148: 46
       152: 41
       155: 41
       164: 50
       169: 42, 50
       238: 70
Unanimity 29, 47ff, 141, 159
Undertakings 54, 59, 124, 133, 138f, 146
       and Eastern Europe 151, 156f, 166ff
Unemployment 33, 88ff, 100
Uruguay Round 35, 54ff, 61, 71, 115, 196, 203
Voluntary export restraints 99ff, 63ff
       country incidence 108ff
       procedure 63, 101ff
       sector incidence 111f
       welfare costs 63, 100
Voters 23, 95, 179, 189
Voting power 47
Welfare costs of protection 3
White Paper, Commission 70, 169
Winners/losers from protection 13ff
       from "Europe 1992" 175ff